Praise for *On All Fronts*

"In *On All Fronts*, [Ward] combines grace, authority, and a humor so dry it evaporates on contact. Whether Ward is fending off the dissolute, lecherous Saif Qaddafi, son of the brutal former Libyan dictator Muammar Qaddafi, in a Moscow Mercedes, or confronting a jihadist leader with video evidence of an execution carried out by his men, she gives off the impression that the story is, above all personal considerations, sacrosanct.... Ward shows an enduring faith in the power of reporting."
—Annalisa Quinn, NPR

"Ward's journalism skills shine, putting readers on the front lines. Readers interested in the life stories of intrepid women journalists and the nature of investigative, international journalism will be captivated by this engrossing account."
—*Library Journal*

"[Ward's] descriptions of her experiences at all the sites are vivid and precise.... A thoughtful account of the excitement and pitfalls of war reporting."
—*Kirkus Reviews*

"Ward details her often harrowing career in this page-turning memoir.... Readers will come away with at least a basic understanding of multiple international conflicts. This is a wonderful addition to the list of recent titles about women working in war-torn lands."
—*Booklist*

"Ward, CNN's chief international correspondent, recounts her life in journalism in this insightful memoir.... She details her often harrowing experiences that eventually took a toll on her physical and mental well-being.... But it's the connections she made with the civilians that really tell the story of these war-torn regions and demonstrate an empathy that makes Ward's work so accessible.... Ward surprises in this affecting insider view of international reporting."
—*Publishers Weekly*

"*On All Fronts* is funny, fascinating, heartbreaking, and heroic. Clarissa Ward doesn't just take us to the front lines of the world's most dangerous places, revealing the pain and pleasure of being a foreign correspondent, she gives us a startling and often hilarious look at her own unconventional, almost unimaginable childhood. How did a continent-hopping Eloise, who was banished at ten to a dismal British boarding school, wind up in Beijing as a stand-in for Uma Thurman on a Quentin Tarantino film, and then break into the news business and become one of the great foreign correspondents of our time? Read on . . . Ward has an extraordinary tale to tell."

—Anderson Cooper, author of *Dispatches from the Edge*

"*On All Fronts* takes the reader on a riveting journey of storytelling as Ward crisscrosses the globe in a relentless quest to become the acclaimed chief international correspondent she is today. From Russia to China to Syria, the reader watches her navigate the most intense of human experiences while finding the tools to stay emotional."

—Lynsey Addario, author of *It's What I Do*

"Clarissa Ward takes us on a page-turning ride through natural disasters and debaucheries, the terror and grief of war zones, and the grace notes of motherhood. *On All Fronts* traces the formation of one of our generation's most dynamic foreign correspondents, and gives us an intimate view of the failures and tragedies of the conflicts that are reshaping our world."

—Megan K. Stack, author of *Women's Work* and
Every Man in This Village Is a Liar

"There has never been a more vital time for journalists who bear witness to crimes against humanity and violations of international law to have a voice to tell the stories of those who cannot tell their own. Clarissa Ward is a reporter I have always admired—for her courage but also her clarity and her willingness to take risks to bring sometimes uncomfortable truths to light. Her memoir is a reporter's story—with all the grit and frustration and triumphs—but also a universal story of a tenacious young woman working in a hardscrabble profession who paved her own way with sheer hard work and a vision. Ward has reported diligently from many war zones, but her work in Syria will go down as a historical record of a country that the international community allowed to bleed. Everyone with a conscience should read this book."

—Janine di Giovanni, author of *The Morning They Came for Us*

"War correspondents have long been caricatured as vain figures of parachutist self-glory. Clarissa Ward, for all her onscreen unflappability, has risked this investigative memoir to reveal herself as a reporter of rare modesty in her courage, rare empathy in her diligence, and rare reflection in her daring. This is a poignant and vigorous self-portrait of a journalist graced and burdened with a supreme sense of duty."

—Gideon Lewis-Kraus, author of *A Sense of Direction*

"An honest, candid portrayal of the making of a journalist and the stories behind getting the story. With great empathy, Ward shows us what her viewers don't see—the logistical, physical, and emotional challenges of going to the toughest places—and the toll it takes. A timely reminder of the importance of bearing witness, and why there is no substitute for gutsy on-the-ground journalism."

—Rania Abouzeid, author of *No Turning Back: Life, Loss, and Hope in Wartime Syria*

PENGUIN BOOKS

ON ALL FRONTS

Clarissa Ward is CNN's chief international correspondent. In her fifteen-year career with Fox, CBS, and ABC, Ward has reported from front lines around the world. She has received seven Emmy Awards, two George Foster Peabody Awards, two Alfred I. duPont–Columbia University Awards, two Edward R. Murrow Awards for distinguished journalism, honors from the Radio and Television Correspondents' Association, the 2016 David Kaplan Award from the Overseas Press Club, and the Excellence in International Reporting Award from the International Center for Journalists. She graduated with distinction from Yale University, and in 2013 received an honorary doctor of letters degree from Middlebury College in Vermont. She lives in London.

On All Fronts

The Education of a Journalist

CLARISSA WARD

PENGUIN BOOKS

PENGUIN BOOKS
An imprint of Penguin Random House LLC
penguinrandomhouse.com

First published in the United States of America by Penguin Press,
an imprint of Penguin Random House LLC, 2020
Published with a new preface in Penguin Books 2021

Mahmoud Darwish, "The Damascene Collar of the Dove V: In Damascus: /
the traveler sings to himself" from *The Butterfly's Burden,* translated by Fady
Joudah. Copyright © 2007 by Mahmoud Darwish. Translation copyright © 2007
by Fady Joudah. Reprinted with the permission of The Permissions Company,
LLC, on behalf of Copper Canyon Press, www.coppercanyonpress.org.

"Fair Weather," copyright 1928, renewed © 1956 by Dorothy Parker; from *The
Portable Dorothy Parker* by Dorothy Parker, edited by Marion Meade. Used by
permission of Viking Books, an imprint of Penguin Publishing Group, a division
of Penguin Random House LLC. All rights reserved.

Photo credits appear on p. 319.

ISBN 9780525561491 (paperback)

THE LIBRARY OF CONGRESS HAS CATALOGED
THE HARDCOVER EDITION AS FOLLOWS:
Names: Ward, Clarissa, 1980– author.
Title: On all fronts : the education of a journalist / Clarissa Ward.
Description: New York : Penguin Press, 2020. | Includes index.
Identifiers: LCCN 2019049839 (print) | LCCN 2019049840 (ebook) |
ISBN 9780525561477 (hardcover) | ISBN 9780525561484 (ebook)
Subjects: LCSH: Ward, Clarissa, 1980– | Television journalists—United
States—Biography. | War correspondents—United States—Biography. |
Iraq War, 2003–2011—Personal narratives, American. |
Syria—History—Civil War, 2011—Personal narratives, American.
Classification: LCC PN4874.W2885 A3 2020 (print) |
LCC PN4874.W2885 (ebook) | DDC 070.4/333092 [B]—dc23
LC record available at https://lccn.loc.gov/2019049839
LC ebook record available at https://lccn.loc.gov/2019049840

Printed in the United States of America
1st Printing

Book design by Daniel Lagin

Some names and identifying characteristics have been changed to protect the
privacy and safety of the individuals involved.

For my mother, who rightly insisted
that this book should be dedicated to her.

And for my beloved Ezra and Caspar.

Preface

We sat in silence parked outside the grim-looking apartment block. I looked at my watch. Six forty a.m.

"Is it too early to try now?" I asked my colleague Dasha Tarasova, who sat in the front seat.

For the past twenty minutes, we had been waiting outside the home of Oleg Tayakin, an undercover Russian operative with Russia's state security services, better known as the FSB. Tayakin wasn't your average stooge or spook. He was part of an elite team that was believed to have poisoned Russian opposition leader Alexey Navalny some four months earlier.

Navalny is Russia's de facto opposition leader, to the extent that any real opposition is allowed to exist in Russia. Forceful and charismatic, he rose to prominence in 2011, with bold exposés of the corruption of Russia's leadership that were pumped out on his YouTube channel. In 2016, he deployed a drone over the lavish country estate of then prime minster Dmitry Medvedev, just two days before parliamentary elections.

While most Russians subsist on the information spoon-fed to them on state-run television, the younger generation began to pay attention. Years of cronyism combined with costly global adventurism had brought the country's economy to a grinding halt. Opportunity was in short supply and patience was wearing thin.

On the surface, the Kremlin feigned nonchalance. But after Navalny announced his intention to run for president in the 2018 election, he was quickly barred from running on account of a prior trumped-up criminal charge.

Still, he continued his anti-corruption campaign. We'd learned that, behind the scenes, Russia's FSB (the contemporary Russian incarnation of the domestic arm of the Soviet KGB) had created a sub-unit of operatives with specialist knowledge of toxins and nerve agents—and they'd been tracking Navalny for more than three years, following him on more than thirty trips across the country.

On August 20, 2020, Navalny was flying back to Moscow from the Siberian city of Tomsk. He boarded the plane in good spirits, but minutes into the flight fell suddenly ill. He went to the bathroom and noticed he was dripping in sweat.

"I get out of this bathroom. I went over to the flight attendant and said, I was poisoned, I'm going to die. And then I laid down under his feet and to die," he would later tell me.

For the previous six weeks, we had been investigating the agents at the heart of this operation. Now it was finally time to confront one of them. So we sat, in the dark hours of a snowy winter morning, in a quiet Moscow suburb, during the COVID-19 pandemic, waiting for the right moment.

"OK, let's go," said Dasha.

I looked over at Jeff Kehl, the cameraman, who had connected a small Osmo camera to his iPhone and was already streaming live to CNN's headquarters in Atlanta. The precaution meant that if for some reason

Tayakin tried to grab the phone and take it, whatever footage we had shot would already be in-house.

Jeff adjusted his headphones and nodded.

I opened the car door and stepped out into the icy air. Jeff came around to my side of the car to get a shot of me walking in. I looked into the camera. "So we're here now at the home of one of the FSB team, and we are gonna see if he has anything to say to us," I said, then walked toward the main entrance of the apartment block.

Dasha hit the buzzer. I felt a familiar queasy feeling seize my stomach. Confronting a state-sponsored would-be assassin was not the craziest thing I had done in my career, but it was certainly up there. By now we had gone over the plan a dozen times. We had reasoned that it was unlikely for the security services to retaliate against us. It would be too crude, too obvious, especially once our story about how the FSB unit had poisoned Navalny, which would publish in two hours' time, had come out.

Dasha rang the bell several times before we could finally hear a woman's voice.

"Sorry to disturb you, but is Oleg Borisovich there, please," Dasha asked in Russian. There was a moment of silence, then, miraculously, a series of beeps that indicated the woman had opened the front door for us.

The building's sickly green walls and musty smell were familiar to me from the years I'd spent in Russia early in my career. Dasha bounded up the stairs ahead of me. I felt suddenly dizzy. I breathed deeply and willed myself to stay focused.

On the third floor, Dasha motioned to the correct door. I walked toward it in a daze.

He was standing there in a camouflage T-shirt and shorts, presumably his sleeping attire. Immediately I knew it was Tayakin. I had been studying his face for over a month. The bald head, the distinctive birthmark just below his left nostril.

My heart pounded as I began to address him.

"Zdravstvuyte, Oleg Borisovich?" I greeted him as Dasha had, using his patronymic, the polite way to address someone in Russian.

His eyes darted away from me as he spotted Jeff's iPhone. Hastily he pulled the door closed. But he didn't shut it all the way, and I could feel his presence on the other side waiting to see what I wanted. I ploughed on.

"Menya zovut Clarissa Ward, ya rabotayu v CNN. My name is Clarissa Ward, I work for CNN. Can I ask you a couple of questions? Mozhno vam sprashovat—eta vasha commanda otravila Navalny? Was it your team that poisoned Navalny, please?"

The moment the word Navalny came out of my mouth, the door slammed shut.

"Do you have any comment?" I asked.

Silence.

I turned toward the camera. "He doesn't seem to want to talk to us."

We stood waiting another minute.

"Shall we call him?" Dasha suggested. She pulled out her phone and we called his number. Incredibly, he answered.

"Sorry to disturb you, but we are outside your door," she said. The line went dead.

By now it was clear that we were pushing our luck.

"Let's get out of here," I said.

Our doorstep made news around the world. It was one of those rare and thrilling moments as an international correspondent when you are able to confront someone in a position of power with their wrongdoing.

The victory was especially satisfying since breaking through international news during the chaos of the Trump presidency had become particularly challenging. The world's attention was understandably firmly fixed on Washington. Even ISIS and the threat of terrorism, which had been the focus of most post–9/11 international reporting, seemed far less alarming than the destruction being wrought in the White House.

The new enemy was harder to pin down. One of the greatest dangers of this new era was the astonishing volume of misinformation, indeed bald-faced lies, being pumped out on social media by various actors—often by President Trump himself—and the readiness with which they were embraced by a growing number of people.

All around the world the very existence of truth was increasingly being called into question. I was reminded often of a quote by Hannah Arendt: "The ideal subject of totalitarian rule is not the convinced Nazi or the dedicated communist, but the people for whom the distinction between fact and fiction, true and false, no longer exists."

It seemed to me that there had never been a more important time to be a journalist. And yet many of the skills I had honed covering conflict and crises around the world seemed inadequate in trying to break down the torrent of falsehoods.

To that end, I began to work on a series of investigative reports with my colleagues Tim Lister and Sebastian Shukla. Investigative journalism is always both humbling and thrilling. It requires deep concentration and reservoirs of patience seemingly at odds with the frenetic pace of news. A dead end was as likely as any breakthrough. I was acutely aware of how woefully ignorant I was of the ways in which technology could help us uncover truths and hold people accountable. And yet never had I been more excited for the opportunities these tools presented.

As the United States learned during and after the 2016 election, few countries were as bold in their use of misinformation as Russia. Ahead of the 2020 election, Seb, Tim, and I began digging into what the Russians were planning. We worked with a pair of star CNN researchers, Katie Polglase and Gianluca Mezzofiore, as well as academics from Clemson

University. Teams from Facebook and Twitter helped corroborate our findings. For a story of this complexity, the burden of proof was high and collaboration was essential. Our team would gather in an empty office, and I would watch in awe as Gianluca and Katie talked us through their latest findings, scribbled on an increasingly chaotic white board.

Ultimately, we were able to expose the existence of a new Russian troll factory, outsourced to the West African country of Ghana and disguised as a nonprofit, that was actively targeting African American voters with incendiary and divisive content.

After the success of our Ghana investigation, Seb and Tim approached the investigative outfit Bellingcat to see if they might consider working together on a project. I had admired the group's work for years. The collective of both paid and volunteer investigators was founded by a Brit, Eliot Higgins, who had made a name for himself covering the conflict in Syria for years from his laptop in Leicester, in the UK, becoming a munitions expert and using sophisticated open-source techniques to poke holes in the lies of the Syrian regime of Bashar al-Assad. Bellingcat had gone on to identify the pro-Russian separatists in Ukraine who had shot down the Malaysian airliner MH17. But it was exposing the Russian agents who had traveled to Salisbury in the UK to poison former double agent Sergei Skripal that had catapulted the group to the next level.

When digital data could not provide a full picture, Bellingcat turned to the troves of personal information, from flight manifests and passport numbers to cell phone metadata, easily purchased on Russia's black market. These leaked databases from government registries were known as *probiv,* a Russian slang term often translated as "look up." *Probiv* were essentially a by-product of Russia's endemic corruption and lax data protection.

"When the government is trying to cover its wrongdoing," the head of Bellingcat's Russia investigations, Christo Grozev, later told the *Washington Post*, "if the only way to prove the wrongdoing by the state is by acquiring data, then we find that ethically justifiable."

One month after we approached them, we got a call from Christo. "I know who poisoned Navalny," he said. He had our attention.

Navalny had indeed been poisoned with a lethal nerve agent of the Novichok family. If the flight from Tomsk had continued to Moscow, about three hours away, he would almost certainly have died. But quick thinking from the pilot saved him. The flight was diverted to the city of Omsk, where medics quickly administered the life-saving antidote atropine. After two days of back and forth, Navalny, by now in a coma, was allowed to be transported to the Charité hospital in Berlin, where German authorities announced that traces of Novichok had been found in his system. His team members had managed to smuggle some items out of his Tomsk hotel room onto the air ambulance to Berlin—water bottles, a towel, and a toothbrush. Independent laboratories in Sweden and France would later confirm traces of Novichok.

It was the most brazen and audacious assassination attempt I had seen in Russia. And given that the opposition leader Boris Nemtsov had been gunned down on a bridge just across from the Kremlin a few years earlier, the bar was pretty high.

The frustration of a journalist when you are covering these types of horrific crimes is that at a certain level it is impossible to prove who is responsible. Everybody intuitively knows who did it and everybody speculates about it, but for the most part the Russians or the Syrians or whomever it might be can just shrug and say, "We didn't do it." And it's exceptionally hard to prove them wrong.

Tim and Seb flew to Vienna to start working with Christo, listening as he talked through vast amounts of data and brainstorming different possible scenarios with him.

I stayed in London, on maternity leave after the birth of my second son, Caspar. I tried to keep up with their progress during regular calls on an encrypted messaging app, Signal. It was the peak of the pandemic lockdown and doing any work from home with a two-year-old and a six-month-old for company was proving challenging, even with a wonderfully supportive nanny.

One day they called as I was carrying Caspar upstairs for his nap. I sat on the stairs, jogging him on my knee, hunching my shoulder up to my ear to hold the phone in place.

Tim was talking about trips to Sochi that some of the toxins team had taken over the summer. The Black Sea resort town was the de facto headquarters for many in the Kremlin, and President Putin himself, during warmer months and for much of the lockdown.

"So do we have any sense of who Tayakin was there to meet?" I asked.

The pneumatic drill from across the street started up again, vibrating through my head. I took a deep breath and willed myself to tune out the noise. Caspar began wriggling restlessly. I jogged my knee more quickly and made silent silly faces at him, while trying to concentrate on Tim's response.

As if on cue, Caspar began crying. Not the sort of whimper that can be mollified by plugging a pacifier in his mouth, but deep, loud wails.

"I'm sorry, guys," I spluttered.

"Totally understand, go, go," said Tim.

"I'll call you back once I settle him," I promised.

I hung up the phone and looked at Caspar.

"Dude, seriously? Mommy has to do her job."

One week later I was on a plane to Germany to interview Navalny.

During takeoff I felt a tingle of elation at being free from my children and being able to focus on work, followed by a pang of guilt and sadness at missing them. By now I had become used to this barrage of juxtaposing emotions.

In our conversation, I was struck by Navalny's defiance. He was charismatic, with steely blue eyes and a wicked sense of humor. I could see why the Kremlin felt threatened. Navalny had his critics both in the pro-Putin establishment and in the liberal intelligentsia, but no one disputed his relentless and single-minded focus.

Toward the end of the interview, I asked him if he planned to go back to Russia. He didn't hesitate.

"I will do," he answered. I had often heard politicians boldly claim that they were willing to sacrifice themselves for the good of their country. This was different. I knew he was telling the truth and I was struck by his bravery.

He went on to explain his reasoning. He was well aware of the risks. But for him to stay in exile in Europe as a Russian politician meant becoming irrelevant to the Russian public. And, he said, "I would never give Putin such a gift."

Our reporting with Bellingcat was a huge success. President Putin himself even responded to the allegations in his annual press conference, saying that it was normal for the FSB to follow Navalny because he was working with Western intelligence agencies, but that didn't mean they had poisoned him.

Four days later, Navalny fired back, releasing an explosive video of him essentially coaxing a confession out of one of the operatives in a phone call by posing as an aide to a senior member of Russia's national security council. The duped agent revealed how the Novichok was placed in Navalny's underwear.

Despite having humiliated some of the most powerful and dangerous people in Russia, Navalny stayed true to his word and flew back to Moscow on January 17, 2021. He was immediately arrested and, as of this writing, sentenced to more than two and a half years in a penal colony.

On All Fronts

Prologue

---//---

NOVEMBER 2011

DAMASCUS, SYRIA

I looked down at the swell of mourners moving toward me. A coffin was held aloft, touched and blessed by a thousand hands as it swayed down the street. The men carrying it were sweating despite the cool afternoon, pressed in on all sides by chanting protestors. Some of them had caught sight of me and my camera as I had tried to catch up with the cortege and they cleared the way. They wanted their story of resistance told. I struggled through the crowd and jumped onto a flatbed truck a few yards ahead of the coffin, which was draped with the flag of the Syrian revolution (three red stars rather than the two green stars of the official flag).

"I can't screw up this shot, I can't screw up this shot," I whispered to myself.

Lying in the coffin was a sixteen-year-old boy who had been shot by Syrian security forces the day before. He had become the latest martyr of the rapidly growing uprising against the regime of Syrian president Bashar al-Assad.

I took a deep breath and balanced the small point-and-shoot tourism camera on top of the cab of the truck, willing my hands to stay completely still as the coffin approached. I could see the face of the dead boy now, smooth and gray, his eyes closed, his lips parted a fraction. And then he was gone, carried off on the wave of angry mourners.

I was on my own in Damascus on my first assignment as a correspondent for CBS News. As a dual citizen with a UK passport, I had managed to obtain a tourist visa, but my producer had not. And I had no cameraman. I had little experience shooting video and did not underestimate the risks of embarking on such an assignment. A journalist traveling alone could easily be disappeared. But I'd been to Syria many times before, spoke enough Arabic to get around on my own, and was desperate to cover the fast-expanding Syrian uprising, which was reaching a boiling point by that fall of 2011.

Opposition activists had brought me to the sprawling suburb of Douma to cover the funeral. I had been in Damascus for a few days before I had managed to slip away from my hotel and the ever-present secret police to link up with them.

Hundreds of people now poured in from all directions. The women marched together at the back of the procession. Rows and rows of them waved banners with slogans demanding justice and the overthrow of the regime of Bashar al-Assad. Someone started beating a drum, and the crowd hoisted a boy onto a man's shoulders so that he could lead the chant. "Oh, Bashar, you liar," he chanted, "to hell with you and your speech. Freedom is at the door."

"*Yalla irhal, ya Bashar,*" the crowd chanted, clapping rhythmically. "Get out, Bashar!" The chant had become the anthem of the revolution, a revolution gathering strength in the suburbs of Damascus and in Homs and in Hama—and posing a genuine threat to Assad's rule.

I looked over the sea of people, cheering and chanting, hands with cell phones raised in the air to capture the protest and beam it out on social media. The crisp November air crackled with the energy and excitement of their voices. Emboldened by their own daring, they grew louder and louder, the clapping thunderous. My foot tapped along with the beat. It was electrifying.

"Bashar, screw you and screw those who salute you."

These protesters had been waiting for their moment since the Arab Spring unfolded earlier that year—knocking over decades-old dictatorships in Tunisia, Egypt, and Libya.

At the time, Assad had told the *Wall Street Journal*: "This is the Middle East, where every week you have something new." But he had confidently predicted that the maelstrom would not affect his country. Instead, it would spur reform. He would turn out to be spectacularly wrong on both counts.

On March 6, 2011, a group of teenage boys, inspired by the wave of protests spreading across the region, had been arrested for spray-painting *As-Sha'ab yurid isqat an-nizam!* (The people want the downfall of the regime!) on walls in Dara'a, a rundown farming town near the Jordanian border. It was the rallying cry of the revolutions in Egypt and Libya and it brought swift retaliation from local security forces. When the boys were released two weeks later, alive but brutalized, their angry families marched on the governor's house to demand justice. They were met with a hail of bullets. Three protesters were killed. And an uprising was born.

By now a pattern had emerged. The funeral of someone murdered by the regime would then turn into a protest against the regime. Security forces would flood in and open fire, and then the next day there would be an even larger funeral. By that November, there were dozens of such funerals across Syria every day.

I watched the crowd as they chanted "*hurriya, hurriya*" (freedom, freedom) over and over. They waved banners calling for a no-fly zone to prevent Assad from murdering his people. They had seen Western jets save Libyans in Benghazi from Qaddafi's advancing forces months earlier and they believed that the West would do the same for them. How bitterly disappointed they would be.

In that moment, though, I felt giddy with a mixture of excitement and fear. Rallies like these were often targeted by pro-Assad militias, infamous for their thuggish cruelty. Known as *shabiha,* derived from the Arabic word for ghosts, these men wore street clothes and seemingly appeared out of thin air. People lived in fear of them, not just because of the brutal beatings they administered, but because they acted as informants, telling the regime which families were involved with the protest movement. Unlike the military, you never knew if the *shabiha* were there or not. Under these circumstances, talking to a Western reporter could be a death sentence. And yet here in Douma, as soon as people saw that I was a journalist, they wanted to tell their story. I marveled at their bravery.

One man had stopped me in the street as I walked past with my camera. He spoke some English and so I stopped to record an interview.

"Please," he implored, "this is the real Syria." His voice quivered with emotion. "If you come you will see real bodies. They are not stones, they are not toys. They are real bodies."

A group ushered me over to the small graveyard designated for those who had been killed in the uprising. They were called *shuhada*, or martyrs, and there were about sixty of them buried in neat rows. A photograph of a young boy smiled out from one of the headstones. I thought of the man's words—"they are not toys."

Each *shaheed* (singular for martyr) left behind the grieving. The day before the funeral, I had been introduced to a tailor who sat on a stool and wept quietly, his eyes fixed on the ground, as he told me about his son's death. He spoke so softly that I strained to hear the details. His son had attended a protest at his university. Security forces arrived. Bullets were fired. His son . . . He stopped speaking and his body shook softly with sobs. I watched his hands, fidgeting constantly with fear and grief. I wanted to take them in mine and hold them, to put down the camera for a minute and be a human being. But I knew the only way I could help him was to make sure that people heard his story. I prompted him to keep going, "*Wa ba'dayn?* And then?"

His son was shot in the stomach on the university steps, he went on. The hospital didn't want to treat him because they feared punishment from government forces. He bled to death. The man's voice cracked. It was excruciating but I held the shot, held the pause as he wiped his eyes.

IT HAD TAKEN ME WEEKS OF RESEARCH and Skype calls to connect with the Syrian opposition, which by the end of 2011 was being relentlessly harried by the regime. Many activists had already been thrown in jails or simply disappeared; stories of terrible abuse and torture were beginning to circulate.

For the first few days I had played the role of tourist, which is what my visa insisted I must be. Then, one morning, I had put on a headscarf, or *hijab*, and slipped out of the hotel—away from the watchful gaze of the chain-smoking secret policemen. With my blonde hair hidden away, I was suddenly invisible. The difference from the previous days, when everyone seemed to be staring at me, this foreigner, was incredible. I would often wear the *hijab* on subsequent assignments in Syria. From a security stance, it lowered my profile significantly. But it also allowed me to stand on the sidelines quietly and take in a scene as it was unfolding instead of becoming its focus. It's never easy as a television reporter, because carrying a camera inevitably attracts attention. Anything I could do to minimize the distraction of my presence was a plus.

I was careful to ensure I wasn't being followed as I meandered through the streets of the Syrian capital on my way to meet an activist called Hussein. We had been introduced through another Syrian activist online who acted as a coordinator in Damascus. The night before we had stayed up late on Skype, discussing where and when to meet. I agreed I would come and find him at Bab Touma, one of the seven entrances to the old city, the following morning at eight o'clock. For the next five days, I would stay with him.

Hussein's face was round and smiling, with a permanent five-o'clock shadow, and he wore the same sweatpants and plastic sandals every day. He looked like a college student who had pulled one too many all-nighters. He shared his small courtyard house in the old city with a litter of white kittens that climbed over him as we chatted and kneaded their paws on the sofas noisily.

Like many of the activists I would meet that week, Hussein was giddy with the excitement of being part of a revolution. In the evenings, he would take me to meet up with his friends in their apartments. For the most part, they were educated and urbane, a mix of Sunni Muslims, Christians, and Alawites. Later on, the uprising would take on a distinctly Islamist hue, but these were the heady early days that burned with idealism. I would sit with them and watch as they smoked cigarette after cigarette and talked late into the night about what their revolution would look like. They spoke with passion about freedom and democracy and human rights and yet, even then, you could sense that they had little understanding of or exposure to the foundations and institutions needed to build and nurture these ideals.

Hussein introduced me to Razan Zaitouneh, a central figure in the protest movement. She was pale and tall and slim with long, wavy, mouse-colored hair and watery blue eyes and a gap between her front teeth. She chain-smoked when she talked and she rarely smiled. Razan was in a different league from Hussein and his friends. She was a human rights lawyer and had been an activist in Syria for years before the Arab Spring began. She spoke with a blunt confidence and she was savvy enough to know how real the risks were. The Syrian regime had been tracking her movements for some time and she was now living in hiding to avoid arrest.

"Are you scared?" I asked her one day as we drank tea together in Hussein's apartment.

"Who is not?" she replied matter-of-factly, taking a deep drag of her cigarette. She stroked one of the kittens absentmindedly as she talked. "But we have to continue. We decided to start our revolution. This is what we have been dreaming of from a long time ago."

She looked up at me as she stubbed her cigarette out. "*Yalla* [Come on], let's go."

Razan and Hussein had taken me to the funeral in Douma and to the protests that were becoming more and more common on Fridays, the Muslim holy day. Often, the demonstrations would begin seemingly out of nowhere, like a flash mob. A chant would start and a crowd would form, only to melt away again just as quickly, their point made: "We are here and we won't be cowed."

One afternoon, they took me to meet a network of doctors who set up underground field clinics to treat those wounded in the protests. We climbed through a hidden passage in the wall that led to a stockpile of medical equipment. Bandages, antibiotics, syringes, and, most ominously, skin staplers.

The courage and determination of the opposition, which at this stage eschewed violence despite the brutality meted out by the regime, were inspiring. At a demonstration late one night in a Damascus suburb, two young women, their faces covered, sidled up next to me and handed me a note. The handwriting was neat and childish. They had drawn the flag of the Syrian revolution in ballpoint pen at the top left-hand corner of the paper. It said simply, "We don't shed tears for the martyrs, we shed tears for the cowards."

Still, by the end of 2011, protest was starting to give way to resistance, and an armed insurgency was beginning to form. Force could only be met by force. At the funeral in Douma, a man had come up to me carrying a sign. It said: "The Free Syrian Army represents and protects me." The Free Syrian Army, known as the FSA, had formed in July and was made up mostly of Syrian soldiers who had defected after refusing orders to fire on the people.

Razan and Hussein had differing views about the inception of the FSA. Hussein emphasized that the militia's only role was to form a perimeter around the rallies and protect the people: "I guess it's some kind of necessary right now." Razan was much more skeptical, concerned that the group would fundamentally change the spirit of their nonviolent movement. Her concerns turned out to be prophetic.

It was the beginning of the militarization of the conflict, one that Bashar al-Assad welcomed. He liked to claim that Syrians and the outside world had a binary choice: him or terrorism. And in a move of callous calculation, that spring he had released thousands of imprisoned jihadis—they would graft themselves onto the insurgency and eventually consume it.

Late one night, Hussein offered to arrange for me to meet members of the Free Syrian Army. While some FSA fighters had been interviewed in Homs, none had done an on-camera interview with a Western journalist in Damascus—largely because very few foreign journalists had managed to get into Damascus, with the exception of a handful of Europeans who had visas from the regime. But they had minders assigned to watch their every move and weren't able to get near the protests. I knew I had a singular opportunity—and I wanted to see how real this armed resistance was.

Hussein drove me back to Douma, and from there I got into another car with a man who apologized before blindfolding me. He explained that he had to make sure I didn't know the location of the safe house where the interview would take place. Hussein was not allowed to come with me.

I willed myself not to panic as the car twisted along winding back roads. I had no idea where we were going. After about twenty minutes, we stopped, and the cool air rushed to my face as the car door opened. Someone helped guide me inside a house, where my blindfold was removed. Standing before me were about a dozen men in military fatigues, carrying AK-47s and RPGs (rocket propelled grenades), their faces covered by checkered scarves known as *keffiyehs*.

My mouth felt dry. I was all too aware of how much of a target they were—and I half expected a bunch of Syrian military commandos to come bursting through the door at any minute, guns blazing.

I cleared my throat and introduced myself while trying to work out how I was going to shoot this interview. The frame needed to be wide enough to get all the men in it as well as me. How I wished for a cameraman and a tripod. In the end, I gave the camera to the man who had driven me there, and he balanced it on a pile of books on a side table. This would not be a beautifully produced piece of television.

"We are fighting those who made our children orphans and our wives widows," the commander began.

I asked if he wasn't concerned that by militarizing the conflict, more people were going to get hurt.

"We didn't choose to go to war," he said. "It was imposed upon us to protect our people and our honor." He sounded stiff and formal. The commander claimed that his men had carried out attacks on military targets around the capital, the heart of Assad's power base, seizing weapons along the way.

I couldn't get a sense of how this contingent of men fit into the hierarchy of the FSA, which was an early clue that there wasn't really a coherent structure to the organization. Any group could make a banner and upload videos to YouTube, declaring themselves members of the Free Syrian Army—but it didn't mean there was communication and coordination between the groups. The Islamist movements that would eventually subsume the insurgency were more disciplined, more ruthless.

As we were finishing the interview, one of the fighters beckoned me over. He was holding up a passport-sized photo of a smiling little boy with chubby cheeks and curly brown hair, his son.

"This is what we are fighting for," he told me with an air of urgency. "So that he can have a better future." His eyes bored directly into mine, as if to say, "Do you get it now? Do you understand?" I nodded slowly. His sincerity was obvious. But it was also clear that the fighters didn't have a real strategy and they were up against an unrelenting enemy.

After a week in Damascus, I wanted to try to get to Homs, where the crackdown had been at its most brutal. I messaged my bosses in New York. "No," came the immediate reply. "It sounds like you have great stuff, don't push your luck."

It's easy, as a journalist, to spend time in a dangerous place and become desensitized to the risks, to want more, to never think that what you have is enough. You rely on experienced colleagues who can check your ambitions. I remember the great CBS reporter Allen Pizzey quoting an editor with the Reuters news agency in Africa who would summon his reporters back from the front lines of far-flung war zones with a simple telegram: "Cannot file if dead."

In addition to the lure of a better story, in those early days of the Arab Spring there was also a hope that a better reality was actually possible. That change was within reach. I hoped that my work could in a small way aid that cause, but in Syria I would come to realize that the idea of "making a difference" in journalism is as seductive as it is dangerous. It encourages hubris and shifts the focus from the actual job. The reality is we are not there to solve the problem, we are there to illuminate it.

On my last night in Damascus, a blackout blanketed the city, one of many small signs that all was not well in the capital. Hussein and Razan and I sat in the darkness in his living room, the glow of Razan's cigarette lighting up her face a little when she took a drag. I thought back to that morning when I had asked her if she had a message for Bashar al-Assad.

"Leave!" she said simply. "Leave now because you know that you will leave at the end but with more victims, with more suffering of the people. So just leave and leave us to start our new future, our new country. You got enough of our blood."

But Assad didn't leave. And within two years of that trip to Damascus, Hussein would be imprisoned and Razan would be kidnapped by armed men. Neither have been heard from since.

One

By the age of eight, I had gone through eleven nannies. Michelle from Singapore was fired because my mother thought she was working for a phone-sex network. Theresa from South Africa was let go after putting my pet bird, Orchid, out in the garden during a snowstorm because he was chirping too loudly. British Debbie started dating my tennis instructor in Florida and then crashed my mother's BMW—that was the end of her.

Often, they simply weren't there anymore when I got home from school. But their short tenures never bothered me too much. I was always excited when the new one arrived.

I was fortunate enough to have both a privileged and a thoroughly unconventional childhood, one that probably made me allergic to routine. It may not sound like the training for a foreign correspondent but it taught me to be adaptable, self-reliant, and curious.

My petite, beautiful, American mother, Donna, has irrepressible energy and a strong opinion on just about everything. In another era, she might have been called "formidable." While pregnant with me, she insisted that she would soon be the mother of a son, whom she referred to as "my Rupert." There was some surprise when I was born on January 31, 1980, at Queen Charlotte's Hospital in London.

My father, Rodney, is a handsome, six-foot-six-inch, British former investment banker who rowed for Cambridge and attended Yale Law School. A workaholic, he is brilliant and charming and also kind and gentle. Both of them were devoted to their careers, and after we moved from London to New York they separated. Later, when I was fourteen, my dad moved to Hong Kong, where he lived for more than twenty years.

For most of my childhood, my parents had other partners, but it was always assumed somehow that these relationships were secondary to the profound bond that they shared and to our small but strong family unit. Divorce never even came up and they are still married to this day.

My mother and I lived in a string of townhouses on the Upper East Side of Manhattan that she would buy and gut and then do up and sell. They were houses not necessarily designed for children. "Don't touch the walls," my mother would yell as I streaked up and down the stairs.

She worked around the clock but did her best to fill my days with ice-skating, ballet, and horseback riding. Still, as an only child, I spent huge expanses of time on my own, rattling around the top floors of New York townhouses. I would spend hours acting out improvised dramatic scenes from television shows like *Divorce Court*, in which I would play all the parts. ("He's my son, goddammit, and you'll have to kill me before I will share custody with that man." "Well, maybe if you weren't so busy sleeping with your boss, Lydia, we wouldn't be in this position." "ORDER, ORDER.")

When I was eight years old, my mother suddenly announced that we were moving back to London. She had been mugged twice on the Upper East Side in the space of a year and she was sick of New York, she said, though I suspect a series of toxic love affairs with men who made her cry a lot were the real reason. She insisted my life would not change at all. My father traveled regularly to London anyway, so I would still see him. I would simply transfer from one elite private girls' school to another.

The doyenne of my London life was my grandmother on my father's side: Granny Greegs, as I called her. At six feet one inch she was an intimidating character, to say the least (though I pity the man who dared ask her how tall she was). She loved my father with a passion, he was her darling boy. Sensing in my mother a woman who was similarly brilliant and complicated, she had taken an immediate disliking to her.

Granny Greegs was a classically trained pianist who spoke four languages fluently and had written seven novels, at least as many plays, and several volumes of poetry—all unpublished. My grandfather, John, was a senior officer in the colonial service, and the two of them had lived in British Somalia and Singapore for most of my father's childhood. In Singapore, my grandfather had fallen in love with his Chinese secretary, Mavis, and Granny Greegs had accepted this as long as he agreed not to ask for a divorce.

My mother told me that the first time she met Granny in London was at the flat where all three of them lived in Warwick Square. A fence had been erected down the middle of the apartment to separate Granny's living quarters from Mavis and Grandpa's. It was an unusual arrangement, to say the least, but for years they got along, as long as Mavis agreed to cook a big curry for Granny's guests when she was entertaining.

Given such a setup, it is perhaps not altogether unsurprising that, years later, Mavis left my grandfather and went back to Singapore. As he grew old and frail, he begged Granny for a reconciliation. "Oh, Vivienne," he sighed, "I want to die in your arms." "Well, John," she retorted, "it's a shame you didn't want to live in them."

At least once a week I would walk around the corner to the duplex that my grandmother shared with a long-suffering young Polish woman called Teresa (who was part protégé, part companion, part dogsbody) and an endless stream of cats and dogs with names like "Delphinium" and "Ksenia" and "Nefertiti." She would sit in an armchair next to the grand piano and I would come in and kiss her on both cheeks. She would squeal with genuine excitement, "Helloooo, my DARLING girl, now sit down and tell me everything."

After about two minutes, she would interrupt me. "My darling, has your mother been feeding you? You look positively bilious. You need some beef tea. TERESA! Bring us some beef tea."

The words would induce instant nausea. It was a simple recipe of hot water with a teaspoon of an unctuous sticky beef extract called Bovril. A hangover from the days of rationing in the First World War, it was positively disgusting. Fortunately, when I was about fourteen, beef tea was replaced by stiff gin and tonics, followed by not-so-subtle probing about my mother. "Of course, she's always been very difficult, how are you coping? You can tell Granny Greegs anything, I won't breathe a word."

Granny had endless enthusiasm for all my passions and curiosities. I was interested in the theater, so she took me to see plays and arranged for me to go backstage. I was interested in writing, so she gave me notebooks and pens and would tell me that my stories were the most wonderful she had ever read. She even supported my efforts as a sculptor. One year I gave her a "Viking mug" that we had made in school. It was the ugliest thing imaginable, but she kept it on the mantelpiece for years and declared it "the most splendid mug" she had ever come across. This was in stark contrast to my mother, who would invariably find ways to hide things I made for her in class or put them back in my room. "I'm sorry, but what can I do with a chartreuse mug when the chintz in my room is blue," she would explain, or, "We only use antique Scandinavian decorations on the tree, darling, you know that."

At the age of ten, I was sent to a preparatory boarding school called Godstowe, about an hour outside of London. I felt huge trepidation about being sent away, not least because my father went to boarding school when he was seven and was utterly miserable (he went home only once a year on a steamer to see his parents in Singapore).

My mother believed that boarding school had left him and an entire generation of Englishmen emotionally damaged. "Your father had a blankie when I met him," she would say. "They're all very repressed." Yet she overcame this belief in order that I might receive what she deemed the best education possible. So she packed up the car and drove me to Buckinghamshire.

I have the photos of my first day at Godstowe and they still make me weep. A tall, gangly girl with blonde hair and buck teeth is wearing a long, itchy, gray skirt and a red V-neck sweater. She has one hand on her hip and is smiling at the camera confidently. What you can't see is how hard she is trying not to cry, the lump at the back of her throat, the determination not to let mother down. I didn't understand why I was being sent away, why my mother didn't want to have me at home, why I didn't seem to make her happy. Was it because I refused to wear skirts and hated that itchy, woolly Austrian cardigan she bought me? "It's Tyrolean and it's very chic," she would tell me, exasperated.

That night, I waited for the girls in my dormitory to fall asleep before letting myself weep into my pillow. My father had told me that whenever I was feeling homesick, I should think of all the fun things we were going to do on my next weekend out. I closed my eyes and imagined him coming to pick me up, driving in the car back to London and playing word games as we always had, and going to eat zabaglione at our favorite Italian restaurant together. Eventually, I fell asleep.

It didn't help that I had little in common with most of my school-mates. They would look on quizzically as my accent swung wildly between American and British English. (It is like being bilingual but in an utterly useless way.) The girls at Godstowe were crazy about horses and spent their vacations doing wholesome educational things with their families. I was more interested in getting my ears pierced. I spent most vacations in the US with my mother, singing along to pop hits like Jon Secada's "Just Another Day" or Michael Bolton's "Time, Love & Tenderness" as we drove to the mall. Still, by now I was becoming adept at learning to fit in with almost anyone, anywhere. So I bought books about horses and rode in gymkhanas and banished my American accent unless I was in the US.

Letters were the only thing that made the Godstowe years bearable. My father was a terrific correspondent. No matter how hard he was working or how much he was traveling, every week I would find a fat envelope stuffed into my pigeonhole. At night, I would take my torch and pore over his long letters under my duvet. Granny Greegs also sent regular missives, detailing the shenanigans of her various animals.

After two years at Godstowe, I was accepted into Wycombe Abbey, one of the top girls' schools in the country. On my last night before leaving Godstowe, I snuck into the shower after lights out and dyed my hair bright orange. As a punishment, I was not allowed to attend my own graduation ceremony, which was just fine by me. Instead, I sat in the sanatorium with the Sister drinking milky tea and watching Australian soap operas and relishing my act of defiance.

When my mother picked me up later that day, she looked displeased but not so much about my act of gross disobedience. "Really, Clarissa," she chided, "orange is not your color."

I would not dispute for a moment that I had a very privileged upbringing, one that threatened to distort any perception of the real world. The only form of discipline from my parents was that I had to get straight A's. And yet, at the time, I never thought of myself as particularly privileged because as a thirteen-year-old, I had no appreciation of what privilege was.

Instead, I was consumed by the sort of angst suffered by every pubescent girl, which was only aggravated by my mother. I seemed to embarrass her and she constantly embarrassed me. She would drag me along to lunch parties, muttering, "For God's sake, put some concealer and blusher on, you look cadaverous"—and then, as I stood sulking, would whisper loudly to her friends, "She's upset because her breasts haven't come in yet."

When I was allowed to leave boarding school at the age of sixteen, I had a well-developed tendency for mutiny.

I became close friends with a ridiculously handsome boy from my new London day school, who was the opposite of everything I had known. Aidan lived in public housing and wore a tweed cap. He was whip smart and maniacally left wing, with a book by or about Karl Marx always tucked under his arm. He drank too much and would tell me angrily that it was "a fucking disgrace how ignorant" I was about the world. But unlike most teenage boys, he was at least interesting and authentic. Instead of smoking cigarettes in cafés along the King's Road with my posh girlfriends, I spent more and more time sitting in smelly old pubs in less savory parts of London with him.

Seeing the city through his eyes, it suddenly became rich and vibrant, full of different communities with unique stories and experiences. We would argue loudly for hours as he set about shattering the fragile ideas I had formulated about the world. Then he would kiss me angrily against a wall before catching the night bus home.

I knew I wanted to go to the States for college. I had long bristled at the way Brits would roll their eyes if I showed too much enthusiasm or ambition and comment on how "American" I was. And I had come to loathe England's insidious class system. It was difficult to escape your bubble or to have a conversation that went deeper than banter.

I was often reminded of the line from Evelyn Waugh's *Brideshead Revisited*: "Charm is the great English blight. It does not exist outside these damp islands. It spots and kills anything it touches. It kills love; it kills art."

I tried to explain this to my mother, who would just roll her eyes and say, "Why do you have to be so intense? It's tedious."

I was accepted at Yale, where I studied comparative literature and was immersed in the more superficial side of self-discovery. I dyed my hair pink and pierced my tongue and belly button. I smoked copious amounts of pot and devoured Russian novels and French new-wave cinema. I acted in student films and published a magazine with my friends. It featured a satirical social column written by Granny Greegs under the nom de plume "Lady Lavinia Lunge." My idea of being daring at college was attending "naked parties" where you disrobed completely at the door and put your clothing in a paper bag until you left.

And then, in the first week of the first semester of my senior year, everything changed. I was in a deep sleep when my best friend, Ben, called me.

"Ward, you gotta get over here," he said. "A plane just crashed into the World Trade Center."

The apartment I shared with two other girls didn't have a television, so I threw on some clothes and walked over to Ben's. By the time I arrived, there were about a dozen people crowded silently around his TV. I stood over them, struggling to fully absorb what I was seeing on the screen. Both towers were engulfed in flames.

The next few days were spent in a kind of fugue state, trying to get through to my mother, who was alone in her apartment on Manhattan's Upper East Side, trying to get through to my close friends studying at Columbia, trying to get down to New York from New Haven, trying to get near the crash site to make it real. Every other waking hour was spent in front of the TV watching the news.

I felt a sense of profound shame that I had not been more engaged, that I had not been paying proper attention to what was happening in the world, that I had been so self-absorbed.

I also felt a sense of purpose and clarity that I had never experienced before. It sounds presumptuous but I knew I had to go to the front lines, to hear the stories of people who lived there and tell them to the people back home. In the process, I hoped to give people over "there" a sense of what people "here" were really like. I wanted to get to the root of the miscommunication that was fueling this insanity, this mutual dehumanization. We didn't understand them and they didn't understand us. That much was clear.

I thought back to one night in high school when my best friend, Chiara, and I sat in her parents' bathroom, high as kites, talking about what we wanted to do with our lives. Chiara was half Spanish and half a mixture of Italian and American. She had grown up in the UK, and we shared a sense of being comfortable everywhere but not quite belonging anywhere.

"I can't create," I explained. "I am not going to write novels or make films or be a great artist. I'm a vessel." I grasped for the right words in my altered state. "I can understand people and convey their ideas. I'm a communicator," I said finally, triumphantly.

In the sober morning light, it was all a bit abstract but it had still felt like an epiphany. And in the weeks after September 11th, the only thing that seemed important or relevant was to communicate.

Of course, I was more than a little fuzzy on the details of "where" I needed to go and who "they" were exactly. There was a significant amount of hubris at play and it was going to be a steep learning curve.

I had no sense at the time of what conflict reporting actually entailed. I didn't understand that straddling different worlds would require taking a wrecking ball to much of what I thought I knew about life, politically and personally. That gradually, but unmistakably, there would be a smashing.

A smashing of my preconceived notions, a smashing of what I thought I knew about history, about myself. I didn't realize that I would have my heart broken in a hundred different ways, that I would lose friends and watch children die and grow to feel like an alien in my own skin. I didn't understand that the privilege of witnessing history came at a price. But in that moment, only one thing mattered to me: I had a calling.

Two

I bombarded media organizations with applications supported by a sparse résumé. I was far from alone in seeking an entrée into journalism. While thousands of Americans had signed up for military service after the 9/11 attacks, many others were inspired to find out more about a world that had changed overnight.

I chose television primarily because I was drawn to its social nature. I loved the idea of working with a big team and collaborating. Writing for a newspaper seemed so solitary. It reminded me of the many nights I had stayed up late in the Cross Campus Library trying to crash a twenty-page paper.

One advantage I did have over other contenders in my search for an entry-level journalism job was my facility with languages. Since my first French lessons at age eight, languages just made sense to me. By now, I spoke French and Italian, as well as basic Spanish and Russian. In the end, though, it was my mother's savvy and a routine visit to the dentist that led to my first gig in journalism. By a stroke of serendipity, my mother's dentist in Palm Beach was also the dentist of CNN's Moscow bureau chief, Jill Dougherty. I was introduced to Dougherty and then was overjoyed to be offered an unpaid internship with CNN in Moscow beginning in September.

I had studied Russian literature at university and had always been fascinated by the country and its history. My father had given me a copy of Tolstoy's *Anna Karenina* when I was a teenager. I quickly fell in love with both the writing and Anna as a character. I remember telling my parents over dinner, with tears in my eyes, that I was devastated by Anna's suicide.

My mother had taken a sip of her cocktail and waved her hand dismissively.

"You have to toughen up, Clarissa. Anna was a slut."

The Russia bug stuck, however, and at seventeen I went on a school trip to Moscow and St. Petersburg. It was a shock—the Russian economy was in freefall during the chaos and gangsterism of the late 1990s. Boris Yeltsin had been elected Russian president after the collapse of the Soviet Union. His heavy drinking and lack of any consistent policies turned Russia's experiment with democracy into a nightmare for many of its citizens. We were aghast at the poverty and desperation we saw: old women shivering in the snow while begging for a few kopeks, pensioners who had nothing to eat but macaroni and ketchup. Years later, a male colleague bragged to me that in the 1990s you could get laid in Russia for a bar of chocolate. The casual misogyny of the observation stuck in my throat.

The grim desperation of Moscow made a deep impression, but so did the resilience of the Russians. Our school group consisted of Chiara and me and a bunch of fifteen-year-old boys who were constantly getting accosted by prostitutes in the bathroom of our hotel—a hideous Soviet-era block called the Rossiya. On every floor there was a "snack bar" where you could go and get pickled herring with boiled potatoes and vodka. Chiara and I would sit there for hours in the evenings watching people as we drank vodka and smoked cigarettes in our newly purchased fur hats. One night, a sweaty man with a round face and a chipped tooth took out a violin and began playing what sounded like folk songs. The snack bar quickly filled with people singing and clapping. It was a beautiful interlude of escapism.

Before I could reacquaint myself with Moscow as a freshly minted graduate, I had a summer to fill. My father was a friend of one of the producers on *Kill Bill*, the Quentin Tarantino movie then being shot in Beijing. Both fascinated by movies and eager to see China, I asked if she could find a role for me on set.

Based on my height and hair color, it was determined I would be Uma Thurman's stand-in. Essentially, my job was to pretend to be Uma while they tinkered with the lighting and perfected the camera moves. Once everything was just right, Uma would come on set and I would sit back down.

Initially, it was thrilling. Quentin was brilliant and warm and friendly and his enthusiasm was infectious. But the job soon became quite tedious. We worked long days, often fourteen hours, and I was never able to venture more than a few yards from the set. It was my first time in China and I longed to be out of the studio, visiting the Forbidden City and Tiananmen Square. Instead, I spent six days a week on a set that was designed to look like a restaurant in Tokyo.

Sundays were my one day to get out. I spent hours walking around Beijing, marveling at the sea of bicycles—the main mode of transport. I would lose myself in the maze of alleyways, called *hutongs,* where people lived in traditional old houses surrounding a courtyard, called *siheyuan.* I would watch the men, shirts pulled up over pot bellies in a style that was thought to be cooling, as they crouched on the side of the street playing dice games and chain-smoking Zhongnanhai cigarettes.

The city was not charming or beautiful but it had grit and character. Walking around, I rarely saw another white face. China was certainly opening up, but expats still gravitated toward Hong Kong and Shanghai rather than Beijing. And if you were an adventurous eater, the food was incredible. Occasionally, the martial arts team on the set would take me along to lunch and watch with glee as I gamely ate duck tongues and chicken feet.

While I enjoyed getting to know the crew, on set it was apparent that Hollywood operated by its own rules and that those rules were written by powerful men. The women seemed largely ornamental.

One day, we were setting up for a scene in which Uma Thurman's character is choked by a meteor hammer, essentially a long chain with a spiked iron ball on each end that offers myriad ways to inflict bodily harm. Tarantino wrapped the chain around my neck and then stood back behind the camera and began pulling on it. I could feel the blood thudding in my ears as the chain tightened around my neck. I looked down the length of it at Tarantino.

"Just relax," he said. He was clearly enjoying himself.

The chain was now tight enough to be uncomfortable. He looked into my eyes searchingly, smiling, as if to challenge me: *Can you go further?*

"Enough," I spluttered, and tried to pull the chain free of my neck. Quentin laughed and let go of the chain. "Ladies and gentlemen, give her a round of applause," he joked. I coughed and laughed shyly.

If anyone else found the episode uncomfortable, they certainly didn't show it. QT was the center of everyone's universe, breathlessly referred to by all, including myself, as a "genius."

One night, my father's friend, the producer, told me Quentin wanted to have dinner with me.

"That's odd," I told her. "I'm often at dinner or drinks with him and the crew."

"I think maybe he wants to have dinner alone . . ." she said.

"OK . . . I think he's awesome but not in that way."

She looked peeved.

"I'm not saying you have to have sex with him!"

I was confused. "Right, but I don't want to make out with him, either."

"Fine," she said tersely.

The fact that she was clearly annoyed disturbed me, but the issue never came up again and I continued to get along well with Quentin. It was clear to me that plenty of other girls working on the set had been given similar invitations and perhaps some had accepted. Frankly, I was just relieved that he hadn't propositioned me directly.

Tarantino's obsession with Uma Thurman was well known to everyone on the set. She used to joke that he was punishing her for marrying Ethan Hawke by making sure her character "got the shit beat out of her in every scene." At the time, most of us just laughed. But many years later, Thurman accused Tarantino of having been abusive to her during the film's production. Uma revealed that while they were shooting in Mexico, Tarantino had pressured her into driving a faulty stunt car, resulting in a crash that left her with injuries to her neck and knees.

Toward the end of the summer, Quentin invited me to join them for the second half of production in LA. I was, he conceded, the worst stand-in he had worked with because I always had my nose in a book and never remembered the blocking of each scene. To be honest, I think he enjoyed the novelty of having a stand-in who didn't want to be a movie star. I briefly toyed with the idea. But it was time to go to Moscow and start my CNN internship.

The CNN office in Moscow was not a particularly invigorating place. The bureau kept itself busy covering President Vladimir Putin's consolidation of power, but there was a sense that the Russia story wasn't hot anymore. Afghanistan and the Middle East were the places to be.

The bureau chief, Jill Dougherty, who had given me the internship, spoke impeccable Russian and was friendly but away much of the time. In addition to Jill, there was a young American producer who was trying to get on television and who reminded me of a paunchy frat boy. I coordinated his first live shot for him when no one else was around. It was a shambles: rambling, inarticulate, incoherent. But it was also reassuring. If they allowed this incompetent on television, then one day it might be me.

I had no idea what I was supposed to be doing with my days, so I started frantically searching for stories that might be of interest to an American network. I had my first win when I pitched a piece on a new Russian board game available for kids called "Capture the Terrorist." For the most part, though, the news was painfully slow and I spent an awful lot of time offering to make people tea and practicing Russian verbs at my desk.

Away from work, there were acres of solitude. I lived in one of the famous Seven Sisters, the huge buildings shaped like wedding cakes that Stalin had ordered built in the 1940s to compete with the United States. I had no friends and spent my time wandering around in the snow or people watching under the jaundiced light of the Moscow metro, listening to Russian singers like Zemfira and Viktor Tsoi and reading depressing poems by Anna Akhmatova, while secretly feeling comforted that I was having such an authentic Russian experience.

I longed for the evenings when, somewhere high in one of the Seven Sisters, I would curl up and watch *Law & Order* reruns, which aired on the Hallmark channel in English at 9 p.m. It was my only connection with home. To this day, the distinctive guitar twangs of the theme song make my heart ache.

The one huge story that fall broke as I was in the sky on my way back to London for a short break. Chechen terrorists stormed a Moscow theater and took hundreds of people hostage. Russian special forces had pumped a mysterious gas into the theater to put everyone to sleep before storming it. But they had miscalculated the effect of the dosage in that space and neglected to tell first responders what the antidote was. By the time I got back to Moscow, all the attackers and more than one hundred and twenty-five innocent theatergoers were dead.

Three different CNN crews had been flown in from Jerusalem, London, and Johannesburg to tell the story of this tragedy on the network. I did whatever I could to be of service—fetching tea, printing out the latest news wires, calling the desk in Atlanta, CNN's hub, to coordinate live shots. This, I knew, was what I wanted to do with my life.

BACK IN NEW YORK, my internship completed, CNN told me I would need to wait a few months before they could hire me full time. A few months? Were they crazy? I would be twenty-three by then. I was desperate to get my foot in the door somewhere.

I went to an interview with Fox News on a whim. Less than twenty-four hours later, I got a call back.

"So, we can offer you $27,000 plus overtime, but you have to start out on the overnights."

The "overnight desk" assistant's job at Fox News was about as low as it gets on the totem pole of journalism, but it was mine.

I wasn't entirely comfortable with Fox's obvious editorial bias but I was in a hurry. And the Fox job was Route One to Baghdad. There was no more exciting story on earth. It was January 2003 and America was poised to invade one of the most important countries in the Middle East.

The hours were midnight to nine a.m. It was brutal, but working the overnights meant you were directly responsible for dealing with the Baghdad bureau as they started their day. I would spend hours every night messaging back and forth with the producers there. I imagined them sitting in the bureau, smoking cigarettes and drinking cups of strong Arabic coffee, as they argued about the lead story. It seemed impossibly glamorous—particularly from the vantage point of the overnight desk, where the delivery of cheese fries from the local diner was the highlight of the shift.

My colleagues on the overnights were an eclectic mix of nerds, misfits, and underachievers. They liked to tease me about going to an Ivy League college and would shake their heads and laugh when I said I wanted to be a foreign correspondent. "Pretty damn confident, aren't we, Yale?"

Of course, I wasn't actually confident at all, just driven and desperate to get out of that depressing newsroom in the basement of 1211 Avenue of the Americas.

As a sign of intent, I had started taking Arabic lessons. Twice a week, I would finish my shift in the newsroom and go straight to see Alia, my Berlitz instructor. Alia was a force. Originally from Yemen, she was the mother of seven children. When she first moved to Bay Ridge, Brooklyn, in the mid '90s, she wore the flowing black gown, known as an *abaya*, that is common in Yemen. But the kids in the neighborhood had shouted at her, calling her "Batman," so she now opted for Western clothes (a long skirt and button-down shirt) and the *hijab*.

When we first began our lessons, she looked at the Berlitz textbook with horror. "I can't teach you this," she said about the Modern Standard Arabic curriculum. "You need to learn Classical Arabic, which you can use in any country in the Middle East."

Classical Arabic, known as *fusha* (pronounced fus-ha), is the formal language taught in schools and used in the media, but it is not what people speak in their homes. It has the advantage of being understood in most of the roughly twenty predominantly Arabic-speaking countries. On the downside, the grammar is a nightmare and people giggle when you speak it because you sound like you're reciting Shakespeare (as I later found out). Still, I figured Alia knew what she was talking about and we threw the Berlitz textbook in the trash.

I loved the lilting flow of *fusha* Arabic. "*Ana ureed an athhab illa mak-tabah law samaht*," I would repeat with flourish (I want to go to the library please). Later on, my Arabic vocabulary would move in a very different direction. I would learn essential words like:

> *shazaya*: shrapnel
> *sarookh*: rocket
> *qunbula*: bomb
> *is-haal*: diarrhea

Alia was the first practicing Muslim I really became friends with. I knew plenty of people who were born Muslim, but none who were devout, wore the *hijab*, prayed five times a day, and abstained from alcohol. She loved talking to me about her passion for her faith.

I will never forget Alia showing me how she performed *wudu*, the ritual ablution required before prayer, in the ladies' room at Berlitz. I watched as she methodically washed her right hand three times, then the left, then rinsed her mouth, her nose, her face. There was no sound other than the water gently running and her whispering "*Bismillah ar rahman ar raheem*" (In the name of God, the most compassionate, the most merciful). She rhythmically washed her forearms three times—first the right, then the left—and then ran her wet hands over her hair and ears. Finally, she lifted her right foot into the sink and rinsed that three times. A French teacher walked in as she washed her left foot in the sink and looked disdainful. Alia ignored her.

Later, when we continued lessons in my apartment, she would take a break from class to pray and I would watch, quietly mesmerized by her graceful movements.

Alia was not afraid to ask personal questions. One day, she was explaining the difference to me between the words "*bint*" (meaning a young girl, implicitly a virgin) and "*sayyida*" (meaning a lady, married).

"*Enti bint aw sayyida?*" she asked me, Are you a *bint* or a *sayyida*? I didn't really know how to answer the question. Alia knew I wasn't married but I wasn't exactly a virgin, either.

"Well," I ventured hesitantly. "I am not a *sayyida* because I am not married. But I am not a *bint* either . . . because, um, well, I have a boyfriend."

Alia's eyes widened and she nodded grimly. Never in my life had I wanted to be a virgin so badly.

"But I hope we will get married," I said, trying to soften the blow.

I did have a serious boyfriend. Maxim, or Max as everyone called him, was a bright and handsome Belorussian who was a few classes below me at Yale, though we hadn't known each other in college. He had gone to boarding school in the UK and then to college in the US. We shared a love of Russian poetry and Arcade Fire and bonded over the acute sense of loneliness that we had both felt as children.

Alia appeared to be somewhat comforted by the mention of marriage and she asked to see a picture of Max.

"He looks like a little boy," she exclaimed as I showed her one of the two of us. "Where is his beard?!"

We both laughed.

WHAT WAS MOST STRIKING ABOUT ALIA was her generosity, a trait among Arab women I would marvel at many times. She would usually arrive at my apartment laden with Tupperware full of delicious Yemeni food. Often, she would invite me to her apartment to meet her family and eat with them. The first time I went, she had set up a little chair and table with a knife and fork and plate for me. The rest of the family ate on the floor together and used their hands. I laughed when I saw the table and sat with them on the floor instead, but I was touched that she wanted to make me feel comfortable. It was a generous gesture of the sort that I would often encounter in the Arab world.

Scarcely had I begun the overnight shift at Fox than I began to pester my boss about going to Baghdad as a producer. He was intensely awkward, with a nervous tic that caused him to clear his throat every few seconds. It made him sound like a car refusing to start.

"You have no in-the-field experience, ahem," he would say without looking up from his computer.

"But I'm a quick learner and I'm studying Arabic in my spare time. Just give me a chance, I won't let you down," I pleaded.

An irritated sigh, then the inevitable response. "Clarissa, ahem, I am not going to talk to you about this again, ahem. No."

I felt frustrated that my work wasn't going in the direction I wanted. Meanwhile, my preoccupation with getting to the Middle East had created a rift between Max and me. He didn't like the idea of me running around war zones, and it was becoming increasingly clear that we wanted different things from life. After we broke up, I spent months walking around in a fog of sadness and confusion.

Around the same time, my beloved Granny Greegs passed away. At eighty-five, she had lived a full life but that did little to soften the blow. I kept thinking of her distinctive smell—a combination of Imperial Leather soap, perfumed silk, and wet dog. I thought of mornings at her cottage in Dorset when I would crawl into bed with her and her motley crew of animals to drink tea and discuss the rabbit at the bottom of the garden (which she swore to me engaged in long conversations with her).

There were so many things I had wanted her to see me achieve, so much I wanted to share with her. I could just imagine her excitement if I managed to become a reporter: "How splendid, you brilliant girl!!!" She had loved me in a way that I felt I might never be loved again—not for who I might become but for who I was.

Then one Thursday morning in late spring, my boss looked up at me through his glasses and cleared his throat.

"Clarissa, ahem. I may have a rotation for you in Baghdad this summer, ahem."

I was ecstatic.

"Thank you so much. You won't regret this. I promise you I will work my guts out. Can I please give you a hug?!"

"Ahem, no, that won't be necessary, thank you."

In the end, it was not my entreaties that wore Fox down but the stark reality that, by the summer of 2005, no one wanted to go to Baghdad anymore. It was getting too dangerous, and the heat of the Iraqi summer was unbearable. Plus the audience had begun to tire of a story that seemed to be on repeat: suicide bombings, American casualties, and offensives in places with unpronounceable names.

Aside from the few shoots I went on during my internship, I had no experience in the field and I had never been to a war zone. Such details seemed unimportant, both to me and to the chain of command. After attending a hostile environments training course, where I learned how to tie a tourniquet and duck for cover if there was incoming fire, I was pronounced good to go.

Three

They called the landing the corkscrew. No gentle glide path but an abrupt series of tight downward circles to avoid being hit by missiles from below. The insurgency against the occupation of Iraq had gained both momentum and some frightening weapons, including missiles capable of hitting aircraft at several thousand feet.

It was Friday, June 10, 2005, two years and three months since the US-led invasion of Iraq to oust Saddam Hussein. I was twenty-five years old and landing in Baghdad for the first time.

I grabbed both armrests and tried some deep breathing.

"It's too late to change your mind. If this plane is going to be shot out of the sky, there's nothing you can do about it now."

Later trips to Baghdad would bleed into a hazy soup of memories: the monotony of the landscape and the food; the military embeds, where tedium would be suddenly interrupted by mortars landing or the reverberation of a suicide bombing; the nights spent drinking and idly speculating about how it would all end. But I remember every moment of that first day.

I was one of only two women on the flight. Most of the other passengers were tattooed Westerners wearing desert boots and cargo pants.

They had leathery, tanned faces and all of them seemed to be wearing the same Oakley ballistic sunglasses that I had bought. They were unfazed by the "corkscrew"; some even had their eyes closed. These were just a handful of the army of contractors and private security consultants who were beating a path to Iraq for the sort of money regular soldiers could only dream of. Perhaps, as they dozed, they were calculating that just a couple more tours would buy that beach house.

They were being paid handsomely by the same government that had botched the invasion, hired to "stabilize" a country it had broken, to make up the numbers because Defense Secretary Donald Rumsfeld wanted a "minimalist" troop presence.

Meanwhile, Iraq was unraveling. The month of May had been among the bloodiest since the invasion. The "coalition of the willing" that had promised to make Iraq safe for democracy was failing a crash course in Iraqi politics: the many shades of sectarianism, the tribes, the hangovers from Saddam's brutal Baathist regime.

A large part of the Sunni minority—horrified that the so-called Coalition had empowered their Shi'a rivals—sympathized with an insurgency that was finding its feet. And a good portion of the Shi'a majority—egged on by Iran—was also resisting the occupation.

The harder the US hit the insurgency, the more vicious and widespread it became.

"Bomb one terrorist and ten come to his funeral," a friend who covered the region once told me.

The elections promised by the Coalition Provisional Authority (which had turned out to be not so Provisional and even less of an Authority) had been held earlier that year amid rampant violence and Sunni disaffection. Another election was scheduled for later in the year, but lofty ideas about transforming Iraq into a shining example of democracy, in a region bereft of it, were quickly melting away.

The previous year, the US had lost any moral credibility it still had left after news emerged that American soldiers were torturing and abusing detainees at the Abu Ghraib prison. If there had been any optimism after the invasion, as defiant Iraqis tore down a statue of the man who had oppressed them for decades, it was a distant memory. There wasn't going to be a withdrawal of US troops anytime soon.

The plane banked steeply to the right and my stomach dropped. I thought briefly of the emergency stash of Valium pills I had stuffed into my backpack, but then remembered the advice I'd received from an experienced war correspondent who had shuttled between Iraq and Afghanistan for the previous four years.

"If you need that shit, you have no business being in a war zone in the first place."

I looked out the window as the plane continued its spiral. For most of the flight from Amman there had been nothing to see but desert—endless, bare, and flat in varying shades of burnt sand, punctuated with the odd dot of white: a car, a shepherd's hut shimmering in the heat. Now we were descending over the sprawling city. I could see streets fringed with palm trees, choked with cars, mazes of alleys, and mosques.

The plane bounced down onto the runway and a South African voice drawled through the intercom. South African crews operated the Royal Jordanian flights to Baghdad from Amman—it seemed they were the only ones willing to risk the corkscrew.

"Welcome to Baghdad International Airport; the time is just after one in the afternoon and the temperature is thirty-eight degrees centigrade. On behalf of Royal Jordanian, we would like to wish you a pleasant stay."

Thirty-eight degrees—one hundred degrees Fahrenheit. A city in the grip of bombings, with no defined future. "Pleasant" was not the first word that sprang to mind.

The plane door opened and I was immediately assaulted by the baking hot air. It was like someone pointing a hair dryer directly at your face. My eyes smarted and my nostrils stung. I looked at the engineer I was traveling with and made a face. He laughed. "Welcome to Baghdad."

The plane was surrounded by heavily armed American military personnel who appeared to be wearing the same ballistic Oakleys as the contractors (I was clearly going to have to find some new sunglasses). They stood silently, eyeing the passengers as we disembarked. I thought how surreal and humiliating it must be for Iraqis coming home, who seemed to attract the soldiers' attention more than we did.

Our security detail met us at baggage claim and gave us flak jackets. I had been instructed to bring a baggy shirt to put on over my vest so that it would be less conspicuous. I also had a dark headscarf to conceal my blonde hair. The overall look was absurd: a gangly, five-foot-ten-inch woman with blue eyes peering out from a black *hijab*, looking distinctly misshapen in a billowing man's shirt over a bulky bulletproof vest. But the calculation was that, at a glance, I wouldn't attract too much attention. Foreigners were a prized target for the insurgency, particularly along the road from the airport into the city. Route Irish, as it was called by the military, had been given the ominous accolade of deadliest road in Iraq.

At that moment, I could not have cared less how ludicrous I looked. From the dusty smell of the hot, dry air to the look of the beat-up, old armored Chevy, and the sound of the crackling two-way radio as we headed out down the airport road—"This is Lima Charlie to Alfa Romeo, Lima Charlie to Alfa Romeo, do you copy?"—everything was thrilling.

BUILT IN THE EARLY 1980S, the Palestine Hotel on the banks of the river Tigris was a hideous concrete monolith rising eighteen floors above Baghdad's hubbub. Apart from us and the Associated Press and the

US-funded Al Hurra television station, there were practically no other guests. Several other news organizations had decided to decamp to the relative safety of the Green Zone across the river, where the coalition and diplomatic missions were based.

I would soon hear from Iraqis how, back in the 1980s, the Palestine would host fabulous parties, how women in miniskirts and jeans would waft through the lobby and expats in the oil business would fill the rooms. Saddam Hussein was already in power then, already torturing opponents—real or perceived—and imposing his secular blueprint on Iraq. No Iraqi dared utter a word against Saddam, but there were few religious restrictions at that time.

Now an elegant manager sat alone in the lobby, next to a shuttered Iraqi Airways kiosk and a very sad-looking souvenir shop. He was there every day and always wore the same brown suit and smiled politely and said, "Hello, madame" when I passed through. But it was unclear to me what he actually did.

To get to the Fox bureau, you had to take a staff elevator to the fifth floor and then walk down a flight of stairs. It was heavily fortified, with armed guards manning steel doors and panic alarms on every wall. There was even a safe room that we were not allowed to enter under any circumstances unless we came under attack. It reminded me of a submarine.

The bureau comprised two of everything to staff the 24-hour news cycle: correspondents, producers, cameramen, engineers. There were also locally hired translators and fixers, who were vital to our journalism, as well as cooking and cleaning staff.

My job as producer was to get up early and print out articles and wire copy, read through them, then put them under the correspondents' doors for them to peruse at their leisure. When there was an attack on US soldiers, I would call the military for confirmation. When there was an attack on Iraqis, I would ask one of the fixers to call their Iraqi sources for confirmation. In my spare time, I would work on long-term projects: applications to embed with the American military, for example, which required reams of paperwork.

I was first assigned to work with a Scottish freelance correspondent, David MacDougall, who had an acerbic wit and ate mayonnaise with everything. In my first few days, there was very little news, which was fortunate as I succumbed to what was affectionately known as "Baghdad belly."

"It's a rite of passage," the Scot told me. "First time you arrive in country, you always end up with an arsehole like a Japanese flag. But once you've had it, that's it."

Everyone else in the bureau had been coming to Baghdad for over a year, and they all had different nuggets of advice. Tip the housekeeping staff if you want them to actually clean your room. Take a cold shower before you go to sleep and then position a fan at the end of your bed and you might just be able to fall asleep before you start sweating again. Avoid bringing important requests to the fixer, Omar. He does nothing but play cards and surf porn sites.

That weekend, we had a small barbecue around the pool to celebrate my arrival. After popping a couple of Imodium tablets, the sealant of choice for exotic places, I went down to join the team. It was a cultural education. On one side, the Westerners were playing music and splashing around in the pool, eating ribs and swigging cold Corona beers. On the other side, the Jordanians and Iraqis sat together and ate steaks, sipping orange Mirinda soda. It reminded me of a toe-curling scene in E. M. Forster's novel *A Passage to India* where one of the British characters hosts a bridge party at his club at which the Indians spend the whole evening standing on one side and the Brits on the other.

I hovered nervously in the middle, not knowing which side to join. As a woman, I felt shy about plonking myself down with the Iraqis and

Jordanians, who were all men. But I also felt uncomfortable with the obvious segregation.

"Come get a steak, Clarissa," one of the engineers shouted. I felt relieved to have the decision made for me, even though my stomach was definitely not ready for red meat.

As the evening rolled on, the Iraqis and Jordanians began to peel away and the Westerners got more drunk. I began by pacing myself in deference to the Baghdad belly, but the spirit of camaraderie was seductive. Everyone was so funny and cool and worldly.

As the sun dipped below the horizon, the heat relaxed its grip and the call to prayer reverberated across the city. I sat with my legs dangling in the pool, breathing it all in, a cold beer in my hand.

"War is hell," someone toasted ironically, and we all raised our drinks and laughed.

"War is hell!"

I had no idea.

THERE WERE TWO DESK SHIFTS in the Baghdad bureau. I preferred the early shift because it began at 8 a.m. and no one else was up yet. I quickly developed a breakfast ritual. Iraqis make a delicious doughy bread called *samoon* that is shaped like a diamond. I would take a piece and cut the pocket open and spread little tinfoil triangles of Laughing Cow cheese on each side. Then I'd cut up two hard-boiled eggs, put them over the cheese, and add salt and pepper and Tabasco, before closing the pocket. I would take this gourmet sandwich onto the balcony and sit on a dusty air conditioner unit. I would eat slowly, sipping sweet black tea and drinking in the relative cool of the morning.

When the news was slow, I would spend my afternoons exploring the hotel. It reminded me of the hotel in *The Shining*—vast, eerie, and empty.

There were banquet halls, covered in dust as if frozen in time. All the windows were covered by sandbags. I happened upon rooftop tennis courts with broken nets. Signs for a bowling alley led nowhere. The rooftop Panorama Bar was sadly padlocked shut.

One day, as I walked through the lobby after one such expedition, the handsome young man who worked in the souvenir shop called out to me. "Please madam, come in."

I walked over to him. He clearly hadn't sold a souvenir in years.

"Hello, I am Ahmed. What is your name?"

"I am Clarissa."

"Kareesa?"

"Sure, that works."

He looked momentarily puzzled.

"Are you Kistian?"

"Christian? *Masihi* you mean?"

"Yes."

"Yes, I am." I had talked about this before with Alia. It's pretty much the last question anyone in the West would ask someone they meet, but one of the first questions people in the Middle East ask. Alia had warned me that saying you were an atheist or agnostic would lead to a confused frown or potential suspicion. So here in the Middle East, I was a Christian. It was easier that way.

"Do you have any of the old Iraqi dinars with Saddam Hussein on them?" I asked. I suddenly felt a painful need to give this guy some business.

"Yes, I do," he said, looking in a drawer under a glass case for them and pulling out a stack.

"Excellent, how much do you want for them?"

"Forty-five."

"Dollars?!"

"Yes."

"What," I snorted. "I will give you twenty-five."

A broad smile. "Madam, madam, thirty-five."

"Well, let me go and ask the Iraqis upstairs how much they are worth."

A frown. "Are you saying I am a liar?"

"Good god, no," I said, suddenly mortified and also surprised he'd been taken aback by what I'd thought to be customary haggling.

"I will give them to you for free."

"No, no." I blushed, panicking. "I will pay, of course. I just meant . . . how much did you pay for the dinars?"

"Ten dollars."

"OK, I will give you twenty dollars."

A broader smile. "But we said forty-five dollars."

"Twenty dollars," I insisted, handing over the money.

"OK, madam, now close your eyes and pick a sweet. Anything you want."

I walked out with my dinars and a dark chocolate, feeling desperately confused by my first experience haggling and hoping that I hadn't caused offense. Back in the bureau I showed my purchase to the Scot, who gave the dinars a withering look and snorted.

"They're fake." He laughed. "You're such a sucker, Clarissa."

One of the highlights of my first trips to Baghdad were my Arabic lessons with a teacher called Hakim. Hakim was a gentle, lovely man in his early thirties, with a big nose and a bushy moustache, a Sunni Muslim whose mother and father had moved from Saudi Arabia in the 1920s and settled in the desert area between Nasiriyah and Basra. Up until the war he had worked as a reporter, covering sports for a government newspaper. It wasn't particularly intellectually taxing for a man as erudite as Hakim, but under Saddam Hussein's repressive regime, the less political a job was, the safer it was.

Like many Iraqis, Hakim had hoped that the ouster of Saddam might bring opportunity, that a thriving, free society might actually develop to replace the police state he had grown up in. But in the face of the daily car bombs and escalating chaos that now consumed Iraq, Hakim was considering leaving the country.

"I don't want to leave this place. This is my life," he told me one afternoon, as we sat at the dining room table. "But my children . . ."

He looked down at the table. Hakim had four children. His two youngest, nicknamed Ulla and Mohammed, were the apples of his eye. He talked about them constantly. Their safety and well-being were his only priority.

"Clarissa, I need to ask you. Can you help me get my family to the West?"

It was a question I would be asked dozens and dozens of times as a reporter working in some of the most dangerous places in the world. And it would not get any easier to answer. There was always the burn of shame—what had I done to deserve the security and privilege that my passports afforded me? In the case of Iraq, that sense was compounded by the guilt of being American. How many lives had been destroyed by this senseless invasion?

I promised to look into it, but I was not optimistic.

Hakim and his family left Iraq for Jordan not long after. For our last lesson, he brought in photographs of his family and a book of drawings that he worked on in his spare time. I was immediately struck by the sincerity of his sketches. One depicted a man and a woman looking at the moon together. In New York or London, the drawing could have been dismissed as trite, but I found it quite lovely and openly tender.

"This is romance," he said as I looked at the sketch. I nodded.

A year later, Hakim would email me to say that after Jordan he had moved to Syria, before managing to claim asylum in Sweden, where he was now manning the cash register in a corner store. He was having difficulty learning Swedish and getting used to the cold, he said. It depressed me to think that Hakim was one of the lucky ones, that he had managed to get his family safely out of Iraq only to find himself a stranger in a freezing country working a menial job that was way below his education level.

With the exception of Hakim and the handful of cameramen and fixers and security guards who worked for us, I rarely had the opportunity to spend time with Iraqis. Perhaps, in 2005, this was inevitable. The security situation was diabolical and we rarely left the bunker that served as our bureau unless it was to go to the Green Zone to cover a political story, or out on an embed with the US military. Even a neophyte could see that this presented a real problem for our reporting. How can you humanize or attempt to explain a war when you're watching it from behind a series of blast walls and concertina wire?

I was desperate to get out. And if an embed with the US military was the only way to do that, then that's what I would do. So I went on every possible one. I visited Mosul and Kirkuk and Taji and Anbar and Diyala, all places where the Sunni insurgency was taking root, as well as the Shi'a stronghold of Basra in the south. I flew in Chinooks with the marines, on Black Hawks with the army, drove in Strykers and Humvees. I dipped tobacco with the 10th Mountain Division and had beers, or tinnies as they called them, with the Brits. I wiped out getting off a CH-46 Sea Knight in Anbar Province, learning the hard way that the helicopters are famous for leaking slippery hydraulic fluid from the fuselage. As I was rendered a temporary invalid by the fall, the cameraman had to carry almost all the heavy gear himself for the rest of the embed. One night, as he dragged three enormous boxes across the gravel by the airfield, he stopped to catch his breath and looked at me. "In the next life, I'm coming back as a piccolo player."

I learned the essentials of living with the military. Eat as much food as you can if you are on a big base with a good DFAC (dining facility). If you're stuck on some remote forward operating base eating MREs (meals in a bag), then don't sift through them all to pick the least hideous combination. Soldiers call it "rat fucking" and it's frowned upon. Bring a Camel-Bak and stay hydrated but not so hydrated that you need to pee all the time. No one wants to stop a convoy in a dodgy area to accommodate the bladder of the female journalist. Always remember flip-flops for the shower. Always remember a towel (trust me, I forgot mine once). And always bring a book or two (you might sit on that helipad for up to 36 hours waiting for a bird to take you where you need to go).

There were more important lessons, too—like, if you hit a roadside bomb, feel all your limbs to make sure they're still intact and then wait for the instructions of the officer in command. Or, don't be a burden on the unit you're embedded with; bring your own med kit and know how to tie a tourniquet.

I enjoyed the soldiers' company. Sure, they used way too many acronyms and generally had little understanding of or interest in Iraqi culture and history, but they were polite and professional and often funny.

I remember walking through an airport hangar in Anbar Province with a public affairs officer from the marines. Anbar was the heartland of the insurgency and the marines had lost a lot of men there. That week there had been terrible sandstorms that had grounded all flights. The hangar was packed with hundreds of marines lying on the floor waiting to get out for their R&R. As we picked our way through the crowd, the media handler aka public affairs officer had a grin on his face.

"What is it?" I asked

"No disrespect, ma'am," he replied, "but every single marine in here is eye fucking the shit out of you."

I laughed, delighted by his candor. It was refreshing after the stiff formality of the military.

While I appreciated the patience and good humor of the troops, I felt depressed when I heard spokesmen deliver canned lines about bringing Iraqis freedom and helping them rebuild their country, because it was obvious that wasn't happening. As far as I could tell, most of them were there for the same reason I was: 9/11 had blown up their world and they wanted to do something to put it right. So they had signed up to serve their country, to ensure that America would never suffer such an atrocity again.

There was no way for them to know then that 9/11 would be exploited by a coterie of "neo-cons" around President George W. Bush, eager to take down Saddam Hussein on the pretext that he was (a) in league with al Qaeda, the perpetrators of 9/11, and (b) amassing a stockpile of weapons of mass destruction. Neither turned out to be true.

Here they were—the soldiers and marines drawn from all fifty states—on a battlefield without front lines, fighting an enemy they couldn't see and didn't understand, getting blown up and shot at every day in a war where progress or purpose seemed unattainable.

The goal of spending more time with Iraqis remained elusive. I did manage to spend some hours drinking tea with Iraqi generals and nodding enthusiastically as they waxed lyrically in Classical Arabic about their hopes for their country and showed me their photographs. "This is me with Rumsfeld, this is me with Casey, this is me with Abizaid." I remember pressing one General Jalil: "But how can you say that the situation is getting better in this area when we still can't go out on a foot patrol with your men here?"

"Ah!" he flashed a smile at me from behind his thick black moustache and sipped his tea. "Of course, for a woman as beautiful as you it is very dangerous."

The closest I got to an encounter with ordinary Iraqis was accompanying the soldiers on raids. I was with the 10th Mountain Division getting ready for a series of night raids to be conducted in Sadr City, a sprawling eastern suburb of Baghdad that was the stronghold of a Shi'a cleric called Muqtada al-Sadr. He hated the American occupation as much as the Sunni insurgents, and his militia—Jaysh al-Mahdi, or JAM—were determined to make their part of Baghdad a no-go zone for coalition troops. Deadly roadside bombs made with molten copper, known as EFPs (explosively formed penetrators), were killing a lot of US soldiers at that time.

We sat in the TOC (tactical operations center) one hour before the raid. I watched as the twenty soldiers prepped for their mission, guzzling an unfortunately named energy drink called Rip It and listening to death-metal music that blared from crappy speakers. The men put their gear on, all fifty pounds of it. One of them asked me to try on his vest. My legs nearly buckled under the weight.

"You're all going to be suing the US government in ten years for fucking up your backs," I said.

"Yeah," one short guy said, laughing. "I used to be six foot."

At one in the morning we loaded into the Humvees. Driving through Baghdad in the dead of night, with a dust storm raging around us and no headlights, it felt pretty damned spooky. Dogs were howling and the stench of raw sewage seeped into the Humvee through the gunner's turret.

"We call this place shit's creek," one of the soldiers grunted.

The first raid was quick. The soldiers stood outside the house and counted silently to three before bursting through the door. Dazed Iraqi men with sleep in their eyes stumbled out of bed, squinting into the bright flashlights shone into their faces and trying to shield the women who were not wearing headscarves.

"Where's the terp?" a soldier asked for the interpreter. "I'm here," came a timid voice. "Tell the men to get down on their knees," the soldier barked. Some of the women began wailing. The interpreter hesitated.

"I said tell 'em to get down on their goddamn knees," the soldier shouted again. And kneel they did, on the ground facing a wall as the soldiers methodically handcuffed and blindfolded them, and then began searching for weapons.

The main room was covered in posters of Muqtada al-Sadr. There were no beds, just a mass of carpets and mattresses and blankets spread across the floor. The wailing was getting louder now as more women joined the chorus and a child had started crying, too.

"Tell them we are not going to hurt them or touch their women, we are just looking for weapons. Do they have any weapons in this house?"

The interpreter haltingly translated for the men. But the women just kept wailing. It was unnerving, for me and for the soldiers.

"Goddammit, get those women into the other room."

I looked at the children, some sobbing, some blinking in confusion into the bright light. Their cheeks were chapped from the dry cold, and thick snot poured out of their noses. My head was throbbing under my helmet. The soldier was still shouting to get the women into the other room.

No one was communicating. The soldiers were hopped up on caffeine drinks and were nervous themselves. The Iraqi men were humiliated and angry, kneeling on the floor; the women were frightened and vulnerable, hastily trying to cover their hair; and the children seemed to be in shock, confused by all the screaming and chaos.

The interpreter and I played peripheral roles, witnesses with one foot in either world. I imagine he felt as I did—ashamed and startled and unsure of how to react. His face was covered in a balaclava to protect his identity. He was probably desperate to make some money and get his family a green card to get the hell out of Iraq. The dangers for translators were growing; the insurgents had begun to target their families.

In the end, no weapons were found, and we moved on to the next house. Same result.

Later, back at the TOC, as the soldiers took off their gear and joked about what a waste of time the raids were, I watched the interpreter take off his balaclava. His face looked crumpled, his eyes tired. "Good work tonight, Mo," one of the soldiers said, slapping him on the back. Most of the interpreters used fake names that were easy for Americans to pronounce. He smiled weakly and nodded, "Thank you."

I felt an urge to go up to him and say, "I see you. I get it. Or at least I get some of it." But the moment passed and I went back to my hooch (hut), crawled into my sleeping bag, and collapsed into a deep sleep.

THE DAYS WERE PUNCTUATED with the sound of bombs going off and rockets hitting the Green Zone, but we were divorced from their real impact and from the chaos that was ravaging the country. About a year into the war, most news organizations had decided it wasn't safe for Westerners to leave their secure compounds, and so local Iraqi reporters were the ones who went to the sites of bomb attacks. They were the ones who saw the bloodied and maimed bodies of the victims.

I remember sitting in the newsroom one evening with the Croatian bureau chief, Zoran. Shostakovich was playing loudly from his computer and we drank chilled white wine from plastic cups. I was reading wire copy about a bombing that day.

"Elsewhere, one car bomber Sunday struck the offices of Iraq's electoral commission in eastern Baghdad, killing five election employees and one policeman," it read. The words felt so remote.

The balcony door was open and Zoran was smoking a cigar, his head bobbing to the crescendo of violins.

I tried to focus on reading the report. But the sun was setting and the call to prayer began, melting over Perlman's solo. If I could feel detached from the suffering that was tearing apart Iraq while sitting in Baghdad, how did Americans watching from home feel after two and a half years of war?

Some journalists were doing great work that punched through, that made the war vivid and real and personal, that told the stories of Iraqis and humanized their suffering. Most were print reporters because they were able to move around more easily than we were, without cameras and other equipment. They could tell stories with nuance and context in a way that was difficult for television. And invariably their deadlines were less demanding than the hourly "live shots" of the all-news networks.

Still, I couldn't escape the sense that the media overall had failed in Iraq from the start. It had been too credulous of the pretext for invasion, and now we were in a sort of purgatory, near the war but still removed from it. So we threw parties and played poker and danced all night and "formed relationships"—anything to distract us from the truth that we were telling only a fraction of the story, that we were complicit.

One evening in October 2005, during Ramadan as the muezzin sang out the *Maghreb* prayer announcing *iftar*, the breaking of the fast, I was sitting in the newsroom with a reporter and another producer when we were almost knocked over by an ear-splitting blast. Running out of the newsroom into the corridor, we saw that the rest of the bureau was running toward us.

Jomana, a young Jordanian producer, was on the verge of tears.

"It's OK," I said.

At that moment, another blast ripped through the air, causing the building to tremble and the hallway to fill with smoke. "Oh my god, oh my god, oh my god," I thought over and over. Our security detail was shouting at us to go to our rooms and get our body armor.

Jomana struggled to open her door. The force of the blast, I assumed the pressure wave, had warped many of the doors. "I have no shoes, I have no shoes," she moaned.

I felt like I was in a fire drill back in boarding school, running to my room in a trance, getting my vest and grab bag, running back into the corridor where the head of security was going to take roll call.

I felt strangely calm. One clear thought went through my mind. "What the hell am I doing here? I want to leave, this isn't worth it."

Everyone was milling back and forth, putting on body armor, trying to open their doors.

Then it came, the third blast, the single most frightening, deafening boom I had ever heard. Surely no building could withstand such a shock. Someone was telling us to get into the safe room but no one could remember where the safe room was. There were shards of metal and glass everywhere, crunching underfoot. Several people were bleeding, my ears were ringing, and it was difficult to hear what anyone was saying.

I remember thinking to myself, "This is what fear feels like."

As the smoke cleared, I began to see my colleagues, looking almost otherworldly, covered in gray dust with large, petrified eyes.

"I have no shoes," Jomana whispered again, as if the thought was the only thing keeping her from hysteria.

With an engulfing sense of nausea, I suddenly realized that we were not collateral damage. We were the targets of the attack. People wanted to kill us. And then I understood that I might die in the next few minutes. I felt no longing for loved ones at that moment, nor sadness. Those were gentle emotions, and they found no space amid the naked pure acid of fear.

"War is hell." I remembered for a furious moment the brash complacency of the expression. But there was no bravado here.

The silence, broken by occasional shouting and a distant siren, was almost as disorienting as the blasts. We found and collapsed into the safe room.

We waited for what felt like an eternity; slowly the fear began to subside. The attack was over. Suddenly, cameramen were roaming around filming, and then we were working again and doing live shots from an improvised position in the newsroom and conferring about how it happened and clustering over CCTV video and then joking and calling loved ones and sweeping rooms and hanging fabric where balcony doors used to be.

In the lobby, people moved around like zombies; there were no doors or windows or lamps—everything was shattered. Incredibly, the elegant manager still sat at his desk, with dust on the lapels of his brown suit, the painting behind him tilted to one side. "Are you OK?" I asked him. He shrugged, but there was more than a hint of bitterness in what he said.

"This is life in the Middle East."

I took my little camera and went out to film the crater in front of our hotel. The first explosion had been a car bomb at the concrete blast wall surrounding our compound. The second blast was another vehicle bomb nearby that created a distraction for a cement-mixer truck packed with explosives to lurch its way through the shattered blast walls and toward the hotel. Some razor wire and concrete troughs of flowers had saved us, preventing the truck from reaching the steps to the hotel. The US military later told us that if the third bomber had gotten twenty yards closer, we would have died.

As I darted around in the aftermath, filming, Iraqis called out to me, eager to point out body parts they had found, most of them belonging to the bomber or bombers. There was unmistakably human tissue smeared among the wreckage, a finger, the top row of teeth, and then a foot, completely black but still perfectly intact from the ankle down. I did not feel anything looking at that foot, just a blank fatigue.

Later, we all sat in the living room and drank scotch and talked animatedly about the attack. We had survived. We were alive. The bile of fear had subsided, subsumed by the adrenaline of living to tell the tale. It no longer felt real or even frightening; there was a veil between the experience and the telling.

At about two in the morning, we all peeled off to bed and I slipped into the room of another producer. He had covered Iraq for years and Yugoslavia before that. He was strong and tall and smelled good and smiled only with his eyes. I felt safe with him. I lay next to him on the bed in the quiet darkness as he stroked my hair.

"How are you feeling, guppy?" he asked me. "It's been a long day for you."

The feeling of elation from earlier slowly drained away. Tears began streaming down my face.

"I don't know why I'm crying." I sniffed. "I'm just tired."

He wiped my tears away silently with his thumbs, waiting for me to finish.

"If any of us had died today, I would never have been able to come back," I said.

But nobody had died and I would come back. I was addicted.

Four

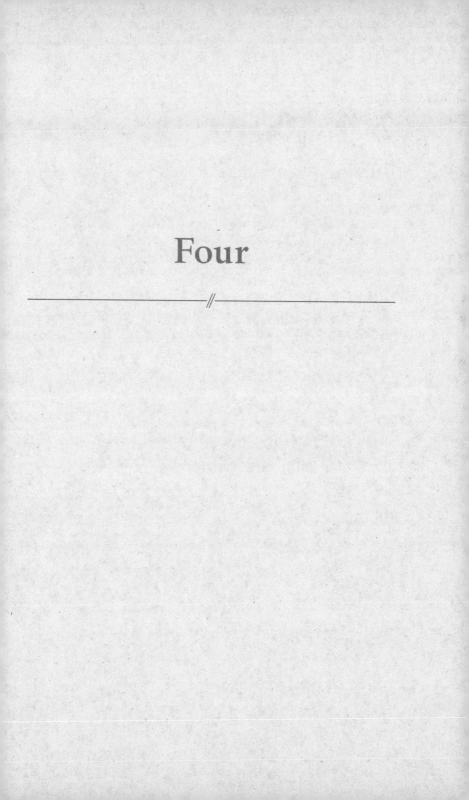

The blast was so loud, it sounded as if the air were being ripped apart. Instinctively, I ducked under the table.

Jonathan Hunt, the wickedly funny British Fox correspondent I had been sent to work with, looked down at me with amusement. "Relax, Clarissa, it's a sonic boom," he said. The rest of the crew laughed.

We were sitting in the restaurant of a small hotel in the Gaza Strip at the end of June 2006. A few days earlier, Palestinian militants had kidnapped a young Israeli soldier, Corporal Gilad Shalit. Israel had launched a large-scale military operation to rescue Shalit and stop the barrage of rockets being fired by Hamas into Israel.

Part of the Israeli campaign involved fighter jets flying low and at supersonic speeds.

"It's the Israelis' favorite tactic at the moment—they're really into this psychological warfare," Jonathan said.

I sat up straight and tried to compose myself. I wanted to take another sip of my Arabic coffee but I was worried my hands would shake.

Over the next 24 hours, we would hear another eight such blasts, mostly between the hours of 2 a.m. and 7 a.m., and every single time, no matter how much I had been steeling myself, I jumped in the air involuntarily.

A young waiter, who had been hovering, came to the table smiling.

"Are you OK, miss?"

"Oh yes, sorry, thank you, I feel pretty silly," I said, blushing. "I didn't realize it was just a sonic boom. How do you get used to those?"

He shrugged. "For me it's OK, but for the children it is too scary."

I tried to imagine what it would be like to experience a sonic boom as a child, given that my pulse was still thudding.

That morning I had been sipping a cappuccino and reading the *Herald Tribune* in the air-conditioned dining room of my hotel in Jerusalem. Ninety minutes later, I was drenched in sweat, lugging a suitcase as well as a flak jacket and helmet, and struggling to wedge everything through the turnstile at Erez, the border crossing that separated Israel and Gaza.

Navigating Erez is a surreal experience. The crossing has to be done on foot, and the walk is over a mile long. The Israeli soldiers who run it do not actually interact with you face to face. Instead, they talk to you over a loudspeaker system.

"Please take off your belt," a voice boomed from nowhere as I passed through the metal detector.

It can take hours to get through the crossing. Sometimes you will find yourself stopped in the middle, penned in, with metal gates in front of you and behind you. There is no one to ask why you can't pass. You simply have to wait until the gates open and a voice tells you to proceed. It is disorientating and, I wondered at the time, perhaps designed to be humiliating.

The year before, Israeli forces had withdrawn from Gaza, which they had occupied since the Six Day War in 1967. Even so, Israel retained control of Gaza's coastline and airspace and most of its border. This tiny strip of land, no bigger than Philadelphia, was often dubbed the world's largest open-air prison. In recent elections, the militant Palestinian group Hamas had won an overwhelming victory and the pace of attacks against Israel had quickened. So had Israeli bombardments, and the one million Palestinians crammed into the Gaza Strip bore the brunt of the suffering. Now that an Israeli soldier had been abducted, the crisis threatened to escalate.

By the time I emerged from the long, lonely corridor into Gaza, I was exhausted. The sun was beating down. I looked around, trying to get my bearings. A car was supposed to pick me up but there was no one around. The quiet was punctuated by the steady thud of Israeli shells landing.

A few phone calls and an overpriced taxi ride later, I found myself sitting with my colleagues at the Beach Hotel. As I gazed out of the bay windows at the Mediterranean, with the gentle breeze streaming in, it was possible to forget the violence for a moment. It occurred to me that Gaza could have been a world-class tourist destination, but another thunderous boom quickly shattered the illusion.

I'd accepted the assignment because I would actually be producing stories in the field, not just printing out wire copy in a bunker in Iraq. My goal was to be in front of the camera, but I didn't have the experience or confidence to push for that yet. Producing was an excellent education, especially if you were working with a veteran correspondent, as it provided a window onto the editorial and logistical demands of reporting.

Jonathan was the sort of reporter I liked. He found live shots boring (though he was very good at them) and preferred to go out and talk to people and put together packages that made the conflict accessible and human. He was also incredibly generous with his time and wisdom.

I was still doing rotations in and out of Baghdad for Fox, but no longer from New York. I had taken a chance on making a career out of journalism in the Middle East and had set up shop in Beirut as a freelancer.

Fox kept me extremely busy, so I didn't have time to work for anyone else. But by hiring me as a freelancer, they were not technically responsible for me, which suited them and me just fine.

Beirut was the perfect antidote to Baghdad. Even if there were daily power outages and you couldn't flush loo paper (there was always a small bin discreetly placed next to the toilet), you could get a great pedicure and buy designer clothes and have sushi delivered to your apartment. It was a city of fun and sunshine and sex and superficiality.

Lebanon was also a great place to learn about the Middle East because it was a microcosm of the region. There were Sunni and Shi'a Muslims and Druze (an isolationist sect of Islam who lived in the mountains); Maronite and Orthodox Christians; Catholics, Armenians, and Assyrians. The diversity made the country vibrant and fascinating, but it had also been a source of misery. The Lebanese had endured a grueling fifteen-year civil war; much of Beirut's downtown had been reduced to ruins and more than 100,000 people had been killed. All the different groups had fought one another in a kaleidoscope of shifting alliances, backed by various outside powers. The Americans had tried to broker peace, and the Israelis had invaded (and would soon do so again).

In February 2005, the former prime minister Rafik Hariri, who had done more than anyone to restore Beirut's fortunes—and made a pretty penny doing so—had been killed in a massive car bombing. Most Lebanese blamed Syrian intelligence, and a spontaneous outburst of popular anger led eventually to the exit of Syrian troops from Lebanon after a twenty-nine-year presence. It was a rare example of the people's will in the Middle East actually counting for something.

The Lebanese (apart from the ascetic Hezbollah militia) had no patience for misery. The war had been over for more than a decade but the mentality was still "Tonight we party for tomorrow we may die." This hedonism was set against a stunning Mediterranean backdrop. The people were warm and charming and attractive, making Beirut an alluring base for journalists covering the region.

I lived in a modern, furnished apartment in a neighborhood called Clemenceau. My mother had come with me when I first moved to Beirut and did it up for me. She would do the same in every apartment I went on to live in across the world, which was a blessing because I didn't inherit her gift for design.

The view from my balcony would have been fantastic were it not for the shadow of the bullet-riddled skeleton of the Holiday Inn. Built in the 1970s, it had become the front line of Lebanon's civil war and the site of some of the fiercest fighting. After the war, it had been stripped of everything but the concrete. Now no one knew what to do with it. To tear it down would be too difficult; to blow it up was impossible without destroying other buildings. And so it stood as a grim testament to a conflict whose underlying enmities remained. The Lebanese acted as if it wasn't really there.

I had never traveled before to Israel or Gaza. When I landed at Ben Gurion Airport in Tel Aviv, I asked the woman at the passport desk not to stamp my passport. Having an Israeli stamp would make it impossible for me to travel to most countries in the Middle East, including back home to Beirut. The woman arched her eyebrow and asked me where I lived.

"Beirut," I answered truthfully.

I was immediately escorted to another room, where I was questioned extensively in Arabic and English. "Why do you speak Arabic?" "Are you Christian?" "Who do you work for?" "What will you do in Israel?" "Who do you know in Gaza?" "Why does your employer send you from Beirut instead of someone from here in Israel?"

I thought the answer to the last question was pretty obvious: my Israeli colleagues weren't exactly lining up to go to Gaza. I was asked the same questions over and over again. In the end, they called the Fox bureau in Jerusalem, before finally deciding that I could enter the country.

In Gaza, we worked out of the Gaza Media Center. The office was on the fifteenth floor, the electricity rarely worked and the toilet didn't flush, but there was a fantastic falafel stand outside and the people who worked with us were wonderful, especially our fixer, Nael. Nael was the same age as me: twenty-six. He was quiet and thoughtful with a sweet, pudgy face and bright green eyes.

A good fixer can make the difference between a hellish assignment and a successful and enjoyable one. Fixers do everything from setting up and translating interviews to sourcing food for the team and confirming reports. The best ones have great local contacts (often kept in a dog-eared notebook) and very understanding families (who they will likely see for only a couple of hours a day when they're working). Most important, top fixers have an acute awareness of local conditions, a sort of mental radar that tells them when a situation is about to go to shit and the confidence to speak up.

Every morning we would bundle into our armored Jeep, which had been fitted with a videophone that gave us the ability to go live from anywhere, and drive out to see what was happening. The bulletproof glass was so thick you couldn't hear what was going on outside, so we would stop periodically and open the doors to listen to where incoming shells were landing.

One of the first things that struck me as we drove around was the vast number of so-called martyr posters, honoring young Hamas fighters killed in battle. Everywhere you looked—on shop fronts, on public buildings, on roadsides—the smiling faces of young men, some just boys, carrying large guns, beamed down, part memorial, part recruitment.

The martyrs (*shuhada*)—those who died defending their homeland or community—were heroes of the cause. Muslims believe that a *shaheed* can intercede on behalf of his family members to gain them entry to paradise. Families who have lost sons or daughters as *shuhada* are treated with enormous respect and reverence. It is a way of honoring their life, of justifying the sacrifice, of coping with the loss.

I thought of all the American families who had lost their children to the wars in Iraq and Afghanistan. It was not so different. They were told that their sons and daughters were heroes, that they died defending freedom, that their sacrifice had meaning.

One day we drove to the northern Gaza Strip, to an area called Beit Hanoun, to get a closer look at the Israeli tanks that were pushing deeper into Gaza. We came off the road into a field and found ourselves about 200 yards away from a tank.

"Should we get closer?" Jonathan asked.

Nael looked visibly frightened. "No, no, they will fire on us."

"Well, it does say 'PRESS' in bright yellow letters all over the car," I said, "so they can see we are journalists."

Jonathan and the Australian cameraman, Mal, both snorted and shot me a look as if to say, "like that makes any difference."

"Let's call Eli and see what he suggests," Jonathan suggested.

Eli was the Jerusalem Fox News bureau chief who had served as a tank commander in the Israeli military. Most US and British media outlets brought their own people into Israel to run their bureaus. So inflamed were opinions in the long-running Middle East conflict that it was assumed that no Israeli, let alone a former military man, could be neutral and balanced. Fox felt no such compunction. They were reflexively pro-Israeli, even by American standards. To give them credit, though, the bosses never interfered with what we were seeing and saying in the field. The spin came from the talking heads and anchors in the US.

Eli's response was "They probably won't shoot you," which was slim comfort. After five minutes of discussion, we inched toward the tank. No sooner had we started moving than a shell exploded just five yards away. I could feel the pressure of the blast wave smash against my inner ear.

"Fucking hell," Jonathan said, "that nearly bloody hit us."

Mal hit the gas and we reversed out of the field quickly. As we came to the road in the village, a large group of Palestinians approached the car and started hitting it with their shoes. They were furious that we had incurred the wrath of the Israelis so close to their homes. It was so easy to get greedy in the moment, to want a better picture, a closer shot—and to lose sight of the fact that for the people around you this wasn't a temporary assignment they wanted to ace. This was their life, their home, their security.

The people of Gaza never had a minute to catch their breath during what the Israelis had called Operation Summer Rains. From sonic booms to shelling and air strikes, they were on edge twenty-four hours a day. One sensed that the purpose of the Israeli operation was as much to exhaust them as to crush the resistance. And yet, day after day, Palestinian militants would come out and fire off their Qassam rockets into Israel. They knew the response the rockets would provoke and they understood the misery the Gazan people would suffer as a result, but still they did it.

Years later, Ben Wedeman, a CNN veteran correspondent who has spent many years covering the Israeli-Palestinian conflict, explained to me that firing the rockets, while ineffectual, was an act of defiance.

"One thing you have to remember about the Palestinians, going back to the 1960s, is their addiction to symbolic acts that remind the world of their existence yet do nothing to advance their cause. It's a rather depressing calculation that inevitably leaves them as losers."

Jonathan and I were on the same page about how to cope with the intensity of the assignment. Having both grown up in the UK, we shared an irreverent sense of humor that manifested itself in merciless and constant ribbing. He would call me horseface and I would tell him he was a grizzled old boozehound, and that was just for starters. In the evenings, we would try to carve out time to sit outside at our hotel restaurant and order the "shrimp special" (shrimp in a creamy tomato sauce served with rice) and decompress. One evening, we all decamped (though not poor Nael) to Jonathan's room to eke out a bottle of whisky that he had managed to sneak in.

After ten days, Jonathan and Mal were replaced by a Chicago-based correspondent, Mike, and a cameraman with a dark, luxuriant moustache, perhaps the only Irishman with the name of Pierre. Staff crews rarely wanted to stay more than a couple of weeks anywhere, and certainly not in Gaza. Freelancers would stay anywhere as long as they were getting paid. We were the vultures of the industry.

The Qassam rockets kept flying over the border and the Israelis were no closer to rescuing Shalit. One day we drove north to the town of Beit Lahiya. Israeli tanks were advancing to create a buffer zone in the fields from which militants had been firing. We had been here before to do live shots and played with the kids and sipped sweet hot tea with local families.

On this day the streets were crawling with militants carrying AK-47s and RPGs. The shelling from the Israelis was incessant and the sound of gun battles reverberated through the cramped neighborhoods.

Suddenly, we saw an older woman, in the traditional veil, walk out into the dusty street and yank something out of the ground. My jaw dropped as I realized what it was.

"Holy shit, it's a bomb," Mike said.

The roadside bomb had been buried by Hamas fighters hoping to hit the Israeli tanks. Within minutes a group of fighters surrounded her.

"What are you doing, Hajja?" they asked, using a respectful term for old people that literally means someone who has completed the Hajj, the pilgrimage to Mecca.

"We don't want these bombs near our houses," she admonished them, brandishing the device.

"It's for the occupiers," they proclaimed.

"These are our homes, we are families living here," she said, growing more hysterical. "We don't want fighting here. Take it away."

"Leave it where it was," they shouted at her, "and go back inside."

Hands on her hips, facing off with the militants, this woman didn't care if it was "the occupiers" with their tanks or local kids with balaclavas and RPGs. She didn't want fighting in her neighborhood and she wasn't afraid to speak her mind. It was resistance in its purest form. But the civilians who were being killed on a daily basis weren't lauded as martyrs of the resistance. It was people like her who were suffering the most, shelled by the Israelis and used by Hamas as cover for their futile acts of resistance.

I felt an immediate urge to tell her story. But as we were shooting the chaotic scene, an Israeli Apache gunship swooped down over us and began spraying .30-caliber rounds and chaff all over the streets to try to disperse the fighters, sending the crowd running in panic. We ran to the armored Jeep to take cover and move to a safer location.

We decided to stop at a nearby intersection to try to do a live shot. Just as we were about to go live, the satellite lost its signal and then, wham, a Hellfire missile hit its target just 50 yards from us, blowing up a car. I stood in absolute shock, looking at the burning vehicle. From what I could see, at least two people had been killed, their charred remains barely visible through the clouds of smoke. A man who had been standing right next to the car began staggering toward us.

His face was contorted with rage and he was pointing at the white dome on the roof of our vehicle that housed the satellite phone. He began wailing over and over again, "*Yahood, Yahood*" (Jews, Jews). Clearly, he thought we were spies or somehow responsible for the strike. I saw that he had a rock in his hand and was heading toward our cameraman.

"Pierre," I shouted. He looked up just as the man cracked him in the head with the rock. Pierre staggered back, dazed as he grasped at his temple.

Nael began trying to talk to the man, to calm him down and buy us some time to get our gear packed up. But now other men started walking toward us.

"Get in the car now," I screamed. I realized later it was the first time I had taken command of a situation as a producer.

We jumped into the back and threw the tripod and camera in on top of us, the legs of the tripod still sticking out of the half open door as we sped away.

Later that afternoon, we went to the Shifa Hospital, where most of the casualties had been taken. There was a huge crowd of people gathered outside, mostly young guys waiting to see whether their friends were OK.

Nael looked at me. His big green eyes were bloodshot from fatigue.

"You stay in the car," he said sternly. As an uncovered, blonde, Western woman, I was frequently being told to stay in the car and it was beginning to piss me off, even though it was for my own safety. Almost every woman in Gaza wore the *hijab*, certainly when they were outside their homes. Later on, I would always keep a scarf with me, sometimes wearing it over the back of my head as a gesture that I was sensitive to a very conservative culture. But at that time, despite my lessons with Alia in New York, I didn't give much thought to the impact of my appearance.

Years later I saw a cartoon that captured the cultural divide perfectly. It showed a Western woman wearing a bikini, sunglasses, and high heels walking past a Muslim woman in a black *abaya* and face-covering veil. They were looking at each other. Above the Western woman was a thought bubble: "Everything covered but her eyes—what a cruel, male-dominated culture." Above the Muslim woman was another bubble: "Nothing covered but her eyes—what a cruel, male-dominated culture."

I sat in the back of the van for a few minutes, exhausted but buzzing from the adrenaline of the day. I wanted a cigarette but I had spent enough time in the Middle East to know that in most places a woman smoking in public was frowned upon and sent a signal that she was of easy virtue. I waited for another few minutes, feeling increasingly irritable.

"Fuck it," I said to myself, and got out of the car to smoke a cigarette behind the back door. No sooner had I lit it than I knew I had made a stupid mistake. Heads swiveled to look at me. I gave a passive-aggressive smile and shrugged.

Someone shouted something at me that I didn't quite catch, and suddenly it seemed everyone was looking at me. People started moving toward the car. I took another drag before hastily putting out the cigarette. One guy reached out and touched my arm, causing me to jump. Men in Gaza didn't normally touch women they aren't related or married to.

"A'atini sigara," he said (give me a cigarette). I shook my head: "Ma 'aindi" (I don't have any).

I turned to get in the car. I could see Nael coming back from the hospital entrance. He saw me and his eyes bulged with anger. A man started hissing at me. I opened the car door slightly and squeezed back in. By now there was a crowd of young men around the vehicle. The one who had asked me for the cigarette pressed himself against the window and put his hands in his pants while staring at me. Another flicked his tongue at me. I moved across the back seat to the other side of the car and looked away, willing Nael to hurry.

Moments later he was there, shouting and shooing the crowd away. "Khalas, ruh"—that's enough, get lost, he said, pushing them back.

I was mortified at the thought that he might get hurt defending me. The men grumbled but began to disperse. Nael got back in the car. He waited until we were safely out of the hospital compound before exploding.

"Why did you leave the car? I told you it's not safe for you. And smoking?! It's a stupid thing for you. Don't you understand?"

He looked exasperated. It was the second time he had had to protect us from an angry crowd and I felt like an idiot.

WE WERE IN GAZA TWO WEEKS before there was a lull in the fighting. Shalit would remain a detainee for over five years.

The journey home to Beirut would have taken about three hours in a car; it was less than two hundred miles north of Gaza as the crow flies. Instead, because the Israeli-Lebanese border was sealed shut, it took more than twelve hours. Drive to Erez, cross on foot, drive to Tel Aviv, then fly to Amman, Jordan, change flights, and fly to Beirut.

By the time I got back home I had lost seven pounds. My jeans were always a little baggy after an intense assignment—the combination of exhaustion, adrenaline, stress, irregular mealtimes, and too many cigarettes. Embarking on such trips was always exciting, but after two or three weeks, home comforts and sleep seemed like a far-off oasis. In Baghdad, we played a game, listing exactly what we would do when we got home: our first drink or meal, what we'd buy, who we'd see. I had done exactly the same at boarding school.

And yet, the first few days of being home were rarely as wonderful as anticipated. Once the adrenaline stopped pumping, my body would just shut down, demanding sleep. I always felt very lethargic and a little blue after a big trip. It hadn't helped that on my way out of Ben Gurion Airport I had been questioned again for more than an hour and then strip-searched by a stone-faced female security guard who pretended not to hear me when I declared I was going to report her for making me take off my underwear. Stories like this were all too common at Ben Gurion and you wondered where legitimate security concerns overlapped with a dislike of foreign media.

I spent three days in my apartment sleeping, watching *Sex and the City*, and exchanging funny emails with Jonathan. After big trips, I usually had no interest in talking to anyone except the colleagues I had just been with. When I could be lured out for dinner or a drink by some friends, I would find it hard to focus. It was some form of Stockholm syndrome, I guess, and reminded me of how US soldiers in a combat outpost in Afghanistan found it difficult to adapt to not being there, bound together in a situation where solidarity meant survival.

My mother called me and I answered her in monosyllables, unable to really engage. She complained that I had what she always referred to as "the flat voice."

"No, no, I'm fine. I'm just tired, that's all," I explained.

"I know my baby and you have the flat voice," she insisted. "I just can't understand why you're blue because you have everything in the world and you have no reason to be upset."

"Mom, I'm not blue," I assured her, trying not to get irritable. "I just spent three weeks sleeping four hours a night and I'm beat. That's all."

"Maybe you should go on antidepressants," she continued, not hearing me.

I laughed out loud. "Stop, you're being ridiculous. It's normal to need to decompress. I'm going to hang up now but not because I am depressed. Love you. Byeee."

I debated whether to call the Lebanese guy I had been seeing on and off for six months. I had broken up with him for the tenth time just before leaving for Gaza, though in his mind we were never in a relationship anyway. Christophe was a Francophone, a Christian Lebanese who loved surfing and spearfishing. He was insanely cute, lots of fun, and a genuinely positive person. He called me his "super badass superwoman" and would tell me how smart I was while covering me in kisses.

He was also a total playboy. We had almost nothing in common, but for some reason he was my kryptonite, and no matter how bad things got, I kept coming back for more. I had never experienced a relationship with a philanderer before, and so I held on to the idea that eventually he would magically fall in love with me, despite all evidence to the contrary.

At the end of one drunken night out, we were sitting in a popular fast-food place with a group of his friends. One of them asked me to explain what was meant by a "fuck buddy" in English. I said that it was basically when two friends are having sex but there's nothing more to the relationship than that.

"It's like you and me, babe," Christophe chimed in, before bursting into laughter. It was like a punch in my gut. I had never felt so humiliated or hurt by a guy in my life, but I was too proud to show it and so I just laughed and said, "Yeah, you wish," or something to that effect.

But Christophe and his circle were a balm for my occasional bouts of homesickness. Like many Lebanese, they seemed closer culturally to the West than to the Middle East. He and his friends listened to the same music and enjoyed the same pastimes as my American and English friends. We would go out on his boat, have lunch on the beach, and go up to his chalet in the mountains. But at the end of the night, or the next morning, I would sense him withdrawing from me and it just felt awful. Just as I resolved not to take it anymore and to stop seeing him completely, my phone would ping and there would be a loving, sweet message from him. And I would be hooked again.

A FEW DAYS AFTER RETURNING FROM GAZA, I needed to visit the Hezbollah offices in the southern suburbs of Beirut. I was trying to set up an interview with a Hezbollah official for a correspondent who was coming in to do some stories on the future of Christianity in the Middle East.

While Hezbollah is considered a terrorist organization in the US, it is very much a part of the fabric of society in Lebanon. The majority of the country's Shi'as (roughly 30 percent of the total population) feel the group and its leader, Sayyed Hassan Nasrallah, represent them. Hezbollah was formed in the slums of southern Beirut with Iranian backing in the 1980s and became an effective insurgency against the Israeli occupation of south Lebanon. After the civil war, it expanded into providing social services and welfare programs and becoming a political party. In 2006, it was still getting strong support from both Iran and Syria and was a major player in Lebanese politics.

The waiting room of the press office was comfortable but sparse, with a sofa and a big Hezbollah flag on the wall. There was usually a handful of Western journalists there, trying to lobby for access. Doing anything in Hezbollah-controlled areas without the appropriate permission was ill-advised.

After waiting ten minutes, I was summoned into the press liaison's office by a dour woman known only as Hajja Rena. I had just begun making polite conversation with the press officer when another man hurried in and began whispering to him in Arabic. The press officer's face registered surprise and then delight. There was a flurry of activity outside. Cars were honking; AK-47s were being fired into the sky; firecrackers resounded.

I wondered if there was a soccer match.

Two Hezbollah officers burst into the room. They had huge grins plastered across their faces and began pouring juice into glasses.

"Are we celebrating?" I asked.

"Yes, Miss Clarissa, we are," the press officer replied. "We have just received the wonderful news that the resistance has captured five Zionist soldiers."

For years, Hezbollah and the Israelis had fought skirmishes on the border, with the militia building an elaborate network of tunnels. The Israeli army patrolled the area aggressively to prevent rocket fire against villages in northern Israel. On this occasion one of its patrols had been ambushed.

This is how it always starts; this is why it never ends. The Israelis had been prepared to demolish Gaza to retrieve Gilad Shalit. Now they had lost five more soldiers. (It would soon emerge that only two had actually been captured in the raid. The other three had been killed.)

"Yes, *alhamdulillah*, this is a blessed day," the press officer beamed.

"How do you say in English? Cheers?"

I laughed nervously. "Will you excuse me for a moment?"

I ran outside and called my bosses in New York.

"You'd better send in an extra crew tomorrow," I said. "There's going to be a war."

THERE ARE TWO COMPONENTS TO COVERING A WAR: editorial and logistic. Of course, the journalism is what we love, producing the words and images that tell a story. But it doesn't happen without the tedious but essential practicalities.

As I left the Hezbollah office, I made a mental list of the things I needed to do. Source cars and drivers, translators and fixers. Book everyone hotel rooms, find a workspace, stock it with food and drinking water in case the supermarkets close. Buy a generator. Make sure there's a good supply of diesel. Organize temporary press accreditation for everyone flying in. Send drivers to the airport to meet them. I would have to buy printers and paper and pens and pencils and electric adapters and flashlights and bug spray and sun cream—the list went on.

All the preparations were necessary. In the next few weeks, Israeli air strikes targeted dozens of buildings in south Beirut regarded as belonging to Hezbollah, as well as roads, bridges—even the airport. After the airport was hit, incoming staff had to fly to Damascus and be driven the three hours to Beirut.

The conflict lasted exactly thirty-four days, but the destruction it wrought was enormous. Power stations and water and sewage treatment plants were hit and much of Lebanon ground to a halt. Tourists and dual citizens were evacuated out of the country. Beirut, normally buzzing during the summer months, became a ghost town as people fled to the safety of the mountains. Two hundred civilians were killed in the first week of air strikes. Another nine hundred would be killed before the war was over.

But this was unlike Baghdad, where being unable to go out made you feel so detached from events. This war was happening where I lived, in a city I had come to love. It was personal. Those fleeing weren't just "displaced people," they were my friends. For the first couple of weeks I continued to stay at my apartment, driving back and forth to the workspace, which we had set up on the third floor of a hotel near the Lebanese parliament. It was surreal to go from the office—impersonal, functional, full of colleagues who had flown in from around the world—to my little apartment. Often, I would arrive home in the middle of the night. There were no cars on the street, no electricity, no sounds, really, except for the periodic "boom" of air strikes reverberating through the air from Dahiyeh, the suburb that was Hezbollah's stronghold.

The park in front of my building was full of families from the south of Lebanon, near the border with Israel, who had fled the worst of the bombardment and were now camping out or squatting in apartments that had been abandoned.

Jonathan was among those sent in to cover the war. Technically, he was based in New York and covered the United Nations, but he was one of a few solid correspondents at Fox with extensive international experience and so they often sent him overseas when things flared up. I was excited to work with him again.

Early in the morning we would roam through Beirut, covering rescue operations at flattened buildings that all too soon turned to retrieving bodies, the overworked hospitals that were running out of medicine, the panicked evacuations. It was an oppressively hot summer, with a cloying humidity thickening the already smoky air.

Jonathan knew that I wanted to be a correspondent and he began pushing me to put together a "clip reel" to show what I could do. Every location we went to, I watched him closely as he did his "stand-ups." They were dynamic and engaging and easy to follow. Then he would make me try one. At first, I felt self-conscious. Who was I, at twenty-six, to presume I could be on television, to pretend I knew anything about anything? What if I sounded and looked foolish?

The key, Jonathan said, was to speak clearly and simply—and to try to sound conversational as if I were explaining things to someone's grandmother or talking to guys in a bar.

"And always find something to do with your hands," he said. Whether it was pointing at something or picking something up or holding your notebook—the hands needed to be involved.

I started to feel more comfortable, even began to enjoy doing stand-ups. I found that it felt instinctive to share what I was seeing and what it all meant with the viewer. Jonathan seemed impressed, or maybe surprised.

"You're a natural," he would tell me cheerfully.

One day, we went to interview the Lebanese president, Emile Lahoud.

After the civil war, it had been codified that the president would be a Maronite Christian, the prime minister a Sunni Muslim, and the Speaker of the parliament a Shi'a. It was a typically Lebanese deal.

To sit down with Lahoud was considered something of a scoop. Jonathan and I had spent some time going over the questions.

At the end of the interview, Jonathan thanked Lahoud. And then dropped a bombshell.

"And Clarissa, my producer, has a couple of questions for the Fox News website," he added, motioning me to his seat. The pages of my notebook turned moist with the sweat of my palms. I glanced quickly at the questions we had discussed, took a deep breath, and looked the president in the eye.

"How do you think the US should respond to Israel's strikes on Lebanon?" I asked, desperately trying to convey the sense of calm authority I had seen on the CBS flagship show, *60 Minutes*.

I don't even remember what his answer was. I was just so relieved not to have stumbled over the question.

As we left the palace in Baabda, I punched Jonathan on the arm.

"You muppet, you could have warned me you were going to do that."

He laughed. "You're welcome. I told you that you would have a killer clip reel by the time I left."

Several days later, as I walked into the workspace, I found Jonathan looking distracted and upset.

"What's going on?"

"It's a grim day," he said. "A bunch of children have been killed in a strike on Qana."

The Israelis had hit a three-story building that they claimed was being used by Hezbollah as a launching pad to fire Katyusha rockets across the border into northern Israel. But the residents of Qana said the building had no military purpose and dozens of civilians had been killed, many of them children. I spent the morning scrolling through footage of their lifeless bodies being pulled from the rubble. They were dusty and gray and rigid—their faces frozen in grotesque snapshots of the moment of death. I felt a wave of nausea and anger rising inside of me.

When people started gathering outside the UN building around the corner from our office, I knew it would deteriorate into a riot. No matter what their political persuasion, most Lebanese shared a deep sense of anger that the international community had done nothing to rein in the Israelis for their regular killing of civilians. I ran over and watched as hundreds of people began streaming into the square, waving Hezbollah and Lebanese flags, chanting "Death to America, death to Israel." When they saw our camera, they grabbed me, begging me to record their thoughts, to give their anguish an outlet. As more and more people poured in, I could feel the emotion of the crowd reaching a fever pitch. The chanting became shouting and wailing. I stood rather precariously on a concrete barrier next to the UN building, flanked by Hezbollah men in black, who had formed a protective barrier around some of the journalists. On the rare occasions when Hezbollah wanted a story to get out, they were very helpful to the journalists who could make it happen.

I watched as someone in the crowd threw a stone at the building, then another and another, until suddenly the whole crowd rushed on the building, taking me with them. They hammered down the doors in a frenzy and started setting fire to whatever they could, wailing all the time. It was the wailing that was perhaps the most disturbing part of it—a combination of pain and humiliation and desperation. It was a desperation that came with knowing that their cries would fall on deaf ears, that they could burn this building to the ground and there would still be no justice for the children of Qana.

A week later, we set out early to visit some of the areas worst affected in southern Lebanon. We were joined by a short, wiry, ginger-haired security guard called Matt. Until recently, journalists in war zones had operated without security protection. But after the invasion of Iraq, most major media organizations had invested heavily in hiring former soldiers as security advisers, renting armored vehicles and ensuring that their staff had Kevlar vests and the right training.

Fox was no exception. It sometimes felt strange, even a little embarrassing, to be traveling with these precautions when local people had no such protection.

The drive south was deceptively picturesque—through quaint mountain villages drenched in hibiscus and bougainvillea, past fig, citrus, and banana trees and tobacco fields.

We stopped in a village called Ansar. Every few minutes the ground trembled and we would look up to see a plume of gray smoke rising in the distance.

As we wandered through the village, we came to a house that had been flattened, killing the whole family of five. I remember looking through the rubble of their home. It felt so intimate, an inventory of their lives. A family album, covered in dust, revealed a smiling couple at their wedding. A math textbook, a slipper, a small blue coat, a piece of children's clothing, spattered with blood and buzzing with flies.

We shot video of the scene and interviewed a neighbor, but I felt frustrated that there was no way of really painting a picture of this family for the viewer. At best, we could maybe signal that ordinary people were being killed in this war, that there was real sadness and loss. We sat in silence on the way back to Beirut. I looked out the window and thought about the little blue coat in the rubble and who might have worn it.

As we drove through the southern suburbs on our way into the city, air strikes began hitting the area and we found ourselves driving too close to the pattern of explosions. Panicked civilians were running, looking for cover. Young Hezbollah operatives, dressed in black, were buzzing around on their mopeds, shouting into their radios and furiously gesturing at us to leave the area.

Our lead car pulled over to the side of the road. Jonathan and the cameraman got out and started filming, just as another missile struck barely 100 yards away. My ears were ringing. I did not want a repeat of Gaza and I knew how hostile Hezbollah could be to foreign journalists who were in the way. Like Hamas and other militant groups, they often saw Western journalists as spies.

"Why don't we get up the hill toward Baabda," I suggested, "where we can see the strikes from a distance?"

Our security adviser, Matt, ignored me. This was his first time in Lebanon. He was in his mid-fifties, and describing him as gruff would be generous. We had never hit it off; someone had warned me he didn't like working with women.

"They're bombing in a box formation," he kept saying, as if that made it safer for us to be standing there.

I began to get impatient. "See these guys on the mopeds?" I said a little too loudly. "They don't take kindly to Americans filming in these parts without permission, especially in the middle of air strikes like this."

My tone was probably a bit brusque but the situation hardly demanded politeness. He kept arguing with me, without ever making a point. I had only been working in war zones for a year, but I wasn't a total rookie and resented his arrogance. I was trembling with rage as I stormed back to the car.

Back at the workspace, Matt wouldn't drop it. He kept blathering on about being a paratrooper and box formations and how I shouldn't have spoken to him that way because he knew what he was talking about.

I pointed out that we all knew the rule—if any member of the team feels unsafe, we get out. But he kept talking right over me, as if he didn't hear me. Finally, I lost it.

"You are a fucking moron!" I said under my breath, standing up to leave the room.

"What did you say?"

"I said, you're a fucking moron!" I repeated more loudly.

Suddenly, he leaped up out of his chair and lunged at me. I jumped back in shock. A couple of colleagues grabbed his arms and pushed him back down into the chair.

"Whoa, whoa, everybody calm down. Clarissa, come with me," the bureau chief, Kim, said, dragging me out of the room. "Matt, I will deal with you in a minute."

I had never spoken to anyone like that in my life.

"I'm sorry," I said, "I should haven't lost it like that. But the guy is a fucking moron. And he's a fucking moron who hates women, which is the worst kind of fucking moron."

Kim laughed. "Yes, he is, but he's not worth upsetting yourself over. Go take the rest of the afternoon off."

I decided I needed some time out of Beirut and drove up to the mountain resort of Faraya to see Christophe. He and other wealthy Lebanese who hated Hezbollah had retreated to the mountains and felt detached from the conflict. I told myself I was going up there to store some valuables, but it was a pretty flimsy excuse. I knew full well that I really just wanted to be held tight.

We met at an outdoor bar perched over an incredible infinity pool that seemed to melt into the mountains. The air was cool and clean. How the other half live, I thought, thinking of the scruffy kids riding mopeds for Hezbollah. I looked down at my jeans and T-shirt and ran a hand through my dirty hair self-consciously.

Christophe was sitting with a woman with long curly hair and big white teeth.

"Hey, babe," he jumped up and gave me a big hug and then turned to the woman with curly hair. "This is my friend, Michaela."

"Hi, Michaela," I said, smiling and shaking her hand. I wondered if he was sleeping with her, then hated myself for going there. The purpose of tonight was to relax and have fun. We sat and drank chilled white wine as the sun dipped below the mountains. People were milling around, swimming and chatting and laughing. For them, this was déjà vu. They had lived through war before and their main focus was to avoid it—to try to lead as pleasant an existence as possible.

I was agitated. The wine tasted sour on my tongue but I kept drinking, hoping it would help me transform from the shivering, exhausted alien I felt like into a beautiful and carefree woman.

Christophe was telling a story in French about his latest kiteboarding accident and I smiled along without really listening. I noticed that he smiled a lot at Michaela and touched her arm as he talked. I felt a pinprick of jealousy. Why had I come here? To pretend to laugh at stories I had already heard and watch him try to bed a pretty girl? We ordered another bottle of wine, and then another, until finally the alcohol began to do its magic and I felt the stress of the past weeks loosen its grip.

We decided to go to one of the trendiest nightclubs in Beirut, Element, which had moved up to the mountains along with all the privileged youth for the summer. I rode with Christophe, and Michaela drove with his friend.

"So, how do you know Michaela?" I asked, once we were in the car. I was trying to sound nonchalant but it was pretty transparent.

"She's just an old friend, babe."

"Are you sleeping with her?" So much for sounding nonchalant.

He smiled. "It's not a big deal, babe. You don't have to worry about Michaela because she is nothing to me. But you, you are my best friend. *Je t'aime. Vraiment, je t'aime*," he said.

He reached out and stroked my cheek. Tears sprang to my eyes and I quickly looked out the window. I felt a pang of longing to be back in Beirut with Jonathan and the rest of my colleagues.

Inside the club, Lebanese girls with perfect French manicures danced on the bar, looking down at me with pity as I sat chain-smoking, emaciated and exhausted. They must have been able to see the judgment in my eyes.

"It's not our war, *hayati* (sweetheart)," one of them said. In other words, it was fine to dance while others lay pulverized under tons of rubble. But by the end of the night I found myself dancing, too. My mind was empty and quiet; my body no longer belonged to me. Maybe this is how you survive decades of war. Maybe it's only when the music stops that it hits you.

Another Lebanese friend would later talk to me about the numbness many of them felt at that time. There was no electricity and we were sitting by candlelight smoking joints. There was never a shortage of hash in Lebanon, even during times of war. Beirut felt particularly spooky that night, all black and empty.

"It's like someone has cut our wrist and given us a shot of morphine," my friend said. "We're bleeding to death, but we can't feel it, we can't even feel it."

I woke up early the next morning. I felt queasy from an excess of white wine and from the lack of sleep. I looked over at Christophe sleeping peacefully and wondered if anything in that pretty head occasionally disturbed his peace.

It was a relief to get back to Beirut, closer to the war, closer to my other life, to real life.

BEFORE THE WAR ENDED, we interviewed the Lebanese prime minister, Fouad Siniora. He might have held that office; he didn't exercise much power. This was a war being fought by a group that ran a parallel state against its sworn enemy. Most Lebanese were bystanders. Some had ridiculed Siniora for weeping during a televised Arab League meeting, in an impassioned plea for an immediate and complete cease-fire. But he was in an impossible situation. Hezbollah was holding the country hostage, and he had no means of stopping them or of protecting Lebanon from Israel.

He understood that nothing good could come of this war. Both sides would claim victory; in reality, neither would taste it. And they would begin planning for the next war.

"Look at how Israel came in last time in '82 to bomb out the PLO [Palestine Liberation Organization]," he told us after the interview. "Well, they bombed out the PLO and they sowed the seeds for Hezbollah."

It was similar to what had happened in Gaza, when Israel had stamped out Fatah, the dominant political faction in the PLO, which only paved the way for Hamas.

Siniora chastised us for the US media's coverage of the war, which he saw as biased. "As if the tears of Israelis are worth more than the blood of Lebanese, as if we are children of a lesser God."

I thought of the day when a large convoy of Lebanese civilians trying to flee from the south had been hit by an Israeli strike. Fox had led every broadcast with reports from Israel, talking about people from border towns being treated for hysteria because of constant rocket attacks. Not for a moment did I minimize the trauma among Israeli civilians living under a barrage of Hezbollah rockets. But on that same day, dozens of Lebanese had been killed—for no other reason than they were Lebanese.

As the war lurched to its stalemate, most journalists were starting to burn out. It had been twenty-eight days of three or four hours of sleep a night, of coffee and cigarettes and chicken kebab sandwiches as the main form of sustenance, of working like dogs, of cracking hangovers, of struggling to find new angles to keep the story fresh, of sifting through rubble until it no longer had any effect, of becoming desensitized to the enormity of death.

I had moved into a room at the hotel by this stage because security (not Matt, thank goodness) thought it wasn't safe for me to keep driving back to my apartment in the middle of the night. I walked out of my room one morning to find Jonathan curled up asleep on the floor. One of the hotel cleaning ladies stood nearby, frowning. I smiled with embarrassment and made a sign to indicate that I would resolve this.

"Jonathan," I hissed, nudging him. "Get up, you old lush!"

"Good morning, dear," he said, blinking open his eyes. "I must have nodded off."

"How late were you up?"

"I dunno, three or four. I think I called Kim at some point and told her I was gay."

"Are you gay?"

"I don't think so."

"Hilarious," I deadpanned. "You better go clean up, you have a live shot in an hour."

Six days later the war was over after both sides agreed to a UN-brokered cease-fire. It felt spectacularly anticlimactic. The only people celebrating were Hezbollah, who promoted it as a major victory with huge rallies and announced the construction of a new museum. And by not losing to a far superior military machine, it was a victory of sorts. But most Lebanese were simply worn out and fed up that their country had been hijacked by a militia and then bombed to pieces by its enemy. The economy was in tatters and there was a Herculean cleanup job ahead of them.

As soon as our operation wound down and the airport finally re-opened, I got on a plane and went to see my parents in the south of France. One war had ended, but I had to dive back into another soon. I was sched-uled to go back to Baghdad in a few weeks and I desperately needed to get some rest before then.

"You've lost too much weight, darling," my mother chastised gently. "It doesn't suit your face."

I laughed. This from a woman who had once told me, "You look bet-ter when you're bony." It must be bad.

My parents had mixed feelings about me spending so much time in war zones. On the one hand, they were incredibly proud. On the other hand, they were constantly worried about my safety. The attack on the Palestine Hotel in Baghdad had shattered the illusion that it was some-how vaguely safe to be a journalist in a war zone.

I spent the week in France stuffing my face with baguettes and not smoking cigarettes and acting like a spoiled teenager. My dad and I played hours of Scrabble and went on walks together. Ever since I was little, we had made a ritual of doing these things together, enjoying long conversa-tions and comfortable silences as we went. My mother fussed over me endlessly and probed me about my career. When was I going to start doing on-air reporting? Why was I doubting my own abilities? Was I being persistent enough? Her nagging often drove me crazy, but it also gave me the push I needed.

I called my boss in New York to ask if he had looked at the clip reel that I put together with Jonathan's help in Beirut. He said that he had and that they were willing to give me a shot at reporting on air, provided I do a six-week rotation in Baghdad over Thanksgiving, Christmas, and New Year's Eve.

"Yes, yes, of course," I spluttered over the phone. "You won't regret this!"

I felt sick with nerves and excitement.

"Mom," I cried, running out to the pool, "they're going to let me do on-air reporting!"

"That's great, darling! I knew they would," she said. "You're made to do this."

Five

I was twenty-six years old and consumed with nerves. I was about to stare into a camera lens and speak to an audience of millions of people whom I couldn't see and try to sound conversational and fluent about important and complex events in Iraq. It was not a moment I could really rehearse. I had stood in front of my mirror in Beirut and practiced talking about a news story for 90 seconds countless times. But I knew that once I had my earpiece in and my microphone on, it would be a completely different experience.

Remarkably, my first live shot as an on-air reporter for Fox went well. I had written simple and clear notes for myself in case I went blank. But once I heard the anchor's voice prompting me, "Clarissa—what's the latest?" the adrenaline kicked in and I started talking and it was over before I knew it.

During those six weeks in Baghdad, I did go blank a couple of times on air. One time, I was talking about an insurgent attack on a mosque that had left the building engulfed in flames, killing the worshippers inside. As I described the aftermath, I could feel myself suddenly become lightheaded and everything going very quiet and my mind just going blank.

"And the people inside were burned," I said, "uh . . . uh . . . uh . . ." I could hear a tiny voice inside my head screaming at me to wake up and just keep talking, just say anything to avoid the deafening silence that is the biggest no-no on live television.

"They were burned to a crisp," I blurted out, relieved that I had managed to finish the sentence and yet utterly horrified that I had said something so awful.

"That's one for the blooper reel," my bureau chief said when I had finished the live shot. I felt so mortified, and yet, incredibly, there was no reaction from our office in New York, nor any from viewers that I heard about. To this day, I am intensely grateful that I came of age as a television reporter before the advent of Twitter.

On another occasion I did an entire live shot with my bra strap showing. A couple of weeks into my first rotation as a correspondent I received a note from a female anchor, with the headline "some girly advice." She wrote:

> You're gonna be a star. And trust me, I know Roger Ailes . . .
> he loves girls to wear their hair down. He once told Megyn
> Kendall [Kelly] (my good friend) not to wear her hair up
> anymore. You guys have similar hair so I know he'd prefer it.
> Gotta look out for you sexy girls!! :) I tell Megyn the same
> thing!

Roger Ailes was the legendary boss at Fox who had turned it into a powerhouse among the "all-news" channels but whose behavior toward female employees would eventually lead to an ignominious departure. And Megyn Kelly would be in the front line of women complaining about his conduct. I never experienced any untoward behavior during my time at Fox, but I could see how pervasive sexism was just by looking at the women on our channel with their seemingly identical uniform: cascading hair (preferably blonde), figure-hugging dress, big smile.

I had always found it distracting when female reporters had perfect blowouts and lipstick in war zones. It was so jarring to watch an immaculately coiffured woman opine about the terrible suffering around her. But if that was what the big man wanted ... So I bit my tongue and tried wearing my hair down for the next couple of live shots even though I knew it didn't really suit me.

My mother, who watched every single one of my live shots like a hawk, called me immediately and said, "For the love of God, you look like SpongeBob SquarePants."

I returned my hair to its usual style. In later years, I would be asked again to wear my hair down, or to cut it short. Wearing your hair up in TV news appeared to be something of a revolutionary act. While Fox was particularly egregious in dictating a "look" that its female talent should embrace, every US television network clearly placed great emphasis on how women should look and dress on air. I would see pretty girls with no real talent ascend to meteoric heights and brilliant women who were less telegenic languish, unused. No matter who you work for or what story you cover, television is at its essence a superficial business.

The timing of my trial stint was fortuitous. A few days after Christmas, Saddam Hussein was suddenly executed. None of the more senior correspondents was able to fly in in time for the story, which meant that I spent the better part of 36 hours propped up in the live-shot position doing wall-to-wall coverage. It was strangely exhilarating—the excitement of sharing breaking news as it's happening, the adrenaline of staying awake for hours on end, the buzz that comes with knowing that you are speaking fluently on air.

At the end of the six weeks in Baghdad, Jonathan Hunt generously put me in touch with his agent, who signed me on the spot (and who is still my agent). I did a couple more rotations with Fox but I knew instinctively that my future didn't lie with them. When my stints in Iraq did not lead to the offer of a contract with Fox, I wasn't particularly surprised. The network was driven by outspoken personalities and red-meat opinion, and its foreign coverage felt more like a token gesture than a sincere effort. I didn't experience any pressure to toe a particular editorial line, but with the exception of a couple of shows, I found its coverage unwatchable. Fox had been very good to me and had given me my first break, but it was time to move on.

My clip reel was doing the rounds. In the summer of 2007, ABC News came calling. They wanted to hire a junior-level Moscow correspondent. None of the other networks had full-time Moscow correspondents anymore. It simply wasn't a big enough story. ABC had been kicked out of the country for nearly two years after airing an interview with a Chechen rebel leader whom the Russians accused of ordering many high-profile terrorist acts, including the one on the Dubrovka Theatre in Moscow. Now the Kremlin was willing to let the network back into the country, but only if ABC installed a full-time correspondent as a gesture of goodwill.

Five years after my CNN internship, I was fascinated to see what had changed in Russia and leaped at the chance to work for one of the big networks. Cable news was all about live shots and breaking news and breathless moments. Working for a network with one or two shows a day brought a different challenge—crafting a piece with strong video, vivid writing, good pacing, and a compelling voiceover. I had to learn how to synthesize complex and often dry events into coherent and gripping stories.

Part of that challenge for me was to settle on an accent. My transatlantic existence meant that mine veered from New England to Old England and places in between. "You don't want the viewer to spend your whole piece trying to work out your nationality," an ABC executive told me.

When a producer asked me where in Canada I was from, I decided to keep my accent more consistently American.

The Russia I found in October 2007 had settled into a state of lethargy. Most Russians had had enough of "democracy." President Vladimir Putin was providing security, a better standard of living (thanks to buoyant energy prices), and renewed self-respect. So people didn't much care that he was also quietly amassing huge power and wealth, and outside of Moscow they didn't see how a small elite was stealing the country's resources. There were Ferraris and Bentleys cruising the streets of the Russian capital, designer boutiques and any number of high-end restaurants with high-end prices. Enough of this new prosperity had trickled down: the pensioners had plenty of *grechka* (buckwheat) and it would take a lot more than a bar of chocolate to get lucky.

Still, something had been lost in the bargain. The people were slightly better off, depending on where they lived and how old they were. The lucky ones could travel for all-inclusive vacations in Turkey and Egypt. But it seemed to me that for millions of Russians life had become solely about acquiring more "stuff." Perhaps it was the inevitable reaction to decades of the Soviet command economy, where drab, poorly made goods were doled out in dreary state-run stores. Russia was now an ideology-free zone; there was nothing to aspire to but getting rich.

Explaining the new Russia to an American audience was never less than fascinating but also devilishly difficult in the 100 seconds you were allowed for a piece (and that was on a good day). To say that Russia was a place of extremes and contradictions was an understatement. There were hot summers and freezing winters, abject poverty and obscene wealth, a harshness that could border on heartlessness, and a love of nostalgia that was downright cheesy. Young Russian women were incredibly disciplined about their diets, yet the supermarkets had aisles groaning with chocolates and sweets. Russians were hard-headed and cynical but also incredibly sentimental and superstitious (spit three times to avoid jinxing something, never buy someone an even number of flowers—it spells death—and for God's sake, do not make the mistake of whistling indoors).

Walking home from the Moscow bureau one evening, I saw the aftermath of a bad car accident. I watched, horrified, as a young woman struggled to breathe on the cobblestones. She had been thrown from a taxi after it collided with another car. A crowd was now gathered around her, watching her twitch and gasp on the ground. Her blouse had been torn, revealing dark purple internal bleeding around her torso. But no one in the crowd knelt beside her or screamed for an ambulance. No one retrieved her bag, or held her hand, or offered to call her loved ones or whispered reassuring words. Instead they stood, observing the scene passively, mute.

Angry tears pricked my eyes. "She's dying—why doesn't anyone help her?" I shouted in English to no one in particular. The crowd looked at me like I was deranged and shuffled away from me. Two ambulance workers arrived on the scene and hoisted her body onto a stretcher. The taxi driver, who appeared not to have a scratch on him, picked up her bag and handed it to them in a daze. Then the ambulance doors closed and the crowd dispersed. Moscow, it seemed, was a lonely place to die.

The next day I related the story to Sasha, one of my Russian colleagues at ABC, still disturbed that no one had tried to comfort the injured woman in what I presumed were her last moments.

"Clarissa, you have to understand," Sasha said with a sigh. "In Soviet times, other people's problems could bring you problems. So you didn't get involved. Even today, people don't want trouble, so they don't help."

In the Soviet era, Russians really had two options. Either you bought into the great myth of the Soviet experiment, or you kept your head down. The elite had been one of intellectuals who distinguished themselves from *narod* (the people) through learning and education, not Lamborghinis and Prada. In the new Russia, getting a PhD and being able to quote the poems of Anna Akhmatova was no longer enough to command respect. Academia was for suckers. The elite were identified by cash and how flashily they could spend it.

One Russian friend had explained this heady transition to me like this: "Imagine you grow up in a religious cult and your life is built around the rules and regulations and culture of that religion. And life is hard but it's also predictable because you have a clear sense of what's allowed and what's not allowed. You're like animals in a zoo and you know the rest of the world is watching you with curiosity, but it's safe in the zoo and there are fences everywhere. And then one day you wake up and you're told there is no God, the whole thing was a lie. And the gates of the zoo are opened and the fences are gone and no one gives you food anymore and you no longer have any idea what you have spent your entire life in service of."

As I'd found out on my internship, for most people Russia was now a place you went to pursue career opportunities at the cost of gut-wrenching loneliness.

It would not be an exaggeration to say that my best friend during those first few months in Moscow was probably Volodya, the ABC driver. He was about five feet seven inches, built like a sack of potatoes, and had a strong earthy smell. When he smiled, which was not that often, you could see his three silver teeth. His face was doughy and pink and his eyes were almost hidden in the softness of it. On one eyelid he had an enormous pink mole that just sort of hung there. I sometimes wondered how he could see properly.

Volodya came from a small town in the Urals and wore a little silver cross on a piece of blue string around his neck, even though he rarely went to church. He drove a VW van that had been purchased sometime in the 1980s, and while we were out on shoots he stayed in the van and listened to business (*beeznees*) FM, drinking kefir (a yogurt-like drink) and eating *kolbasa* (a bologna-like sausage). The van always smelled a little sour.

We would spend long stretches sitting in Moscow's notorious traffic. Volodya never drove faster than 30 miles per hour and never changed lanes, even if we were at a standstill while the next lane was whizzing by. He had a sort of patience about life; he just accepted things for what they were.

Volodya didn't speak a word of English, which meant that I was less shy about speaking Russian to him and so we would chat for hours. He told me proudly that he used to be the captain of a riverboat police unit. He had worked as a driver for the past ten years to subsidize his meager pension, like millions of other elderly Russians. In his spare time, of which there was little, Volodya told me he liked to play with his grandchildren and read Agatha Christie novels.

I would ask him if life was better in 2007 than it was under Communism and he would shrug fatalistically, as if to say, "a bit." But he had no interest in politics and no faith in the New Russia.

One day, as I wrestled to pull a heavy bag out of the van, he pushed me aside to do it himself. "*Chto stoboy?*" I asked (What's up with you?) "Clarees!" he said, almost angrily (everyone in Russia called me Clarees for reasons I still don't fully understand). "How will you have babies?" I burst into laughter.

He decided that I was too thin and he frequently brought me hunks of gag-inducing fatty meat smeared on bread, which I obediently ate in front of him while his three silver teeth beamed with satisfaction. There were countless other small acts of kindness. He took me to the circus with his grandchildren; he bought me a pair of *valenki* (Russian wool boots that are warmer than anything else in the world) out of his modest wages. He potted my plants, gave me music, and burned four CDs of pictures from the Urals so I could see what his hometown was like.

Whenever he dropped me at the airport, I would embarrass him greatly by making him hug me goodbye. *"Obnimaem?"* I would say (We hug?), and he would roll his eyes and blush before obediently giving me a squeeze.

To thank him for his kindnesses, I took him and his granddaughter to a popular Russian chain restaurant called Yolki Palki (which roughly translates as something between "holy cow" and "oh crap"). It was the little girl's first trip to a restaurant, and the two of them took four trips to the salad bar. I felt a pang of guilt: how we took such simple treats for granted in the West.

Perhaps the most remarkable thing about Volodya, though, was that he never wore gloves, no matter how cold it was. I frequently chastised him for this, but he just dismissed my protests with a swipe of the hand and a grunt, *"Ne nada, Clarees, ne nada."* (I don't need them.)

SOON AFTER I ARRIVED IN MOSCOW, I was invited to dinner by an exceptionally wealthy Russian-American acquaintance called Alex.

I was mildly intrigued and a little apprehensive about the invitation. I had been introduced before to members of Russia's *novi russki* (a moderately pejorative term meaning nouveau riche or literally new Russians) and had found that, while some enjoyed the attention of a journalist, most viewed me as a pathetic curiosity rather than a strong, independent woman.

I arrived at Alex's triplex apartment overlooking the Moskva River at exactly 8:00 p.m. Naturally, I was the first to arrive, and I cursed myself for being slavishly punctual. A butler let me in and took my coat as I stood in the hallway and surveyed the overwhelming morass of black marble before me.

I smoothed down my dress in an attempt to stop my hands from sweating. Alex came bounding down the stairs with friendly confidence. He was curious and engaging, peppering me with questions as he poured me a glass of Cristal champagne, all the while giving a ream of instructions to the butler in rapid-fire Russian.

"How's your Russian?" Alex asked with a smile before continuing. "We are having a special guest tonight and he requested Uzbek food, so my kitchen staff have been busy all day cooking."

"Delicious," I said. "I love samsa [a savory meat pastry]. Who's the special guest?"

"My good friend Saif Qaddafi," he said.

It certainly wasn't going to be a boring evening. Some of the other guests began to arrive. For the most part, they were not as sociable as Alex. There was a deputy minister who was polite but clearly uncomfortable at the prospect of an evening with an American journalist. There was an immaculately dressed real estate mogul who appeared to spend more time in the gym daily than I had in my entire life. He was accompanied by his girlfriend, who wore skintight leather pants and pushed a piece of lettuce sulkily around her plate for hours in an elaborate charade designed to create the illusion of eating.

In general, I had struggled to bond with young Russian women. The older generation was tough but at least they had grit and soul. Many in the younger generation appeared to be focused on looking perfect, finding a rich man, and limiting their caloric intake. If there was a mantra that seemed to unite them, it was "You can never be too rich or too skinny." They wore high heels at all times: on the subway, even to carry bags of groceries through the winter slush. On one level, I admired their ability to withstand intense physical pain. And they definitely looked amazing. At the same time, it irked me that it all seemed to be done to please men. Being honest with myself, I think their impeccable appearance probably made me feel unfeminine and unattractive. I could almost see them whispering about me with pity. "Look, she is wearing sneakers and not for the gym. It is very sad."

By 9:30 p.m., the guest of honor had yet to arrive and Alex was growing irritated. Apparently, Saif Qaddafi was running late because he was meeting with one of Russia's best-known "oligarchs," as the super-rich had become known. Oleg Deripaska was the second-richest man in Russia, an aluminum magnate with close ties to Putin. The following month, I would attend a party thrown by Deripaska. We stood talking by the side of the roomful of "models" who had been hired for the event. I was struck by how intently he listened, as if he were making a mental note of everything I was saying. Clearly, you didn't make it to the top of the rich list in Putin's Russia without being astute.

Sometime after 10 p.m. Qaddafi finally arrived with a gaggle of bodyguards. He was dressed in Western clothes, clean-shaven and handsome. He wore glasses and seemed very distant. During introductions he shook my hand but barely seemed to register my presence.

"Let's eat," said Alex. "My chef has prepared an Uzbek feast."

"I'm not hungry," said Saif thoughtlessly. "I ate something earlier."

Alex gritted his teeth and smiled. "Come, sit down, you can just taste it."

While Saif might not have wanted to eat, he certainly seemed happy to drink. After an initial dispute over whether his bodyguards could sit at the table with us ("Absolutely not," said Alex. "They must," insisted Saif. "You are in my house, they will eat in the kitchen with the drivers," Alex declared), we all sat down.

I could not help but admire the firm way that Alex handled this manchild. I was seated directly across from Saif but he had little interest in talking to me. Instead, he addressed the men at the table, sinking glass after glass of red wine. His teeth turned dark gray and his gestures became more exaggerated as he rambled about the plight of his Palestinian brothers (speeches I took with a grain of salt given that our host, whose hospitality he regularly accepted, was a major supporter of Israel). He knew how to solve the Israeli-Palestinian crisis, he said, by uniting Israel and Palestine into "Isratine," a secular, federalized, republican state. His father would later champion the idea at the UN.

I think I managed to get in one question during the meal, which Saif barely acknowledged before returning to his meandering geopolitical diatribe. Was I even actually there? I felt a familiar burn of indignation. Whether it came from arrogant teenaged Etonians in the UK or the sons of brutal Middle Eastern dictators, misogyny provoked a feeling of impotent rage in me. Anger at being so easily overlooked or dismissed because of my gender. And anger at myself for being unsure of how to respond to it. Push back too hard and you are labeled as aggressive, or chippy, or a bitch. Don't push back enough and you are condoning it.

I fantasized about calling Saif out for the bullshit he was saying. Isratine? It sounded like a bedtime drink. But in the presence of this gilded set, I also felt clumsy, unattractive, and dumb, tongue-tied and embarrassed, like a little girl who had no business sitting at the grown-ups' table.

At about midnight our host suggested that we all head to Diaghilev, an impossibly lavish nightclub modeled on Paris's nineteenth-century notorious cabaret, Le Moulin Rouge. This was a place where Moscow's elite hid behind a velvet rope to compete among themselves with displays of decadence. There's a very fitting Russian *anekdot* (basically a joke) about two *novi russki* men meeting at a party. They are both wearing the same Hermès tie. One says proudly, "I got mine from Harrods in London and I paid four hundred euros for it." "Ha," the other retorts smugly, "I bought mine in Paris for six hundred!"

It was decided that I would ride in Alex's car with Saif and his bodyguard. I hopped into the back of the armored Mercedes and Saif slid in beside me. I was surprised that he immediately pushed his body right up against mine. Then, having barely said a word to me all night (I am certain he didn't even know my name), he lunged for me, moaning "baby" as he tried to stick his tongue in my mouth. There was no preamble, no pickup line even, no indication that he had been contemplating making a move. My first reaction was to honk with laughter.

"Whoa—what are you doing!?" I asked incredulously.

He put his hand up to cup my head and pull me in for a kiss, moaning "baby" again in a ridiculous way so that I couldn't stop laughing.

"Whoa, wait, stop," I protested, pulling back.

Alex, who was sitting next to Saif, was embarrassed. "Saif, stop, brother. What are you doing?"

For a moment Saif pulled away and we began to drive. I tried to change the subject, but Saif started stroking my fur coat (a mink of my mother's from the '80s that I had brought to Russia as a buffer against the frigid winters).

"You're so soft, baby," he whispered as he petted me. I could feel his stale breath, sour and hot on my face. I wanted to burn the coat.

"I'm a journalist, hello!!" I said, trying to strike a balance between delivering a stark warning and defusing an awkward situation with humor.

"Such a smart baby." He licked into my ear.

"*Khalas*," I hissed at him (it means "enough" in Arabic). He looked momentarily thrown that I had spoken to him in Arabic. See, I thought to myself, if you had bothered to talk to me you would know that I'd lived in Beirut for the last two and a half years, you asshole.

"Saif, cut it out," Alex barked. But Saif didn't stop. And I realized that he wouldn't stop because he couldn't quite grasp the possibility that I genuinely had no interest in having his tongue in my mouth. It simply never occurred to him that I didn't automatically want to be touched by him. Why wouldn't I? His father was one of the most powerful and

wealthiest dictators in the Middle East and he was the anointed successor. His hand began rubbing my leg.

Enraged, I spat at him, pushing his hand away, "*Khalas, ya ibn shar-
mouta*" (it means "enough, you son of a whore"). He froze for a moment,
shocked, then broke into a leering smile.

"I love you."

At this point, Alex had had enough.

"Saif, this woman is a friend of mine. You are disgracing me. Stop it
immediately."

Apparently, something in his words succeeded in penetrating Saif's
alcoholic haze. He finally backed off. Or at least, he stopped trying to jam
his tongue into my mouth. For the rest of the drive, he contented himself
with leaning his head against my shoulder and stroking my fur coat.

Once we arrived at the nightclub, he passed out on a sofa in our VIP
area. Later on, he left with a striking young woman with a dark bob and a
skintight dress designed to showcase her permanently erect nipples. She
had a smile frozen on her face and giggled at everything Saif said, even
though by this stage he was almost entirely incoherent.

It reminded me of another typically Muscovite evening of debauch-
ery some years earlier. I had made a point of visiting a strip club with some
male expat friends. In part, I went to show how open-minded I was, in part
to show that anything they could do, I could, too. And, anyway, strip clubs
were a fixture of Russian culture. I made a big show of finding the whole
thing hilarious and great fun. I drank vodka shots and cheered on the
dancers. See, I'm one of the guys, too; see how OK I am with this, I practically screamed.

But as I watched those women closely, I became depressed. Because they weren't really women. Most of them were barely twenty, and
some perhaps even younger. And every night they danced, with their
fake laughs and empty eyes and emaciated frames, gyrating against my

friends, tossing their hair and giggling at jokes in English that they couldn't understand.

When I made eye contact with the girls, I could sense how my presence flummoxed them. They didn't want me there because we were both in on the lie. I knew they weren't having fun, I knew how cheap they felt, I knew they were probably repulsed by most of the men in this club, and perhaps most poignantly, I knew that many of them felt shame. I knew that they had grandparents back home in the Urals who thought they were working as models in Moscow. And they probably had the goods on me, too. They knew I wasn't having fun, they knew how cheap I felt, engaged in this over-the-top show to appear empowered when in actual fact I was merely proving the opposite. I wonder if they realized I felt their shame, too. That almost all of us have at some point. The shame of pretending to find a man funny because he's in a position of power even though he creeps you out. The shame of being touched by someone you don't really want to be touched by but don't know how to say no to. The shame of being leered at by someone you don't want even to glance at you, but you're wearing a tight dress so deep down you feel responsible for it. The shame of being lunged at by the son of an Arab dictator, who doesn't even know your name.

Salman Rushdie writes in his novel *Shame*, "But shame is like everything else; live with it for long enough and it becomes part of the furniture." Later in the book he warns, "Humiliate people for long enough and a wildness bursts out of them."

The book is about Pakistan and the sexual repression that Rushdie sees as ingrained in Pakistani culture. Yet, as I read it, a Western student at Yale, I found I could perfectly relate to the feeling his female protagonist described. This emotion, supposedly handed down to us from Eve, isn't limited to conservative societies and isn't the exclusive domain of any particular creed or religion. Often it is in the most permissive societies that we feel shame—and ours is compounded because we are not supposed to feel it. We are supposed to enjoy this "liberation," this equality, this freedom to have our bodies commented on and viewed as if they were public property. So we hide the shame behind big smiles and high heels and trade bawdy stories about our sexual experiences over Manhattans with our girlfriends.

Years later, I saw that Saif Qaddafi had been captured by rebels after the Arab Spring swept through Libya. I felt a delicious prick of schadenfreude. At the time of writing this, he's safe and sound, sitting in some opulent villa, reportedly in the Emirates, and waiting for his moment to waltz in and save the day in Libya. And so it goes.

ON AUGUST 7, 2008, I was sitting in the Moscow bureau killing time before my vacation, which was due to begin at the end of the week.

For several weeks there had been skirmishes between Russian-backed separatists and Georgian forces in South Ossetia, a small region that claimed independence from Georgia after the collapse of the Soviet Union and had received some support from Russia. I'd been keeping an eye on the violence as it escalated, though I wasn't sure that ABC News would be terribly interested in a place few of their viewers knew existed.

Vladimir Putin intensely disliked Georgian president Mikheil Saakashvili. The Columbia Law School–educated Saakashvili spoke perfect English and had branded himself as a champion of Western democracy—right on Russia's border. Under his leadership, Georgia held joint military exercises with the US and was pushing for NATO membership. Since the collapse of the Soviet Union, Russia had become obsessed with what it saw as NATO encirclement, as the Western alliance crept closer and closer to its borders.

That morning the separatists had broken a ceasefire that had been declared just hours beforehand. If the Georgians responded, it would give the Russians the perfect pretext for intervening, something they were itching to do. That night, Georgian forces began shelling South Ossetia's capital. A column of Russian troops had been staged near the border and was expected to be mobilized soon.

My vacation was starting to look like a pipe dream.

I got a call from the desk at 2 a.m.

"You're flying to Tbilisi in the morning."

"I think the Russians are really pissed off now," Max, the bureau cameraman, said hours later as we checked in our fifteen cases of gear at the airport. "They had enough of this Saakashvili."

If only I could just say it like that in my reports.

Max was a lovely, even-tempered man who shot beautiful pictures. He was Russian but spoke excellent English and had worked in news for decades, so he could take on the role of a translator and producer as well.

By the time we landed in the Georgian capital, the Russian air force had begun bombing targets inside Georgia. Their tanks had crossed into South Ossetia and surrounded Tskhinvali, the tiny capital. Suddenly, every show wanted me.

The pace of work was unlike anything I had ever experienced. Max and I raced to meet the demand. There were three shows a day: *Good Morning America*, which was at 3:00 p.m. local time; *World News*, at 2:30 a.m. local time; and then *Nightline*, at 7:30 a.m. local time. This meant that I slept a maximum of three or four hours a night. The time we had between *Nightline* and *GMA* had to be spent shooting material for the next day of shows.

I felt permanently jittery, with a sour taste in my mouth. If Saddam's execution had been my crash course in doing live shots, this was baptism by fire as a network correspondent.

"Your track could be faster to give it energy," one well-intentioned producer advised me.

The next day, I tracked the piece as quickly as I could, then fed it to the editors in London. I was worried it was too fast, but they said it sounded good. Minutes after it aired on TV, I got five emails telling me I sounded like Donald Duck on crack.

I ran into the bathroom of the hotel room that we were using as a workspace and burst into tears before calling my parents. How many hysterical calls they would receive from their strung-out daughter over the years!

"Everyone must be laughing at me, the track sounded so bad," I sobbed. "I am so tired, I can't think straight."

"You can do this, Doondle," my father said, using the nickname he had used for me since I was little. "It's not forever and you're doing so well. Just take a deep breath. Mum and I are so proud of you."

"You will laugh about this soon, I promise," my mother added. "Just learn to trust your instincts in the future."

The next day I had an opportunity to redeem myself.

"Diane [Sawyer] really wants to hear you speak Russian," one of the *GMA* producers instructed.

"No problem," I said. It would show that I could communicate first-hand with people affected by this sudden explosion of conflict.

We went to a school that was housing displaced Georgians from South Ossetia and I interviewed them in Russian. We came back and fed in the material and then waited to see if Diane liked the piece. After it aired, I got a call from the same *GMA* producer.

"Why didn't you speak Russian after I specifically asked you to?"

I felt a flush of panic. We had fed tons of material of me speaking in Russian.

"What? I did."

"Well, it wasn't in there."

I hung up and got on the phone with the editor who had put the piece together in London.

"Oh, yeah, I cut out the bits of you speaking Russian because I didn't have a cutaway shot to edit it with."

I was learning that getting your journalism to air is a multilayered process.

I ran back into the bathroom and had another cry. In later years, I would get a little better at dealing with the intense emotional roller coaster that comes with sleep deprivation, but even today I get stressed out on big stories when I haven't slept enough. I think for all journalists in the field, the lack of sleep is enemy number one. Not only does it slow you down editorially, but it affects your judgment, and that can be critical when split-second decisions about your safety are needed.

After a couple of days, ABC News sent a producer in from London to work with me and I finally started to hit my stride. When the Russians launched a major bombing campaign on the city of Gori, just an hour and a half northwest of the capital, we raced to the city and followed the story of the last civilians who were fleeing. When Russian tanks, days later, advanced to just twenty-five miles from Tbilisi, I marched up to them with a microphone in my hand.

"*Chto vi delayete zdes?*" I asked the Russian soldiers (What are you doing here?). Max looked mortified by my boldness.

"The language you used was very direct, Clarees," he explained. "Sounds more like 'What the fuck are YOU doing here?'"

"That's about right, then," I said. We both laughed.

If Saakashvili was waiting for the US to help defend his country, he was going to be waiting a long time. While American officials publicly made bombastic statements voicing support for Georgia's sovereignty and calling on Russia's military to pull out immediately, privately, many were irritated that the Georgian president had allowed the Russians to provoke him into starting a war.

On August 12th, the Russian president Dmitri Medvedev announced that Russia had successfully completed its "peace enforcement" operation. You had to give it to the Russians—only they could come up with such a paradoxical term.

Days later, Saakashvili stood before a crowd of journalists with US secretary of state Condoleezza Rice and fulminated about how Europe had essentially appeased the Russian barbarians. It was a hot day and I hadn't slept in a week, but as I watched him ranting, it was pretty clear that he had gone way off script. This was supposed to be a boilerplate press conference announcing a ceasefire agreement. Instead, it turned into an erratic, rambling broadside on the failure of the international community to protect Georgia. Rice stood next to him glowering silently. Years later she would write that she "was so mad at Saakashvili [she] couldn't even speak."

BY THE TIME I GOT BACK TO MOSCOW I was hallucinating from sleep deprivation and had completely missed my vacation, but I felt elated. I had received a very positive response from management in New York. And I had a newfound confidence that, having survived the intensity of that news cycle, I could handle most situations. But the main reason for the smile that spread across my face as I touched down in Moscow and turned on my phone was quite different.

"Welcome home, darling. So excited to see you," the message read. I was in love.

After several months of self-imposed solitude in Moscow, I had finally cracked and arranged to have dinner with some expats who were friends of friends from London. I had few expectations of the evening. I imagined a group of self-confident, witty young Englishmen and women who had all sorts of clever lines and would drink a surfeit of booze. It would be amusing but empty.

I arrived at the restaurant and was greeted with kisses from David and Giles and a girl called Jessie who had been at my boarding school.

The boys wore dark jeans and Oxford shirts with V-neck cashmere sweaters and suede moccasins from Tod's. It was exactly what I had expected. And then—after we'd begun to eat—someone else arrived. He had come directly from an office party and his face was flushed from drinking, but he was very cute, with soft brown eyes and a shock of curly hair that he had unsuccessfully tried to gel into submission.

He sat down next to me and introduced himself as he kissed me on both cheeks. "Hello, I'm Philipp."

"Hello, Philipp, I'm Clarissa—do I detect an accent there?"

"Indeed you do, I'm from Hamburg. What are you doing here in Moscow?"

"I'm a reporter for an American TV network here. I spent the last few years covering conflicts in Beirut and Baghdad."

He didn't miss a beat. "I think war correspondents are egomaniacs," he said, smiling.

I laughed out loud. It was immediately clear to me that there was something different about Philipp. He exuded a thoughtfulness and sincerity that I rarely encountered among the Moscow expat community. He was also exceptionally elegant and well-mannered in an utterly unpretentious way.

After dinner, everyone bundled into cabs to go dancing. But at the club we struggled to chat above the noise.

"Let's go have tea," he suggested.

We went to a Moroccan restaurant called Chaikhana where you sit on cushions on the floor. One of the many wonderful things about Moscow is that most restaurants are open 24 hours. It truly is a city that never sleeps. It was snowing heavily outside and we lay on our sides facing each other and drank mint tea and talked for hours. He was curious and sincere and loved Russian literature. We connected immediately.

Philipp had grown up in the rarefied world of Germany's old aristocracy. But he had left Germany when he was seventeen and studied in the UK and Spain and Israel before moving to Russia. He spoke slowly and deliberately, as if he were really thinking about everything he said, choosing every word.

By the time I finally looked at my watch, it was starting to get light. I was hoping he would try to kiss me but he didn't. Instead, he put me in a cab without so much as asking for my phone number. I was delirious with exhaustion and elated by our connection, but now felt panicked that we had no way to see each other again. Christmas vacation was about to start and who knows what would happen by January.

I needn't have worried. We returned from the holidays one month later and Jessie organized a dinner where we reconnected. A few days later, I sent this email to Chiara.

"The German and I kissed for the first time on Friday night and have been sort of inseparable ever since . . . I find him incredibly cute and intriguing and he is very affectionate and loving . . . I feel safe and I feel that he really likes me and is not going to hurt me . . . but at the same time I find him mysterious. . . ."

We laugh to this day at my description of him as "mysterious."

It did not take long for me to begin thinking that this relationship was different from previous loves. I used to joke that Philipp moved into my apartment after our second date when he discovered that I had a large number of German cable channels. But it was basically true. We were so happy and at ease in each other's presence that spending all our time together seemed completely natural.

Philipp's calm self-assurance softened my edges, and he had a remarkable tolerance for my itinerant lifestyle and nervous energy. His steadiness was the perfect tonic for my highs and lows.

I remember coming back to our apartment in Moscow after an exhausting trip to Iraq in 2008. I sat in the kitchen and drank a bottle of wine on my own. Then I planted myself in front of him while he was trying to watch television and danced to Chris Isaak's "Wicked Game" on repeat for two hours. He looked bemused and mildly irritated. Finally, I screamed that he didn't understand me and stormed out of the room.

"Drink some water and go to bed, darling," he called gently.

Within a few months, ABC News offered me a position in Beijing as their Asia correspondent. It wasn't officially a promotion but it was a great opportunity with a much larger coverage area and more chances to get on air. I knew I wanted to take it, but I dreaded how Philipp would respond. It had become increasingly clear to me that few men could handle being with a woman who traveled all over the world and regularly put herself in danger, let alone one who upped and moved to China.

"You've got to take it," Philipp said simply. "Don't worry about us, we will be fine."

Six

By 2009, seven years after my *Kill Bill* experience, Beijing had changed beyond recognition. China was enjoying nearly double-digit growth, and gleaming new towers adorned every other block. Luxury apartment buildings beckoned the thousands of foreigners now living in Beijing with names like "Central Park" and "SOHO."

I found a spacious but soulless apartment in the Central Business District, or CBD as it was known. The building was called Fortune Towers—"a most auspicious name," my colleague Cao Jun congratulated me. I knew well the role of superstitions in Chinese culture. When my father moved to Hong Kong when I was fourteen years old, his bank had sent a feng shui man as a welcome gift. He nearly came to blows with my mother because he insisted on moving all the furniture. And in my new apartment building, there was no fourth floor, just a third and fifth. My colleagues explained that the number 4 is considered unlucky because it sounds the same as the word for death.

I was less worried about superstitions than about leaving Philipp in Moscow. We had made an agreement that we would not go longer than two months without seeing each other—whether in China or Russia or

Europe. And, of course, we would Skype every day. I came to realize that the biggest challenge was missing out on the shared silences, the moments of comfort and joy just being in each other's presence. We compensated by spending hours on Skype together over the weekends just reading the papers and puttering around, often without speaking for twenty minutes.

I soon received my first assignment. Riots had broken out in Urumqi pitting Uighur Muslims, who are natives of the area, against the dominant Han Chinese, who essentially rule the region. Urumqi is the capital of Xinjiang, a vast autonomous region in the far northwest of the country that is rich in natural resources and has borders with eight countries. Parts of Xinjiang are closer to Damascus than they are to Beijing, and the old Silk Road trading route that linked China to the Middle East runs through its expanse.

The Chinese had effectively colonized the province in the eighteenth century and began a steady process of importing Han Chinese to dilute the majority of the indigenous Turkic-speaking Uighurs. There is, unsurprisingly, huge tension between the two groups. A separatist movement of Turkic-speaking Uighurs call the province East Turkestan. The Chinese authorities view this separatist movement as a terrorist threat and have responded by cracking down fiercely on religious freedom. Recent restrictions include a ban on long beards and women not being allowed to wear veils that cover the face. The Chinese government has also introduced reeducation camps where hundreds of thousands of Uighurs have been detained for "extremism eradication."

In China, all aspects of organized religion must be monitored and sanctioned by the government. If you are Christian, you must attend a state-sanctioned church. Bibles can be sold only in church bookstores. This has led to a proliferation of so-called house churches, underground places of worship where the liturgy is not dictated by the censor's stamp;

the Chinese government has recently been trying to clamp down on such spaces, too.

As I sat in the taxi on my way to the airport to fly to Urumqi, I thought of a saying in Arabic: *"kul mamnou' marghoub,"* meaning that which is forbidden is desired or, more colloquially in English, you always want what you can't have. If my experiences in the Middle East had taught me anything, it was that this type of repression always came back to haunt the society in the end.

At the airport, I linked up with the Beijing producer, Beth Loyd. Beth was my age and from Marietta, Georgia. She was feisty and beautiful with bright blonde hair and striking, doll-like blue eyes. We had met a couple of years earlier in Baghdad and I had been impressed then by her sharp mind and no-nonsense attitude.

By the time we landed in Urumqi, nearly two hundred people had been killed in the clashes, most of them Han Chinese. The city of 2.3 million had been largely shut down. Roads were closed, internet and cell phone service were cut off, and a curfew was imposed.

Authorities had issued an edict that all journalists stay in one hotel in the center of town, the only place with a working internet connection. The hotel lobby was bustling with teams checking in, laden with camera gear, talking loudly into their cell phones. Clusters of hacks sat around smoking cigarettes and drinking coffee and exchanging carefully curated scraps of information. Harried bellboys pushed overloaded carts, weaving through the crowd to get to the elevators.

No matter the conflict zone or the story, the hotel lobby is the hub. It's the place where journalists meet in the morning before setting off for the day; it's where they congregate to make a plan with their fixers; it's where they stop to have a coffee and a chat, to work on their laptops, and after filing for the day, to drink. It's the place where you bump into old friends and vent about the frustrations of covering the story or share a helpful tip or a good angle, while holding back some nuggets that give you a competitive edge.

After crossing paths in dodgy places over the course of several years, I had developed real friendships with my colleagues from other networks and print outlets. Much of the job entails sitting around and waiting—waiting for press conferences to start, waiting for fixers to arrive, waiting for offensives to kick off—so there's lots of time to get to know one another.

I spotted an old *New York Times* friend from my Baghdad days across the lobby, and he told us that there was some kind of standoff happening nearby.

I promised to buy him a drink later and we dashed out the door, our twelve boxes of kit now pared down to the minimum: camera, tripod, and a run bag with some extra batteries and a basic light.

Half a mile down the road, we could see some commotion. We ran up to an overpass overlooking the street, where we could get a better shot. A group of rubberneckers had already gathered on the overpass to observe the scene below. I was relieved to see that no other journalists were there yet. We pushed through the crowd to position the tripod so we could get a good shot of what was happening below. I could see a Uighur man being savagely beaten by a group of six or seven Han Chinese, armed with sticks and bats.

I stayed deliberately quiet and out of the shot as the cameraman set to work. Partly because I didn't want to attract too much attention to the fact that we were filming. And partly because it drove me insane when correspondents felt the need to insert themselves into every scene and start talking over what was happening. I preferred to listen first and try to understand what was going on. There were times when it made sense for the reporter to be part of the story, to point out things that might not be obvious, even to show sympathy or compassion. But the sight of a man being beaten to a pulp by an angry mob spoke for itself. I wanted the viewer to see the ugliness of the moment with no filter.

The blows made a sickening blunt pounding sound against the Uighur man's flesh. His attackers' faces were contorted with rage. They were no longer individuals, no longer people with families and jobs—they were a mass of pure fury.

For years in the Middle East I had seen people killed and maimed by bombs and shells and bullets, but there was something uniquely disturbing and frightening about watching men beat someone to death. In most conflicts, there is a front line that provides some physical separation. The aggressor rarely sees the victim's face, doesn't look into his eyes. The act of firing a shell and the havoc that is wreaked upon its impact are impersonal and indirect. The same cannot be said of hand-to-hand combat.

The group had torn off the Uighur man's shirt. One side of his body was dark purple, presumably from internal bleeding. The crowd kept beating him. I could see that they were intent on killing him. I wanted to scream at the top of my lungs, to stop everyone in their tracks for one moment, one beat, a pause just long enough to break the trance, for them to remember that they were human beings. It was a familiar feeling that I strained not to act on—the urge to be a human instead of a journalist, to intervene, to help. I looked over to a long line of armed policemen who stood just a few hundred yards away, but they did not move.

Eventually, a lone police car pulled up and a couple of officers began trying to wrestle the Uighur man from the crowd and into the safety of the car. Even as they pushed him into the back seat, the men kept pulling at his legs, trying to tear him out again. Finally, the policemen successfully slammed the door and drove off, with the crowd shouting at them.

Suddenly the crowd on the overpass, who had been watching the beating, turned on us.

"Where are you from?" one woman shouted.

"Canada," Beth lied. Admitting to being an American crew was liable to get you an ass-kicking in many places.

"Why were you filming? Give us your camera," someone else chimed in.

Beth shouted back at them in Mandarin, "*Wo-men shir jizhe!*" (We are journalists!)

"This is your fault, the media doesn't tell the truth," another man shouted.

A man pushed our cameraman. Beth shouted at them again, "Don't touch us!"

I took a step back, looking around for an escape route. The men tried again to grab the camera. Cao Jun, our Chinese producer, was trying to calm them down, to no avail. Someone in the group had a baton that he brandished above our cameraman's head while screaming in Mandarin. I looked over toward the line of policemen for help, but they continued to stand passively.

"Come on," Cao Jun shouted, and we all started running. The crowd began chasing us.

"Where's the car?"

The crowd was still behind us.

Finally, the car was in sight. Our driver got out and looked at us in shock.

"Start the engine," Cao Jun shouted.

We jumped in as the driver pulled into reverse. The crowd was banging on the windows and yelling, their eyes still on fire. As we pulled away, I turned back to watch them receding into the background. They still stood there shouting.

I had never imagined I would see that kind of violence in China. It contradicted so many of the preconceptions that I had about the country.

This wasn't a war zone. It was tightly controlled, disciplined and orderly. This was a country that was growing at breakneck speed, nipping at America's heels, and lifting millions of people out of poverty as it did so, building high-speed trains and investing billions of dollars in green-energy technology. More relevantly, this was a country that went out of its way to avoid conflict. While the other world powers jockeyed for power and prominence on the international stage, weighing in on various conflicts and supporting different actors, China kept a quiet and disciplined focus on its sphere of influence. And yet, beneath the cool pragmatism, the country was seething with discontent, a response perhaps to the political and religious repression and rampant inequality that had come with the economic miracle. The Communist Party had inculcated a strong sense of Chinese nationalism, but it was a volatile, chauvinistic emotion. Over the next two years, I would repeatedly encounter this simmering rage in an array of different contexts: at demonstrations against low wages, in traffic jams, at sporting events, and more.

We returned to an excited gaggle of journalists at the hotel. Word had traveled that we had footage of a beating and that we had narrowly escaped one ourselves. Colleagues wanted to know if they could buy or share our video. Our primary objective was to get the pictures back to New York before the evening news broadcast. The time difference gave us a good head start, but we still had a long night ahead.

We went into the conference room allocated for journalists' use. There must have been about sixty people in a room designed to seat ten. And there was just a single internet connection designated for everyone's use.

We picked our way through the people sitting on the floor with their laptops and finally found a free patch.

"Dammit," Beth said, looking at the internet speed. "There's too many people on here."

I glanced over at the guy next to me who appeared to be mindlessly surfing the net and debated asking him what the hell he thought he was doing sucking up precious data checking his damn email.

As we crouched over the computer, trying to send our pictures, a balding, paunchy British guy approached us. It was clear he had been drinking.

"Hello, ladies," he said. "How are we doing this evening?"

Beth shot me a look as if to say, the last thing we need is to have this drunk dildo hitting on us for the next hour. He introduced himself as Henry, a freelancer working for France 24.

"You looked stressed, ladies. How can I be of service?"

"Why don't you go find us some beers," Beth suggested without looking up.

Henry obediently went off to find the beers and returned twenty minutes later with two Tsingtaos. I noticed the leering smile he gave her when she thanked him.

"Someone's got the hots for you," I said when he had gone.

Beth wrinkled her nose. "I know, right. He's so annoying."

Over the course of the next few hours, Henry came back regularly with fresh beers. Each time, Beth would roll her eyes and take the beer before thanking him and telling him to get lost so we could finish our work. Six years later, Beth and Henry would get married. But at that moment, we had a deadline to make, and we were going to miss it if we didn't get a better internet connection.

Beth looked at her watch nervously. "Should we get out the BGAN?"

The BGAN is essentially a portable satellite terminal; it came with us whenever we traveled. It has to be set up outside and it can be an infuriating process to lock in a good signal. Even when you succeed, it still takes a long time to feed video. But given the hotel's dilatory WiFi connection, we didn't have a choice.

The July evening air felt cool and refreshing after the stale conference room. Beth set up the BGAN and I tried to stay calm as it searched for a signal. There was nothing I could do but watch Beth and pray that we made it. I paced up and down the sidewalk, willing myself not to ask her every five minutes whether the feed was in yet.

Just as I was about to collapse with anxiety, Beth announced that everything was in. We packed up the satellite and went into the hotel lobby. It was empty at 4 a.m. We flopped down on a sofa and ordered two double whiskies.

At the end of a long day on a breaking news story, there's usually a short window where you get to sit and savor a hard-fought victory before your body demands sleep. It is a sweet moment as the days can run 18 hours. Inevitably, there is a lot of stress, and often you've seen some of the darker elements of humanity.

"Cheers," I said, "we made it."

"Werq!" Beth replied. "*Ganbei*" (Chinese for "cheers"; literally, it means "dry glass").

THE CHINA BEAT WAS COMPLETELY DIFFERENT from anything I had covered before, and it required new skills. First, to understand China's place on the world stage, I would have to become *au fait* with terms like sovereign debt and currency manipulation and tariffs.

During my time at Yale my father had practically begged me to take basic economics classes so that I would have a better understanding of how the world worked. Of course, I dismissed him scathingly, saying that I never wanted to be "a wanker banker" so why should I bother. Now I cringed at my arrogance. To understand the relationship between China and the US, I would have to learn about the financial choke hold that bound them together.

China's massive trade surplus with the US—all those plastic goods and cheap electronics crammed onto the shelves at Walmart and the like—had been weaponized. Beijing had gone on a shopping spree for US government debt in the mid-2000s, and by fall 2008 it had become the largest non-US holder of Treasury bonds. Many in the US government worried that the size of its holdings gave China a strategic advantage. Should it sell or even threaten to sell some of its holdings, it could destabilize the US bond market.

The terms of trade were seen as unduly favorable to China, a position exacerbated by the perception that China manipulated its currency to lower the renminbi and strengthen the US dollar—making all those exports crossing the Pacific even more competitive. During my time in Beijing, these issues were less fractious than they are today. China's markets had only recently been opened up to international investors, and much of the attention was on the opportunities offered by this rapidly growing market, not on the longer-term challenge.

In addition to the economic learning curve, I also lacked a facility with Mandarin. Beijing was the first assignment where I landed with a total ignorance of the language. Almost immediately, I began Mandarin lessons with my teacher, Mr. Bai.

Mr. Bai—or Bai Lao Shi as I called him (teacher Bai)—was a tall, smooth-faced, soft-spoken man.

During one of our first lessons, I was learning how to say where I lived.

"*Wo ju zai Tsai Fu Zhong Xin*," I said shakily. I live in Fortune Towers.

"*Tai gue le!*" he said (too expensive), before adding in English, "How much do you pay for rent?"

I squirmed in my seat. I was pretty sure whatever I paid in rent was more than Mr. Bai made in a year. I halved the number and changed the subject. Mr. Bai didn't take the hint.

"How much money do you make?" he persisted. By now, I felt very uncomfortable.

"I would rather not talk about it," I said.

Like the vast majority of Chinese under the age of forty, Mr. Bai was an only child, a product of the one-child policy that had been in place since 1980. He explained to me that he felt overwhelmed by the responsibility of taking care of his parents on his own. He had a serious girlfriend but said he couldn't marry her because he didn't have enough money saved.

It didn't help that popular culture in China—as in formerly Communist Russia—was obsessed with the country's newfound wealth. One reality show contestant infamously confessed that she would "rather cry in a BMW than smile on a bicycle."

While China was still officially a Communist country, Deng Xiaoping had famously declared that to get rich was glorious. "Socialism with Chinese characteristics," as the Chinese government called the current system, was not very socialist at all. The two great pillars of Communism in the twentieth century were now hell-bent on the creation of wealth. But unlike the Russian elite, who reveled in conspicuous consumption, most Chinese saved assiduously.

One day Mr. Bai and I were talking about a new burger restaurant that had opened. He wanted to take his girlfriend but said it was too expensive.

"Come on, live a little, Bai Lao Shi," I cajoled him. "Don't put so much pressure on yourself."

He smiled and chuckled nervously.

"No, no," he said, shaking his head. "We have to."

Pressure, it was becoming clear to me, pervaded Chinese life. Nearly a billion people were working around the clock to improve their lives; their extraordinary work ethic had catapulted China into the second-largest economy in the world. It had turned China's students into some of the most accomplished and competitive anywhere. But with that pressure came exhaustion and burnout and sometimes a breaking point. At times, it felt like the country was ready to explode, which may explain why the government kept such a tight lid on all forms of dissent.

Whether it was censoring the internet or imprisoning human rights activists, the Chinese authorities weren't leaving anything to chance. And that made it a very difficult place to work as a journalist. We would turn up in the city's Tiananmen Square to shoot elements for an anniversary piece on the Tiananmen Square massacre and find ourselves surrounded by security services in a matter of moments. On one occasion, plainclothes policemen began opening umbrellas in front of the camera on a clear day to prevent us from shooting any material.

One Sunday afternoon, journalists around the city were alerted to anonymous letters on a website telling them to go to the central Wangfujing street to witness the beginning of an uprising in China, a "Jasmine Revolution." We obediently all turned up, only to find a thousand policemen and a mere handful of protesters. But instead of dismissing the abortive demonstration as irrelevant, the police began pushing journalists around. Later they came to our houses individually to make sure we understood Chinese law and the repercussions of attending an illegal protest. The heavy-handed tactics inevitably became the story.

Though I was based in Beijing, I was responsible for covering the whole of Asia and, as a result, spent much of my life those years on an airplane. There were regular trips to Seoul to cover tensions on the Korean Peninsula; there were earthquakes in Indonesia and New Zealand and rotations in Kabul and Helmand province, Afghanistan.

Getting stories from the region onto the American evening news agenda wasn't easy and I would spend hours researching feature stories that could be shot on a shoestring. We went to the farthest corner of

Mongolia to follow nomadic reindeer herders whose way of life was in danger of extinction. We camped out on the edge of a volcano crater in Vanuatu to track the work of an eccentric Kiwi explorer. We spent a surreal twenty-four hours in General Santos City, in the Philippines, shadowing the boxing legend and aspiring politician Manny Pacquiao.

ONE MARCH AFTERNOON, Beth and I were returning from a late lunch when we got a frantic call from the foreign desk in New York. A massive earthquake had precipitated a tsunami in northern Japan. We watched as the first images were broadcast showing a wall of water engulfing large swaths of the coastline. Terrifyingly, the quake had also damaged a nuclear power plant in Fukushima and a nuclear meltdown now seemed imminent.

One hour later we were at the airport, our bags hastily packed. I tried to bury thoughts of a potential nuclear disaster in the back of my mind. One step at a time. The airport in Tokyo was shut and all flights were canceled following the earthquake, so we booked ourselves on a flight to Seoul, South Korea, which was at least closer to Japan. From there we managed to find a flight to Niigata, Japan, that was still scheduled to take off.

Niigata was on the western side of Japan but still relatively close to the hard-hit city of Sendai. Beth went out to smoke and call the foreign desk to let them know our plan. Ten minutes later she came back.

"Well, the good news is that we might be the first journalists to get anywhere near the tsunami site because no one can get flights in. The bad news is that there's no way to organize a car for us because the bureau is slammed and phones are down in a lot of places."

ABC News had a small bureau in Tokyo. There was no correspondent based there, just a producer and a couple of interns, who probably wouldn't have a chance to eat or sleep for the next three days. I had worked in Japan before; it was the kind of place where you needed to organize things in advance.

"What about a translator?" I asked.

"They'll try to send someone to link up with us."

Beth and I didn't speak a word of Japanese, nor did our Filipino cameraman, Gamay. And Japan was one of the few countries in Asia, along with China, where few people spoke any English.

We landed in Niigata late that evening. The airport was deserted. I ran out to the taxi area to see if I could find a driver while Beth exchanged some more money and Gamay picked up our bags. It had been snowing and was bitterly cold. A few taxis were parked, waiting for passengers. I approached the first one.

"Sendai, Sendai," I said, giving the name of the city near the epicenter of the quake where we wanted to go.

The driver shook his head as if to say no, no.

"Please, we are journalists, we need to show the world what happened here in Japan today."

He continued to shake his head, not understanding a word I was saying.

I gave up and went to the second taxi. I got the same response. In exasperation, I reached into my bag and pulled out a wad of hundred-dollar bills.

"Please, we need to go to Sendai. We can pay you well."

He only looked down and shook his head more firmly. Frustrated, I called the Tokyo bureau and asked them to help persuade one of these drivers over the phone to take us.

After what seemed like an eternity, the third taxi agreed to do it. He wouldn't take us all the way to Sendai because his shift was ending soon but he would take us most of the way. My American brain couldn't quite comprehend that the driver wouldn't take our thousands of dollars in return for forgetting that his shift was ending and driving us all the way to Sendai. It seemed absurd to refuse the chance to make a month's money in one night. But there was something dignified about his refusal to take our gobs of cash. I felt gauche for having offered it in such a coarse way.

We managed to pack our gear into the small sedan and set off. The streets were completely deserted and eerily quiet but there was no damage to be seen. The western side of the island had been largely spared.

"Do we have anything to eat?" Gamay asked.

I looked at my watch. It was about nine o'clock. There was no question of getting any food tonight. I was OK because I had eaten on the plane. My mother had always instructed me to eat plane food. "You never know when you're going to eat next," she would caution me. I fished through my bag and found a half-melted Snickers bar for him.

The drive was a few hours long, and most of it was spent trying to write a script. In an ideal world, you write your story based on the pictures that you have shot that day. But often on breaking-news stories, you have to file as soon as you land, which means someone in London or New York edits the piece using agency pictures that you can't actually see. It's frustrating as all hell, but in that situation you just have to remind yourself that perfect is the enemy of good and the most important thing is to get the story out.

Our BlackBerrys didn't work and cell-phone reception was out, so we had to stop and use the satellite phone and dictate my script to the desk in New York for approval. I stood on the roadside shivering as I read out loud from my notebook. Once we were given approval, we had to record the voice track, which I did sitting in the car with a heavy coat over my head to muffle out any background noise. Then we fired up the BGAN and sent the track and my piece to camera, recorded in the dark many miles from the earthquake zone, to New York.

By the time everything had been sent in, the driver wanted to go home. We were still about forty-five minutes from Sendai, but we could easily cover that ground in the morning. So he dropped us at a small "love hotel," which is really a motel that rents out rooms by the hour.

I looked at Beth. "Don't get too excited because you're not getting lucky tonight."

She and Gamay laughed.

"You neither, Gamay!" I added.

It was three in the morning by the time we collapsed into bed with exhaustion. I fell into a restless light sleep. I was in the middle of a vivid dream when I began to have the sensation that I was floating on the ocean, being tossed up and down by the waves. The waves were getting bigger and bigger. The whole bed was shaking.

I opened my eyes and felt a jolt of panic. Where was I? I was used to waking up in strange hotel rooms feeling utterly disorientated but not when the whole room was rocking.

I blinked in the darkness, before remembering I was in Japan to cover the earthquake. This must be an aftershock.

The shaking stopped abruptly. I rubbed my eyes and looked at my phone. It was six thirty. I desperately wanted to go back to sleep but the fear of another aftershock that could be as strong as a major quake made it impossible. I only had another hour before I had to be up anyway.

I knocked on Beth's door and found her and Gamay going through the gear.

"I have some amazing news," she told me. "Haru [a producer in the Tokyo bureau] has sent his niece to come work with us. She's a student in college but her mom is British so she speaks perfect English. She should be here in an hour."

I went back to my room and opened my small wheelie bag. Whenever possible I traveled with only carry-on luggage because checked bags often get lost or take hours to lurch onto the conveyor belt. I rifled through the case looking for a change of underwear but there was nothing to be found. I had three clean shirts, an extra bra, some cargo pants, plenty of socks. But no underwear.

Along with making me eating airplane food, my mother had always taught me to handwash my underwear every night when staying in a hotel (presumably because the hotel laundry was a complete rip-off, though I'm not really sure—she said it was what ladies do, whatever that means). But this time, exhaustion had overcome my lingerie duties. And it was extremely unlikely there would even be any hotels to sleep in as we got closer to the epicenter of the quake. I shrugged to myself and put on my underwear from the previous day inside out. It was a futile gesture to maintaining standards.

We stood outside the hotel with all our gear waiting for Haru's niece to arrive.

"I need to stop and try to buy some underwear today," I told them.

Beth snorted. "Good luck with that!"

A taxi pulled up in front of the hotel. We threw our bags in the back and poured into the cab.

Her name was Noriko and she had never worked with journalists before, nor had she experienced a natural disaster. But she was nice and spoke English and Japanese.

As we drove down toward the coast, the tall pine trees cleared, revealing the city of Sendai down in the distance on the water. We drove past a convenience store, where a long line of people waited patiently to buy some food and water.

"Can y'all imagine if this was in the US?" Beth said. "These people would be going nuts."

The closer we got to the city, the more damage we saw. But it was only when we entered the city that we saw the true scale of the devastation.

The earthquake had triggered waves more than 130 feet high that swept six miles inland. Cars had been tossed onto roofs by the strength of the tsunami, boats flung through shop windows several blocks away from the coast. Traffic lights and signs had been simply swept away, the ground floor of almost every building battered. Many smaller structures were demolished.

As we approached the port, the driver stopped abruptly and said something to Noriko.

"He won't go any closer to the water. He's afraid of another tsunami," she translated.

We took out the camera and tripod and some spare batteries, left the driver with the rest of our gear, and walked the remainder of the way. The streets were still ankle-deep in water in some areas and covered with debris. As we approached the water, we reached what appeared to have been some kind of a parking lot. There were cars everywhere, strewn like toys. Gamay got out his camera and started filming the scene.

Out of nowhere, a lone rescue worker appeared at the other end of the lot and began gesturing at us.

"What does he want?" I asked. "Keep shooting," I told Gamay.

It was a reflex action, after years of working in China and Russia and the Middle East, to ignore police and keep filming until they actually forced you to stop. Noriko walked over to talk to him. From his posture he looked exhausted. His head hung down as he spoke to her.

"He asked to be careful when taking video of the cars," she said when she walked back over to us. "A lot still have bodies in them that the rescue workers haven't been able to get to yet. He doesn't want you to show the bodies out of respect."

"Will he do an interview?" I asked, and then hated myself for it. The poor guy had spent the past sixteen hours pulling dead people out of cars. A freak natural disaster had eviscerated his entire community. The last thing he wanted was to have a camera pointed in his face while I questioned him.

"I don't think so," Noriko said, looking mortified at the prospect of asking him. Even at the best of times, the Japanese were very sensitive about going on camera. You couldn't just go up to someone on the street with a camera. There was a protocol to follow first.

Suddenly, a siren began wailing. I froze.

"What the hell is that?" Beth asked.

I glanced over to where the rescue worker had been standing, but he was nowhere to be seen.

"It's a tsunami warning," Noriko said, looking like she was about to cry.

We grabbed our kit and began hurrying toward the car.

If a tsunami comes right now, we are all dead in a second, I thought to myself.

It comforted me somewhat to know that I had no real agency in the matter. If it was going to happen, it was going to happen.

As we approached the car, the driver was shouting at us to hurry up. The siren was still wailing. It reminded me of those air-raid sirens in movies about the Second World War. We picked up the pace and ran to the car, bundled into the back, and drove to higher ground.

"Now I definitely need to go and buy some new underwear," I joked.

We all laughed except Noriko, who still looked like she was on the verge of tears.

The next morning, she announced that she wanted to go back to Tokyo. Our plan was to head north of Sendai after filing, to get to some of the worst-hit areas that rescue workers hadn't been able to reach yet. But the tsunami warning and the regular aftershocks had shaken her. She would find a taxi to take her back and leave us with her driver.

Beth called the Tokyo bureau to ask for another translator but was told there was no one available. Diane Sawyer was flying into Tokyo to anchor *World News* and all resources needed to go to her.

The only solution I could think of was to get Noriko to translate a bunch of questions into Japanese for me from English. Japanese is a phonetic language, I figured, so I would be able to pronounce the questions fairly easily.

"Where were you when the tsunami hit? *Tsunami ga osotta toki, dokoni ita nodesu ka?*"

"What happened to the people living here? *Koko ni sumu hitobito ni wa nani ga okotta nodesu ka?*"

Noriko translated each phrase for me and I wrote it down in my notebook.

As we drove farther north, the roads became deserted. In Sendai, we had seen mile-long lines of cars waiting to fill up with gas. We had passed convoys of rescue workers. But less than half an hour away it was eerily quiet, a series of ghost towns, some still submerged under water. The road became increasingly difficult to navigate. Landslides had dumped huge piles of earth onto some stretches. At one point, we came across an enormous oak tree slumped across the road, felled by the strength of the quake. The driver shook his head and muttered something as he inched around it.

After driving for an hour, we stopped in what appeared to have once been a quaint town. It was about a mile away from the ocean, but much of it was partially submerged. Cars sat deserted on the roadside. A handful of stragglers pedaled by on bicycles. A clutch of houses near the road had been demolished—the roofs ripped off, windows smashed through, debris strewn all around. As we approached them, the salty smell of the air gave way to a putrid stench. Gamay tied his scarf around his nose and mouth.

I coughed and gagged. It was disconcerting because you couldn't see the bodies but you knew they were there somewhere amid the debris.

"Sweet Jesus," Beth said, lighting a cigarette to mask the smell. "Let's just get some B-roll and we can go buy some masks later."

From the wreckage, it was clear that the first house had been a family home. A soccer ball, a fridge, a potted plant, a clock that had stopped exactly at 2:46 p.m., the moment the quake hit, a Hello Kitty toy house poking out of a pile of wet clothes and bedding. I reached down to pick it up and stopped myself. I felt suddenly exhausted and depressed. It seemed indecent to be picking through these people's possessions. I stifled a sob.

I could taste the pungent decay on the back of my tongue. I told myself to calm down and take a deep breath.

We moved on to the next house and found a woman and two girls standing where their front door had once been. The woman looked dazed as she surveyed the wreckage of her home. I took out my notebook with my list of Japanese questions.

"We are ABC News. I am so sorry," I said in halting Japanese, "but may we ask you some questions?"

She looked at me and blinked, then nodded her head slowly. Gamay quietly approached us and turned the camera on.

"Where were you when the tsunami hit? *Tsunami ga osotta toki, dokoni ita nodesu ka?*" I asked, trying not to stumble over the words.

Amazingly, she appeared to understand me and began answering. I could not understand a word she was saying, but I held her gaze and nodded to at least communicate that I had a sense of her distress. It was the first and only time I had ever conducted an interview like this but somehow it did not feel as awkward as it might have. The horror of what had happened was palpable and evident all around us—one almost didn't need language to communicate it.

I glanced at my list of Japanese questions.

"What happened to the people living here? *Koko ni sumu hitobito ni wa nani ga okotta nodesu ka?*" I motioned toward the house next door where we had been filming as I said it to make it clear that I was asking about her neighbors.

Her face crumpled and she sobbed. She spoke for a bit, then paused and wept. I stood silently, waiting for her to finish. Later, a translator confirmed she had said that the family in the house next door had all died.

By the time we headed back to the car, it was getting dark. The driver was agitated and kept saying something to us and shaking his head. We took out the Thuraya satellite phone and called the Tokyo bureau to translate. We handed the phone to the driver and he talked to them for a few minutes before handing the phone back to us.

"Hi, Clarissa, sorry, but the driver says he has to leave now to go home."

"Go home? We're in the middle of nowhere, we can't be without any vehicle. Where will we sleep?"

"He says he will drive you to a rest stop near the main road and Haru-san will drive up from Tokyo to meet you tonight."

"But Tokyo is five hours away!"

"I know, but you can wait at the rest stop. It will be safe there."

It wasn't even dark yet and there was already a chilly bite in the air, but there was no other choice. I knew by now that wads of cash would have no effect on the driver's decision. There were aftershocks every fifteen minutes and there was a reason no other people were on the streets anywhere. The whole place smelled of death.

The driver took us to a rest stop by the side of the road. It was essentially a public toilet. We unpacked the car and then sat on the curbside as he drove off.

Beth lit a cigarette and took a long drag.

"Gimme one of those," I said.

"I thought you don't smoke anymore," she said. I had stopped smoking when I left Beirut, but periodically I would start again, usually during a big story.

"Looks like I picked the wrong week to quit sniffing glue," I joked, quoting *Airplane*.

Miraculously, the rest stop was the only place for miles around that had electricity, so we were able to set up the BGAN and our laptops and file for *Good Morning America* from the roadside. I could only imagine how desperately frightening it must be for the people who were still stranded, shivering in the pitch black, waiting in the debris of their destroyed homes, some half underwater, for rescue workers to find them and help them.

Haru-san finally arrived at midnight and we jumped up in the air with excitement as he pulled into the rest stop. His car was at least warm and comfortable. We bundled in and tried to catch a few hours of sleep. Gamay was snoring like a sailor and my legs were cramped in the back seat. Beth was next to me so there was no space to lean down. I sat in the inky darkness trying to ignore the flutter of panic in my chest. The better I got at my job, the higher my anxiety levels became. I felt a strong sense of pressure to do justice to the story.

I bundled up my scarf and leaned against the cool window and imagined being with Philipp and my dogs at my parents' house in France, hoping the thought would relax me. But my mind was racing.

By the time we got back on the road, I had probably managed about twenty minutes of light sleep. But there was nothing to do except push on.

We went and shot in a gymnasium where thousands of evacuees were now sheltering.

In the middle of the room, there was a large message board where lists of the confirmed dead and injured had been pinned alongside notices from people looking for help finding their loved ones. I watched as people gathered around it, scanning the names. I imagined waiting to learn the fate of the people you loved, then the all-consuming agony of finding their name there.

A woman told us it was impossible to sleep at night in the gymnasium because of the sound of people weeping for the dead.

"A little boy was crying all night—where's my daddy, where's my daddy?" she said.

I knelt next to an eighty-one-year-old man who told me he had clung to a floating log for hours before rescuing his wife. She lay asleep next to him, her face swollen and bandaged. He tenderly stroked her hair, and I felt tears well in my eyes.

After filing for *Nightline*, we kept pushing north. Our goal was to reach the devastated town of Minamisanriku for *Good Morning America*, but when we were just twenty minutes away the desk suddenly called and told us we needed to go back to Tokyo.

"What the hell are they talking about?" I practically shouted. "We are getting fantastic stuff and no one else has got this far north."

Messages had been rolling in from our bosses in New York who were delighted with our coverage. It didn't make any sense.

The answer was that our parent company, Disney, was worried about the risk of a nuclear disaster at Fukushima, and that if there was a meltdown there would be no way to get us out of the country.

"It's some corporate BS and we're not going to be able to fight it," the frustrated news desk told us.

More than eighteen thousand people had been killed as a result of this disaster. It was our job to tell that story, it was our job to get to the most dangerous and difficult places. Otherwise, what the hell were we doing? The fact that the decision was made without consulting us, without talking to people who were actually on the ground, made it all the more galling. It didn't feel like a genuine attempt to keep us safe. It felt like a crude attempt at ass-covering from a parent company that was allergic to risk.

On the drive back to Tokyo I felt defeated. I desperately needed to sleep because I was expected to be live on *World News* when we arrived in Tokyo early in the morning. But I couldn't let go of my bitterness. It was just as well that I couldn't sleep because, about halfway to Tokyo, the car suddenly swerved and was careening toward the barrier in the middle of the highway.

"Haru-san!!!!" I shouted, grabbing his shoulder. He woke up with a start and quickly pulled the car back.

By the time we arrived at the plush five-star hotel where Diane Sawyer was staying, I was a mess. I hadn't slept in days and I had to be on live television in front of six million people in an hour. I felt sick with nerves and exhaustion. All I wanted to do was crawl into bed and have a weep and then sleep for twelve hours. Instead, I took a shower, drank some instant coffee, and put on my makeup.

Miraculously, I managed to get through the show. Afterwards, Diane took us all to breakfast. There were about twenty people from ABC News who had been flown over from New York. It was exhausting pretending to be a normal person talking to them.

"How are you doing? You've been getting amazing stuff!" one of them said to me.

"Thanks so much," I replied. "I've been wearing the same underwear for four days."

They all looked momentarily taken aback. I started laughing hysterically. Beth caught my eye across the table and shot me a look that said it was time to go to bed.

The next day we were all told to get on a conference call with ABC News people in Washington, who said that the Pentagon believed a nuclear catastrophe was imminent. It would be very difficult to extract us from Tokyo in a timely manner, so the suggestion was that we move even farther south to Osaka. Other teams were leaving Japan altogether. We were all completely exhausted and confused and a little freaked out, so we agreed to pull back.

The catastrophe never came, of course, and Beth and I began lobbying fiercely to get back up to the north. Eventually we were allowed to return, but we never quite recovered the momentum we had going those first few days.

When I arrived back in Beijing, I talked to my agent. My contract was coming up and I wanted to explore my options. I had received effusive feedback on my tsunami coverage from all the bosses, including the head of Disney, Bob Iger. Yet I still felt frustrated and underutilized. The Arab Spring had begun earlier in the year and I was desperate to cover it. I had lived in the region for three years but was being told by ABC there was no need for me to go.

Since Diane Sawyer had taken over *World News*, the broadcast felt more like her former show, *Good Morning America*. Packages were super short, loaded with graphics and effects, and written entirely in the gerund. Once, while working on a script about North Korea's Kim dynasty, they wanted me to add a line, "It's like *Dallas* but North Korean style," and play the theme tune to *Dallas*. I explained that a brutal, nuclear-armed dictatorship that was responsible for starving a million people to death should perhaps not be trivialized with such a comparison. My piece didn't get on. Another time, I was embedded with the marines in Helmand province for a week, doing a story on female marines who were being sent to the front lines to engage with Afghan women, whom their male counterparts couldn't get close to. It was a dangerous and grueling embed. *World News* never ran the piece.

My agent told me CBS News wanted to offer me a job. They had seen my work and liked the fact that I had such a wide array of experience in different regions. And they were willing to double my salary. I would be based out of London and travel to cover stories from there, as many foreign correspondents did. After years of living in Beirut, Baghdad, Moscow, and Beijing, the thought of living in a city where I could drink the tap water was a tantalizing prospect. Most importantly, I would have a chance to contribute to *60 Minutes*, widely considered to be the holy grail of journalism.

And it was great timing. CBS was enjoying a new lease on life after the departure of Katie Couric and a bunch of executives. Jeff Fager, the executive producer of *60 Minutes*, had been appointed chairman of the news division. At the time, he was one of the most well-respected men in news, known for his sharp editorial sensibility and genuine interest in international stories. ABC had shied away from airing foreign news unless the story was too huge to ignore. The legacy of the late, great anchorman Peter Jennings, who was known for his overseas reporting, had been usurped by an obsession with minute-by-minute ratings and reams of demographic data that reportedly showed Americans as uninterested in the rest of the world.

Perhaps because CBS was already in third place in the morning and the evening, they were less concerned about ratings and more concerned about journalism. They believed that a great story was a great story, whether it took place in Tallahassee or Timbuktu. The award-winning

60 Minutes correspondent Scott Pelley had been announced as the new anchorman. And my first-ever boss, David Rhodes, who had hired me on the overnight desk at Fox News, was now the new president of CBS News, after running Bloomberg's television operations for several years.

David was nerdy and a little awkward but incredibly smart and funny. He sent me a screen grab of the phone numbers he had accumulated for me over the years from New York, Moscow, Beijing, and my parents' house in France.

"This is why you're perfect for this job," he said.

I was sold.

Seven

As we approached the border, I adjusted my underwear one last time to make sure the memory cards couldn't slip out of the small compartment I had sewn into the crotch.

"Sorry, Waleed, avert your eyes," I joked to the driver.

He shrugged nonchalantly.

My hands were clammy. I was longing to be on the other side of the border, out of Syria, to smell the sweet salty air of Beirut, to be reunited with my producer, Randall, over a cold Almaza beer.

"Five more minutes and we are in Lebanon," Waleed said as he handed me a cigarette. I paused before lighting it. On the one hand, I knew the nicotine would only make me jumpier. On the other, it would give me something to do as we passed through the border. I lit it and breathed in the acrid smoke. I had given up smoking more times than I could count, but this trip had been particularly nerve-shredding and I was having a temporary relapse.

We pulled up at the border guard hut. Waleed gathered my papers and passport and opened the car door.

"You stay here," he warned.

I did not need convincing. The cigarette was making me nauseous so I stubbed it out.

After a seemingly interminable fifteen minutes, Waleed reemerged and got back into the car.

"*Tamam*," he said, all good.

"One down," I whispered to myself. We drove on a hundred yards to the customs post and turned off the engine. I looked out the window at a Syrian family sitting on the curb as soldiers rifled through every inch of their vehicle.

It was November 2011, and Syria was galvanized by a popular uprising that was growing by the day. The Arab Spring had set the entire region on fire, knocking over decades-old dictatorships in Tunisia and Egypt and Libya.

So far, Syrian authorities had mostly managed to contain the protests in the big cities. But the police state had gone into overdrive, arresting anyone who so much as lived in the same building as an activist. Moving in and out of the country had become more difficult, even for Syrian and Lebanese citizens, who traditionally didn't need a visa to cross the border.

I had been working at CBS News for more than two months but this was my first real assignment. ABC News had held me to a non-compete clause in my contract, which meant that I could not appear on CBS's air for three months after joining. To most people at CBS News, I was still a relatively unknown commodity. This was my first chance to prove myself.

For the past week, I had been embedded with a network of brave Syrian activists, watching the uprising against the regime of Bashar al-Assad firsthand. If I managed to get through this border crossing with my underwear (and memory cards) intact, I would have a fantastic story on my hands.

A Syrian guard came up to our car. "*Sabah al khair, ya watani,*" Waleed greeted him, "Good morning, patriot." "*Sabah al nour,*" he replied without smiling, his eyes immediately drawn to the blonde foreigner in the passenger seat.

"Hello," I said, smiling enthusiastically. The soldier ignored me and turned back to Waleed. *"Min wayn hiyyi?"*—Where is she from?—he asked. I pretended not to understand and kept smiling sweetly. Waleed told him that I was British. The soldier finally addressed me in broken English: "Why you come Syria?"

"For tourism," I explained. "I'm a designer and there are many beautiful Syrian antiquities." My cheeks were beginning to hurt from smiling so much. I was definitely babbling. "Get a grip, Ward," I told myself. Waleed passed him my passport.

He arched an eyebrow, fanning through the pages. All it would take was one Google search for him to realize that I was not an interior designer but an American TV reporter.

"Pull over," he told Waleed.

I willed myself to stay calm as he and two other soldiers began sifting through the contents of the trunk. I had purposely bought a large Syrian chest inlaid with mother-of-pearl and also some smaller boxes and the obligatory backgammon set to back up my story and consume their attention. It seemed to be doing the trick. If they asked to see my handbag, they would find a point-and-shoot tourism camera filled with some awkward, hastily taken selfies at various Damascus sites. All the real memory cards were nestled in that little compartment in my underwear.

My throat was parched. "Don't look back at them," I told myself, "just keep smiling." I heard the car boot slam down. The Syrian guard was once again at the window looking at me. He seemed to sense that something was up. There weren't a lot of blonde tourists in Syria these days. In fact, based on my experiences over the past week, there weren't any. And it was hard to fathom why any interior decorator would be traveling solo to Damascus in the hunt for cheap tchotchkes when the country was convulsed by protests. On the other hand, the car was clean and my paperwork was in order. I glanced down at my watch: 12:56, lunchtime. "Please let him be hungry," I thought. He seemed to pause for an eternity.

"*Tfaddal*," he grunted finally, "go ahead."

Waleed started the engine and the car rolled on into no-man's-land. Relief washed over me. We breezed through the Lebanese border crossing and drove out into the Beka'a Valley, a majestic carpet of vineyards and fields below us. I opened the window and stuck my head out. "Woooooo hoooooo!" I cheered. Waleed laughed and shook his head.

I picked up my cell phone and called Randall.

"We're out!"

I HAD FALLEN IN LOVE WITH DAMASCUS six years earlier, in 2005. I was twenty-five years old. I found ordinary Syrian people to be courageous, compassionate, funny, and cultured, despite the suffocation of decades of dictatorship.

The Palestinian poet Mahmoud Darwish wrote:

> In Damascus:
> the traveler sings to himself:
> I return from Syria
> neither alive
> nor dead
> but as clouds
> that ease the butterfly's burden
> from my fugitive soul

My fugitive soul—leaving the decadence of Beirut behind—was quickly seduced by Damascus. It was like stepping into another age. Unlike so many other Middle Eastern cities that had diluted their history and culture, frantically building shopping malls in a pale imitation of the West, Damascus had retained its character and remained majestically aloof.

In Lebanon, I had danced on tabletops and drunk tequila and flirted in French with cute boys who were not afraid to trash their politicians and speak their minds. Syria was much more conservative. Few people spoke English and even fewer French. And under the rule of the Assad family, dissent meant disappearance.

A Syrian taxi driver had helped me fill in the immigration form. "What is your work?" he asked me. "I'm a journalist," I replied proudly. He scowled. "Don't say this." I blushed, how stupid of me, of course I can't say I'm a journalist.

"I'm a producer," I tried again. He nodded in approval. We drove toward Damascus. The spectacular sea views and lush green valleys of the drive from Beirut had given way to a bland highway surrounded by stark, rocky slopes. As we approached the city center, he turned toward me again. "Don't say to people here you're a journalist. OK?"

The old city was unlike anything I had ever experienced. In the covered souk, I relished the pungent smell of assorted spices, cashews and pistachios and perfume oils. The stalls were jammed with dried flowers, gold and velvet, embroidery and mother-of-pearl, sabers and swords. Boys stood beside rusty bathroom scales, charging a penny to weigh people. Old men smoked *nargileh* and played backgammon. Young men leered at me and said, "Bonjour, I love you." Young women shyly smiled at me and said, "You are welcome!" The birds twittered in their cages as I passed the tiny barbershops, from which Arabic pop music poured into the street, competing with the muezzin's call to the final prayer of the day.

In the evenings, the air was cool and thick with the scent of jasmine. The streets hummed with people: Sunni women in full *niqab*, black veils totally obscuring their faces, even eyes, from view; men from the Gulf in their billowing white *dishdashas* and red-checkered *keffiyehs*; shop owners hawking watches and mobile phones, fresh fruit and baklava; beggars missing legs and arms and eyes, reciting the Koran; younger women with kohl-lined eyes and colorful headscarves matching their elegant outfits.

At the heart of the old city was the Umayyad Mosque, one of the holiest sites in Islam, a gleaming oasis of white stone and marble. It was built in the eighth century on the site of a Christian basilica dedicated to John the Baptist, who is seen as a prophet by both Muslims and Christians. In the afternoons, I would take sanctuary there from the heat and watch people come and go through the courtyard.

At the mosque, people dressed according to religious requirement, but they didn't dress up (unless it was a celebration like Eid). Often they brought food with them—fruit and nuts. They would sit in contemplation in the immaculate courtyard or wander inside to the vast carpeted prayer hall and pray or read or often just have a nap. The only formal congregation was for Friday (*Juma'a*, the Muslim holy day) afternoon prayers, but there was a steady stream of visitors every day of the week.

While the mosque was exquisitely beautiful and built on a grand scale with three minarets and a soaring dome and arches, it was somehow quite cozy and very peaceful. Perhaps it was because shoes are forbidden in mosques or because there were no chairs to scrape along the floor— just the soft pad of bare feet on the cool stone.

After leaving the Umayyad Mosque, I would amble over to my favorite chicken shawarma stand and order a sandwich "*ma'a kabees wa toum*" (with pickles and garlic mayonnaise) and freshly pressed pomegranate juice. I would find a place to sit and eat while watching the bustle of daily life, the rich and beautiful moment mingling with a familiar sense of loneliness.

The main purpose of this first visit to Damascus was to improve my Arabic. I began lessons with a lovely young woman called Hala. Everything about Hala was long and gray—from her pale, thin fingers that fidgeted incessantly as she talked, to her soft eyes and drab skirts. She was tall and thin with a sweet face but seemed embarrassed by her height, stooping and often looking at the ground. As she walked into my hotel room for our first Arabic class, she seemed to radiate a soft, nervous energy.

We sat down together at the desk and I began delivering my sermon about Syria—how excited I was to be there, how beautiful Damascus was, how delicious I found the desserts. It was a speech designed to break through the polite suspicion that usually greeted foreigners. "I come in peace," was the intended subtext, "and I don't think your country is any worse than mine and I have no intention of patronizing you."

Hala laughed nervously as I extolled the virtues of her country's rich history. And then she suddenly interrupted me.

"I think you will not love it if you are living here."

I apologized for talking too much. "Why do you say that?" I asked, excited at the possibility that I might have a real conversation with a Syrian.

"It is very hard for the women. She has not good life."

From that moment on, Hala and I spent very little time discussing Arabic verbs. Instead, we would take long walks around the old city of Damascus and she would tell me all about her life. She was from a poor family who lived in the bland, beige sprawl of the Damascus suburbs. They were from the same Alawite sect as the Assad family, but they did not appear to enjoy any of the privileges that more-connected members did.

When Hala was eighteen years old, she was married to a man she barely knew. "My parents wanted it, he had a big house," she explained. Up until her wedding night, she had never even spoken at length to a boy other than her brother, and she told me it was months before she was able to let her husband touch her. Her innocence infuriated him, and he would frequently grumble about what an inept wife she was.

"I was so scared. I was so small, so small," she said in English, using the direct Arabic translation for young.

Within two years of marriage Hala bore her husband two beautiful girls. She fought bitterly with her husband and family to be allowed to attend university part time, while continuing to work and take care of her children. She did not love her husband. She resented his ignorance, his lack of curiosity, his brutishness.

"Education, it is everything," she told me one day as we sipped mint tea in a courtyard café. All around us young students worked away on their laptops.

"Why don't you try to do a fellowship in the US or in Europe like Fadi?" I naively suggested. Fadi was Hala's beloved younger brother, who was studying in Texas on a scholarship. She talked about him incessantly. Anything that Fadi told her about his life in the US, she wanted to experience, too. He told her about digital cameras. She saved up for a year and bought one.

She looked down at her tea as she stirred the spoon around and around. I knew at once that I had upset her, that by suggesting the impossible I had only reminded her that the world she so wanted to see was not really open to her, that her lot had already been cast.

"*Insh'allah*," she said softly, meaning "if God wills it." The conversation ended.

One day Hala invited me to meet her family. She lived in a simple but comfortable apartment with her parents and sister, her husband and their daughters. Her mother was a tough-looking woman with wiry gray hair and dark circles under her eyes. She eyed me suspiciously when she thought I wasn't looking and smiled politely at me when she knew I was. I could see her trying to calculate whether my presence in her home was going to create problems for the family. She was from the older generation that had spent their entire adult lives under Hafez al-Assad, who had sided with the Soviet Union during the Cold War and railed against the West for its colonial legacy in the Middle East. She had been raised on a diet of fear and paranoia and propaganda.

She knew how serious the consequences were for being associated with any form of dissent. In the early 1980s, a rebellion against Hafez al-Assad's secular regime took hold in the central city of Hama, led by Sunni Islamists who chafed at being ruled by the Alawite minority. Assad's forces responded by pounding the city with artillery, before bringing in bulldozers to raze entire neighborhoods. Nobody knows how many people were killed, but it is estimated to be in the tens of thousands.

Being naive and curious, I decided to ask Hala's family what they thought had happened in Hama. Her mother looked at me and pursed her lips disapprovingly. There had been no official media coverage of the crushing of the insurgency, but people in Syria didn't get their news from the papers. They got it through word of mouth, or from listening to international radio broadcasts. Hala's mother likely had a good idea of what had happened in Hama, though, like most Syrians, she was wise enough to pretend not to. Honesty only got you in trouble in Syria. Hala squirmed in her seat.

"We don't know anything here," she said, laughing uncomfortably.

Thanks to the Assad family, Syria had been a police state for decades. After the First World War, Britain and France had carved up the carcass of the Ottoman Empire with the notorious Sykes-Picot agreement. The seemingly arbitrary straight lines had very little regard for the ethnic and sectarian divisions that would haunt the region for generations to come.

Syria fell under the control of the French until it gained independence in 1946. Over the next two decades, a series of coups eventually brought the socialist Ba'ath Party to power. A stern-looking former commander of the Syrian air force, who belonged to the minority Alawite sect, became president in 1971. Hafez al-Assad went on to rule the country for nearly thirty years, consolidating power by populating the security and intelligence services with fellow Alawites and containing the majority Sunni Muslims.

In 2005, long before the protests began, the secret police were omnipresent. The lobby of my hotel was full of gray-faced men in ill-fitting polyester suits who sat and smoked cigarettes and avoided eye contact with me while following every move I made. Every scene seemed to be an elaborate tableau, as if all the guests and businessmen in the lobby were really intelligence operatives, known as *mukhabarat*, sent to watch your every move. The *mukhabarat* were feared and reviled. They inhabited a shadowy underworld where there were no rules, no recourse. You could be swallowed up and disappeared at any time. I could feel their eyes boring into my back and sense their gaze abruptly shift when I turned around. They were spies and probably thought I was a spy, too.

BASHAR AL-ASSAD WAS NOT SUPPOSED TO BE PRESIDENT. The heir apparent had been his brother, Bassel, Hafez's oldest son, until he was killed in a car accident in 1994. After the crash, Bashar was groomed to take over, and when Hafez died in 2000, Bashar was instated as his successor. By 2005, Bashar had been in power for five years, enough time to consolidate his rule and dominance over national life. At the hotel, a large portrait of the young president loomed over the check-in desk. The artist had downplayed his elongated neck and elfin ears and painted his features in a stern expression. The intended effect was: "This is a serious leader." Every single establishment I visited in Syria had a photograph or portrait of Bashar hung in a prominent position. The poses varied. Bashar the beloved leader, arms outstretched to his people. Bashar the commander in chief, standing to attention. Bashar the adventurer, in aviator sunglasses. Bashar the family man. Bashar gesturing defiantly. Bashar contemplating, hand on chin. And so on.

There were whispers about liberalization. Perhaps Bashar—just about to turn forty—would eventually show himself to be a man of the twenty-first century. With his experience as a student in London and a glamorous British-born wife, Asma, he hinted at a more modern Syria. A handful of internet cafés had opened, where more-cosmopolitan Syrians mingled with Western tourists and talked on cell phones and drank bad cappuccinos. Of course, the new, hip Damascus was just a small piece of a state that was still profoundly old-fashioned. But there was a tantalizing sense of potential, of development, in 2005.

The prospect enthralled Hala. At the end of our lunch at her family's apartment, Hala had taken me into the living room and wedged a chair under the door handle so that no one could come in. She gripped my forearm and led me to the sofa. There was a solemn look on her face and she kept glancing up at the door. She pulled her cell phone out of her bag and whispered that she had been receiving text messages from an admirer, her daughters' doctor. They were written in English, which she could not read well.

"Please," she breathed, handing me her cell phone, "tell me what they say."

"Of course!" Smiling, I took the phone and looked down at the messages.

"Hala, my dear," I read out loud.

"Shusssssshhhhhh," she hissed, looking up at the door. Then she gestured to continue, quietly.

"I dream of kissing your neck and lips," I whispered, pointing to my neck and lips. Hala squealed in shock.

"It is dirty?" she asked, blushing furiously.

"No, it's not dirty," I assured her. "It's romantic."

There was something profoundly moving to me about the text messages. They were at once cheesy and over-the-top and, at the same time, so innocent and romantic, in a way that reminded me of being in middle school and having butterflies in my stomach.

Hala's eyes filled with tears as I continued translating them. "I long to hold you and smell your perfume."

"I never have romance. And now I am big, I have . . ." She trailed off, suggesting the impossibility of ever acting on this romance.

"Enough!" I said. "You hate your husband. You should leave him and get a divorce and go on some dates with the doctor."

She laughed and looked at me with the same sad eyes as at the internet café. Once again, I had dared to tempt her. Once again, she was left only with her own disappointment.

"I mean it," I continued. "Women in Syria get divorced, too. You have the support of your family, you can get a full-time job."

She dabbed her eyes with a tissue and put the cell phone back in her bag.

"He will kill me maybe," she said of her husband, ending the conversation. And then she stood up and moved the chair back and opened the door.

SIX YEARS LATER, in the maelstrom of the Arab Spring, I was desperate to know how that faint hint of the future that Hala dreamed of was being snuffed out, to see how Bashar, far from embracing modernity, had copied his father's brutality in dealing with the protests. I wondered what had become of Hala. Had she left her husband? What was her family's view of the protests occurring daily in Damascus? As an Alawite, did Hala fear that the overthrow of Assad would bring chaos, or did she hope for the freedoms dreamed of by the activists I met? While most Alawites supported Bashar al-Assad, this was before the poisonous sectarianism spread across the country. Some younger, educated Alawites were joining demonstrations against the government crackdown. Hala and I had stayed in touch over email for several years, but reaching out to her now was out of the question. I was, after all, supposed to be passing myself off as a tourist consumed by a passion for Syrian art and antiquities.

Getting into the country had not been easy. I had spent weeks trolling Lonely Planet chat rooms to see if any Syrian embassies were still issuing tourism visas. Finally, I came across a couple of posts from adventurous travelers who had managed to get them in Oman.

In a fit of benevolence, CBS had let the "new kid" try her luck—and allowed me to go to Oman. So I flew to Muscat and applied for a tourism visa with my British passport (as a dual national, I have both American and British passports). The benevolence paid off, because several days later I was in possession of a Syrian tourism visa. As I walked out of the embassy, the ambassador himself came running out after me. My heart stopped.

"Excuse me," he said, "I just want to know what is your program in Syria. As you know, the situation is quite difficult in some parts of the country."

I tried to keep my voice calm. "I am going to meet up with my Australian friend in Damascus. We might go to Aleppo, too, but that's it."

He nodded thoughtfully before smiling. "That's fine. Take care."

Two days later, a CBS producer, Randall Joyce, arrived in Oman to try the same tactic. He had worked as the legendary Bob Simon's *60 Minutes II* producer for years, traveling all around the Balkans and the Middle

East and winning awards along the way. He was soft-spoken, thoughtful, and a genuinely nice person—in other words, nothing like most conflict reporters. I was thrilled that he'd been assigned to the story.

Unfortunately, his visa application was rejected. I would go to Syria alone or not go at all. I had been waiting for an opportunity like this for a long time. A big news story, in a place that I cared deeply about, that few others could get to. I wanted to prove myself to CBS but, more important, I wanted to witness this extraordinary moment in history. I had watched the revolutions in Egypt and Libya unfold from Beijing—growing more impatient by the day to be there. I wasn't going to allow that to happen in Syria.

Returning to Damascus presented a very different kind of danger to the kind I had experienced in Iraq and Afghanistan, where the biggest fear was getting blown up. This time, I would be alone. Protests were routinely being met with a hail of bullets. What would happen if I was injured? Where would I go? Who would look after me? Certainly, if I was caught, I could be arrested or roughed up and all my material seized. I sat up late into the night, gaming out different possible scenarios.

I already knew my decision. I would go alone.

Randall and I flew to Beirut; he would wait for me there while I was in Syria. "I'll stock up on Cafe Najjar and do some reading," he joked.

In the days before I crossed into Syria, he went over my kit with me again and again, making suggestions about how to get at the story. The most important thing, he reminded me, was to protect the people whose story I was telling. It was not safe enough to simply blur their faces in post-production. I would shoot every interview without showing their faces, so that they would be unidentifiable if authorities somehow got hold of my raw footage.

Before setting off on my trip, I had reached out to a prominent Syrian activist who went by the pseudonym Malath Aumran. He had been forced to flee the country after it appeared that authorities were poised to arrest him. But he remained in touch with the network of brave Syrian activists operating underground. He introduced me to a woman online who was in charge of coordinating activists in the Damascus area. She explained to me that Skype, which is difficult for authorities to intercept, would be my primary method of communication once I arrived. Another activist called "blue star" would be awaiting my message.

I was still a little worried about my cover story and so, before leaving Beirut, I wrote a semi-cryptic email to Sarah, a school friend of mine who was posted in the British embassy in Damascus. Without giving too much away, I wanted to find out what she thought of such a trip and hoped she might be able to meet me and offer some advice. I knew that I would have to spend a couple of days posing as a tourist before I could slip off and meet opposition activists. Any foreigner would almost certainly be followed at first and I didn't want to risk exposing anyone in the opposition. But I was also nervous about the prospect of posing as a solo traveler. Would I look suspicious? Would people buy my (faintly implausible) cover story? If Sarah was there, to have a coffee or dinner with, I might attract less attention.

Her reply was almost immediate: "Can I suggest that looking around, it isn't the best time for tourism? Perhaps a week or so would be better? Twixt the lines my darling."

I slumped over the keyboard. Unsurprisingly, she thought I was rash for coming, but I was grateful to her for warning me off seeing her. Clearly, as she was one of a handful of diplomats still left in Syria, her every move was being followed. I was going to have to spend a couple of days alone.

I scanned my Beirut hotel room and went over my packing once again. A brand-new Olympus automatic tourist camera sat on the desk with five memory cards next to it. My iPad had been wiped clean and VPN software installed on it that would allow me to go online in Damascus while appearing to be in Hong Kong.

I had prepared two sets of outfits: normal clothes for my "tourism" stint and a headscarf with a long-sleeve sweater dress over jeans (as I had seen many Syrian girls wearing) once I was ready to slip out for the real business. I had bought the headscarf the day before and spent some time watching YouTube videos on how to tie it correctly, before practicing in front of the mirror. I thought back to Alia, my Yemeni Arabic teacher. She had once taught me how to put on the *hijab*, pinning it carefully near the ear. With my hair completely hidden, I looked inconspicuous. Many Syrian girls have blue eyes, especially in the north of the country.

Arriving in Damascus, I was shocked to see what had happened to the city I once knew and had come to love. It felt lifeless, hollowed out. The souk was now half empty, many of the stalls closed. Some restaurants were still open but there was no mirth. People viewed me with suspicion more than curiosity. It was a city of tension and rumor. There seemed to be even more *mukhabarat* lurking in the streets and hotels; blackouts were becoming more frequent.

The first couple of days were quite painful: going out to eat alone in the evening, pretending not to speak any Arabic, lying all day about why I was there. I spent my mornings drinking tea and haggling with antiques dealers to make my cover story more convincing. In the afternoons, I would walk the narrow rabbit warren of streets in the old city, looking behind me regularly to check if I was being followed. On my second day there, I was walking down the famous Straight Street in the old city when I saw a blonde head bobbing down the road toward me. Another Western tourist! Finally, someone whom I could have dinner or a drink with, who might make me look less conspicuous.

I stood on the street waiting for the figure to get closer so I could say

My father rowing for Cambridge University in 1965. Despite being an intimidating six feet six inches, he is one of the kindest, gentlest souls I know.

My mother and me at our old house in Florida in 1988. She is a force of nature—brilliant, beautiful, and opinionated. There are many similar photos from my childhood.

Granny and me at my christening. She was endlessly enthusiastic about all my endeavors. I still desperately wish she could have seen my career unfold.

My first day of boarding school, age te was trying hard not to cry in this pho None of my American friends wen boarding school, and I didn't underst why I was being sent aw

One of the iconic Seven Sisters buildings, als known as the "wedding cakes," built by Stali the late 1940s. This one, in Barrikadnaya, w my home as an intern for CNN in fall 2002.

Arabic lessons in Baghdad with my wonderful teacher, Hakim. I have always loved learning languages and have formed close bonds with my teachers. As the situation in Iraq unraveled, Hakim was desperate to get his family out. It was the first of many times I would experience the frustration of being powerless to help.

Taking cover from the scorching sun under a mortar shelter in Mosul, Iraq, June 2005, while working as a producer for Fox. This was my first trip to a war zone and one of the most exhilarating periods of my career.

Standing in front of the rubble of a building in Beirut's southern suburbs in 2006, weeks into a w
between Israel and Hezbollah; Beirut had been my home for over a year.

Beirut was the chosen base for many journalists. When you weren't covering war, you could
indulge in all the decadence Lebanon has to offer.

Goofing around with Jonathan Hunt in Gaza, June 2006, while working for Fox. Jonathan was a great friend and mentor.

Gori, Georgia, August 2008. Covering the Russian incursion into Georgia was a baptism by fire, my first big story for ABC News.

With Beth Loyd in Helmand, Afghanistan, in 2010. Beth and I worked together all across Asia for two years. The producer-correspondent relationship is hugely important both personally and professionally, and I have been blessed to work with some of the best in the business.

My ABC colleagues and I were among the first reporters to get to the hardest-hit areas of northern Japan after the March 2011 tsunami. After several days of reporting, we were pulled out early because of fears of a nuclear disaster in Fukushima.

With the men of the Syrian Martyrs' Brigade in northern Syria, February 2012. Producer Ben Plesser and I had illegally crossed the border from Turkey and were full of nerves. Sitting across from me is the group's self-proclaimed leader, Muhanned. Our host, Abu Ibrahim, is the second on the right.

My friend and colleague Ayman Youssef al Haji bearing ice cream cones for the team outside Aleppo in 2012. Ayman was a kind soul who could make me smile in the most petrifying circumstances. He was killed in an air strike in 2015 while visiting a friend of his in the hospital.

With Scott Munro, Haithem Moussa, Ayman, and Ben on our way out of Syria in 2012. We had just shot my first story for *60 Minutes*.

This cartoon was sent to me on Twitter by a talented cartoonist. It is always surreal and gratifying when strangers reach out to me.

Austin Tice is a freelance journalist, former Marine Corps officer, and Georgetown University law student. Though we never met, he became my close friend online. He was captured in 2012 in Syria.

At the 2013 Emmys, Ben Plesser and I won two awards for our work in Syria. Coming off the stress of the Syrian assignments, I spent half the night sobbing because I forgot to thank the editor in my acceptance speech.

Israfil was a Dutch jihadi who went to Syria to fight against Assad at the end of 2012. The arrival of foreign jihadis quickly changed the dynamic of the Syrian uprising. After months of talking online, I interviewed him in northern Syria in 2014, before he moved to Raqqa, ISIS's self-declared capital.

With a Kurdish female fighter in northeastern Syria in 2015. The Kurds were a crucial ally for the US in the fight against ISIS.

Dr. Mazen al-Saoud outside the remnants of a hospital in Ma'arat al-Nu'man, Syria, in 2016. Hospitals and schools were regular targets of Russian and Syrian regime jets.

Writing up notes before a CNN live shot near the front lines of the battle for Mosul at the beginning of the offensive.

Eastern Aleppo, February 2016. Producer Salma Abdelaziz and I were among the last Western reporters to visit rebel-held Aleppo.

As one of the last Western reporters to visit Aleppo, I was invited by US ambassador Samantha Power to address the UN Security Council about what I had seen.

Among the happiest days of my life. After twelve years together, married the love of my life. We met in Mosco in 2007 and spent nea a decade long distance before settling in London. Philipp is the most patient and lovir man I know. I love hin with all my heart.

I was two months pregnant when this photo was taken in Greenland, and I was petrified about how having a child would change my career. Over the following few months, I would cover Hurricane Irma in St. Martin, the Rohingya crisis in Bangladesh, and the civil war in Yemen.

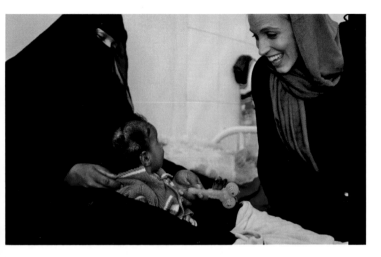

Visiting a malnourished child while heavily pregnant in Aden, Yemen, November 2017.

Palm Beach, Florida, December 2018. I joke to my friends that having a baby is like falling in love but without the stress of worrying about whether they will text you back.

By 2019 most of the media attention in Syria was focused on the battle to defeat ISIS. I visited the front lines of that fight in January, ten months after giving birth to my son. The pressure to come back safe is significantly elevated once you are a parent.

The way the light falls on the olive trees of Syria moves me to this day.

Wearing the full facial veil on an embed with the Taliban in northern Afghanistan in 2019. This was one of the more fascinating trips of my career and took months of preparation.

In August 2019, I finally visited Tehran after years of trying to get an Iranian visa. CNN has given me incredible global resources and support.

My beautiful smiling son, Ezra, in our home in London.

hi, then squinted to make sure I wasn't hallucinating. It wasn't a tourist, it was Sarah! I panicked, certain she was being followed. By this stage, I was pretty sure I was not, and the last thing I needed was to attract the attention of Syria's security services. "Shit, shit, shit," I cursed, looking around.

I was standing next to a shop selling backgammon sets, so I dived inside and crouched behind the window display, peeking out to watch as she ambled down the street.

"Please don't come in here, please don't come in here," I whispered to myself.

Fortunately, Sarah walked right past the shop. I exhaled a huge sigh of relief. Once she was a good distance past me, I stood up and turned around. The shopkeeper was watching me with curiosity. "*Ahlan*," he said, welcome, "can I help you?"

"I would like to buy your best backgammon set." I smiled.

The following morning, I left my hotel early and headed out to meet up with Hussein and Razan, the activists I had been connected with, who would facilitate my reporting.

Over the course of the next four days, they took me into the heart of the activists' world. We went to the funeral of a sixteen-year-old boy in Douma and to protests in and around the city. Through Hussein, I visited an underground clinic. I was even able to interview a contingent of fighters with the Free Syrian Army in Damascus.

Toward the end of my trip, Razan took me out to interview some people who had been seriously injured in the crackdown.

We visited a middle-aged man whose left leg was grotesquely swollen, with a crude jagged scar running down his shin, the result of a bullet wound that had become infected. Going to an ordinary hospital was out of the question, so he had been treated in a makeshift clinic. The man's family was clearly petrified about letting a journalist into their house. They looked searchingly at Razan as I moved around the room with my little camera. I asked the man to lift his pant leg again so I could get a different angle of the injury.

"No," Razan told me abruptly. "It's enough."

In another house, we found a bedridden nineteen-year-old boy who told us he had been shot by regime forces while attending a protest. His mother hovered nervously, her eyes brimming with tears, as he pulled back the bedsheet to reveal a bullet wound in his hip. He looked at me and said simply, "*An-nizam huwe al-shaytan*"—The regime is the devil.

These were ordinary people who had paid a horrific price for the crime of daring to demand a better future. They were incredibly brave but also desperately afraid and therefore relatable. Their stories needed to be heard.

When CBS told me to leave before something could go wrong, I did so reluctantly. I felt that the country was on the cusp of historic change, energized by the idealism of the young activists determined to see Bashar al-Assad toppled. But I was also fearful of the journey out. I had precious material on the memory cards that contained the video I had shot.

After the border crossing, my next greatest anxiety was that once we reunited, Randall would scroll through the footage shot by his rookie camerawoman/correspondent and declare there was not enough usable material. But we were both excited by what I'd managed to gather, and after a week of shot-listing, writing, and editing we dispatched the finished product to New York. The pieces were powerful and the reception to them was extraordinary. I was live on the set around all three pieces. Charlie Rose invited me to come on his talk show. I was bombarded with calls and emails and messages on social media, many of them from Syrians who were sharing the stories online.

And yet a niggling question would not leave my mind. Outside of the media bubble, would the pieces have any meaningful impact? I desperately wanted to believe so. I imagined the *CBS Evening News* audience watching my stories from Damascus in the comfort of their homes. Perhaps they were cooking dinner and had the news on in the background. Or maybe they had just finished eating and were settled in front of the TV, their thoughts turning already to the prospect of another day at work. Perhaps they'd find my reporting moving. Who knew about this brutal repression in Syria? they might say to each other as they removed the dinner plates. Who can understand why there are so many problems in that part of the world, how awful it all is? In any event, what could they do about it?

And yet, could they really understand that those bodies were real? Or was it all impossibly abstract, incomprehensible? Perhaps, in the great majority of American households, the tragedy of Syria was a momentary distraction before the trash was put out and the kids were told to finish their homework. I told myself that if just ten people saw my story and felt moved to care about Syria, then it was worth it.

I was determined to go back and do more.

Eight

I stood pinned against the wall of the small farmhouse, the air crackling with gunfire. The assault on the Syrian army checkpoint had started five minutes earlier. Rebel fighters from the "Syrian Liberation Army" were crawling on their bellies through the mud of an olive grove just in front of where I was taking cover.

When they got within a hundred yards of the checkpoint, they began shouting to their fellow Syrians inside: "You are surrounded. Defect and join us."

There was no response and the attack resumed. One of the rebel fighters lobbed a grenade over the small berm that provided their only cover. I could hear the gunfire intensifying and the cries of the fighters growing louder. A light drizzle slightly muffled the sounds.

In the two months since my visit to Damascus, the situation in Syria had deteriorated dramatically. The uprising had spread further and was gaining momentum in central Syria and in the north. In response, forces loyal to the regime of Bashar al-Assad had gone on the offensive. The dictator was using artillery shells against the people he claimed to protect in all those hagiographic murals.

For the past week, the regime had been brutally bombarding opposition areas in the city of Homs with artillery. They called it an anti-terrorist operation, deliberately using the same language that the US had used for years to justify its military misadventures. It didn't matter that most of the so-called terrorists in Homs were actually civilians. The only criteria for being branded a terrorist was that you opposed the regime of Bashar al-Assad or lived near someone who did. And once you had been branded a terrorist, you ceased to be a human being. You were nothing more than a scourge that had to be eradicated by whatever means necessary.

The crackdown on Homs had attracted an international outcry but no material response. America, it seemed, did not see the Syrian conflict in the same way it saw Libya, and there were no signs of any intervention on the horizon. If the regime could get away with using heavy weapons in Homs, what would stop it from doing the same in Idlib?

In response, there had been a huge wave of military defections. The Free Syrian Army was gaining recruits by the day. But not all of them were former soldiers. Many, especially in the north, were farmers, carpenters, and grocers—ordinary workers, mostly from the countryside, with little to no military experience.

Given the inaction from the West, there was a strong desire among Syrians to get the truth out. After seeing my Damascus stories on the *CBS Evening News*, a Syrian-American called Haithem had reached out to me. His friends had formed a rebel group in Idlib province in northern Syria, he told me, and they could arrange for me to be smuggled across the border from Turkey. They called themselves the Syrian Liberation Army, and Haithem assured me that they would guarantee my safety. He arranged for me to meet with one of the group's leaders in Turkey before I agreed to go in.

The risks were considerably greater than they had been for my trip to Damascus. Then I had entered the country legally on a government-issued visa. Now I would be illegally crossing the border of a sovereign state and hanging out with armed rebels whose abilities and credentials were at best murky. Once inside Syria, I would be relying on my hosts for everything from food to accommodation to transportation. But this was now the only way to cover the incipient revolt that was taking hold in one province after another and beginning to pose a real challenge to Assad's rule.

I had made the crossing from Turkey with an experienced CBS News producer called Ben Plesser and an Egyptian freelance stills photographer called Nasser whom we had never previously met.

Ben was like a character in a movie about journalists. He chain-smoked Camels, loved to argue, and invariably believed he was the smartest person in the room (usually he was). He was cynical, skeptical of authority, and often grumpy. But beneath the curmudgeonly demeanor he was fiercely protective and loyal and kind. Like Randall, Ben was a great writer with a ton of experience in the field. I soaked up everything he had to teach me about what the story really was and how to go about telling it.

Crossing into Syria had been relatively straightforward. We'd picked up Nasser and met the smuggler who would take us across. We walked down to the no-man's-land that separated the two countries. After a month of heavy rain, the area was flooded, and so we had to get into a rowboat to cross. Our smuggler used a broken road sign as a makeshift oar. On the other side, a large unshaven man was waiting for us.

He looked at my flak jacket and laughed, then pulled out his handgun. "Shall we test it?" he joked.

I laughed weakly. He threw an *abaya* at me to cover myself with and motioned at me to hide my blonde hair. We began the journey into the heart of the insurrection, to Idlib city—still a substantial place with nearly 165,000 inhabitants—where different rebel factions were beginning to emerge, testing their military prowess against an increasingly beleaguered Syrian army presence. This part of northern Syria was already becoming a patchwork of fiefdoms, many of which combined opposition to Assad with a streak of opportunism. There was money to be made and power to be seized from the chaos.

The self-proclaimed leader of the Syrian Liberation Army was called Muhanned. Until a few months before, he had been living in South Korea, exporting cars. Like many Syrians overseas, he had watched the uprising closely, seeing an opportunity not just to get rid of Bashar al-Assad and his cabal of corrupt Alawite cronies but to become powerful in his own right. So he'd taken the thirty grand he had saved up and come back to Syria to fund this motley group.

He loved the limelight. We had spent two days shooting a story that focused on him: Muhanned wearing a *keffiyeh* over his face as he read a garbled mission statement to the camera—three rows of stone-faced gunmen standing to attention behind him. Muhanned in the passenger seat of the car stabbing at the landscape with his cigarette—"This all my area . . . this my area. . . . All this, mine."

We had stopped at the side of the road to talk to a group of men. On the ground in front of them was a body, an activist from a neighboring town, they said, who had been dumped here by the regime as a grim warning. His face was bloated and covered in dirt. Muhanned had turned white and looked away. He was clearly terrified of death.

Nor did he exude any authority. At a supposedly "friendly" checkpoint, Ben's camera was ripped out of the car and angry men waved guns in our faces and barked at us, demanding to know who we were. Muhanned tried to charm the fighters and then pleaded with them to let us pass, but they apparently had no idea who he was. His brother Bassel, who was in the car in front, had to mollify the group. He spoke softly and shook hands with the men, and within moments the group was laughing and smiling and shouting "*ahlan wa sahlan*" (welcome) to us.

Bassel Issa was the real leader of the group, but he was a quiet man who didn't care about titles. So he let Muhanned pretend to the blonde journalist that he was running the show. We sat on cushions in the house where we were staying as he held court late into the night, blathering incoherently about religion and democracy and the world. He often appeared to be high, his eyes red, his smile leering, his mood erratic. Invariably he would revert to his favorite topic: women. How Muhanned loved the ladies.

"Before I get married, I was a very naughty boy," he confided to me with delight late one night. His breath was stale with cigarettes as he leaned in closer to me. "So, so naughty!!!!"

He began giggling maniacally. I smiled politely, resisting the urge to punch him in the face. In another world, I would tell him he was a douchebag and walk off. But here in rebel-held Syria, I held my tongue and indulged him.

"Russian girl, wow," he declared, kissing his fingers. "Korean girl, like doll," he pulled his eyes up with his fingers to imitate Asian eyes.

The house where we were staying was deep in the old city on a tiny street, too narrow for a car to squeeze through. It belonged to a great bear of a man called Abu Ibrahim. He was nothing like Muhanned. Before the uprising began, Abu Ibrahim had been a carpenter, making beautiful tables and chairs of olive wood—simple, clean designs. He had large calloused hands and a big bushy beard and dark, expressive eyes. He wasn't the type to talk much, but he went out of his way to make Ben and me feel welcome and comfortable in his house. At night, he would drive us out to a workshop he had in a cherry orchard where we could get a signal for our BGAN. As we worked late into the night, he would make tea and burn branches in a large metal drum to keep us warm.

I felt safe with Abu Ibrahim. He was not a pretender. He did not need to fill the air with the sound of his voice. He was humble and brave and interested in learning from Ben and me. What did the world think about the Syrian situation? Would America help the rebels? Did we think they had any chance of beating Assad?

We would answer his questions as honestly as we could. Yes, the world was horrified by what was happening in Syria, but that wouldn't necessarily translate into action. In Libya, the West (and the Gulf states) had come together to help the rebels in the face of a likely massacre by Muammar Qaddafi. But Libya was desert and oil; Qaddafi's rule had relied on scheming and patronage. Assad's Syria was a much more complex prospect, a large, multi-sectarian country with a significant army and serious international backers, principally Russia and Iran, who were already supplying the regime with weaponry, cash, and geopolitical support. The rebels had none of the training and weaponry that Assad's forces did. Educated professionals were pouring out of the country in large numbers by the day. Without outside assistance, it would be very difficult for them to win. Abu Ibrahim would sit and listen, nodding thoughtfully as he took it all in.

Abu Ibrahim's mother and father lived in the house next door along with his two brothers and their families. One of them was hugely fat and aptly nicknamed the Buffalo. The other, Azzu, was tall and skinny with an extraordinary bushy moustache that he twirled proudly at the ends. His wife and the Buffalo's wife and Abu Ibrahim's wife would spend most of their time sitting together upstairs and taking care of the children. As well as being family, they were one another's only real companions. Women in this part of Syria didn't go out much. It was a conservative society and their role was to take care of the house and the children, to make coffee and clean and now to prepare huge trays heaped with delicious food for the American journalists living downstairs. I would often go up there to chat with them and play with the kids.

Abu Ibrahim had four beautiful sons. The youngest, Bilal, was just three years old. He was intrigued and a little bit frightened by this funny woman with yellow hair who was sleeping in his house and spoke his language with a weird accent. Our favorite game was a sort of hide-and-go-seek that would culminate in me scooping him up and making monster noises as I smothered him in kisses. Being an only child, I bathed in the coziness of such a big, loving family.

Next to the house was a large space that looked like some kind of workshop, full of tools. Members of the Syrian Liberation Army would meet there at night to discuss upcoming operations. One day, Abu Ibrahim proudly showed us a secret project they had been working on. The men only had light weapons and they were no match for the machine guns and artillery of the Syrian army. With that in mind, they had built themselves a catapult. I stared in disbelief at the crudely improvised weapon—it looked like a child had built it. The story of David and Goliath immediately leaped to my mind. I felt a twinge of sadness that they could do nothing but put their faith in such a contraption.

We joined Abu Ibrahim as he led a few training sessions in the cherry orchard. It was clear that learning the basics of how to handle an AK-47 was not going to transform a few dozen farmers and grocers into a functional, fighting force.

Despite their lack of equipment, the men were sustained by their knowledge of the terrain, faith in their cause, and sheer blind courage. Or most of them. Muhanned embodied everything that was wrong about the Syrian opposition and especially its self-proclaimed leaders. In his mind, the revolution was supposed to be fun and easy. He would be the alpha male and ride into Damascus on the back of a pickup truck, basking in popular adoration before being lifted up on the shoulders of the crowd and inaugurated as Syria's next leader.

"A lot of chiefs and no Indians," Ben would say.

Standing now on that hillside in the drizzle, with bullets whizzing by and a growing sense that no one had a clue what was going on, Muhanned looked like a little boy wishing he'd stuck with selling cars in Korea. He flashed demented smiles at me and brandished a handgun he had clearly never used. To demonstrate his bravery and stealth, he crept toward the edge of the house and peeked around the corner—a bullet hissed past him. Muhanned's head snapped backward in shock. He lit a cigarette and drew heavily. This was not what he had signed up for.

"I do not want to die with you, my friend," I thought to myself.

Ben had run off to shoot some video, instructing me to stay put and Muhanned to keep an eye on me. That seemed like hours ago. The gunfire was relentless.

A few men had already started running up the hill back toward the town. No one had two-way radios. No one knew how to fight.

Moments later, the rebels took their first casualty. A twenty-three-year-old mechanic called Fouad Khashan was shot in the head. Abu Ibrahim struggled under gunfire to pick up the young man and carry him away from the front line but he buckled repeatedly under the weight of Fouad's body. Another fighter came and tried to help. They each grabbed an arm and began to drag him, stumbling in the thick, slippery mud as they tried to duck beneath the hail of bullets.

Ben came running toward me, panting. "They're bringing the guy who got shot around this way to get him out to a hospital. Stand in front of the camera and I'll tell you when they're behind you. And then do a piece to camera and don't screw it up because we can only do it once."

I looked behind my shoulder and saw the men running toward us, carrying Fouad. He was wearing a turquoise bomber jacket. His bloodied head lolled back. He showed no sign of life.

"Go!" Ben shouted.

I looked into the camera and began talking. "They tried to reclaim this checkpoint, they haven't been able to do it yet, and now there is a casualty. Someone has been hurt very badly, they're trying to take him to a hospital."

It was a very basic account of what was going on, but events behind me were telling the real story. Fouad's limp body was stuffed into a car, which screeched off out of sight.

"Nice job," Ben said.

I looked around. Muhanned was gone. He had jumped into the car with the dead guy to catch a ride back to safety. Thanks a lot, asshole, I thought to myself. More and more of the men were now running back up the hill toward the town.

I looked at Ben with panic. "What do we do now?"

"They're retreating so we have to run back."

I surveyed the olive grove sloping up toward the town. There was a road that cut it in two, but that wasn't safe to use. Every fiber of my being wanted to go inside the farmhouse and hide under a bed until it was all over.

"Can't we wait here for a few hours and then go back once it's quiet?" I suggested lamely.

"Nope, we're about to be on the wrong side of the front line. We have to run."

The rain seemed to be coming down harder, churning the earth into thick mud. I felt like I was moving in slow motion under the weight of my body armor, plunging in and out of the mud, trying to run, tripping constantly on the long *abaya* I was wearing. Away from the farmhouse there was no longer any cover. Ben tried to guide me as bullets continued to whiz overhead.

"Come on, keep moving. You're OK, that's outgoing, that's outgoing, too."

More bullets, a different sound, a hiss. "OK, that's incoming. Run with me, Clarissa. Come on."

My chest was on fire. I couldn't breathe. Goddamn cigarettes, I swore to myself. I didn't even smoke in my "real life," but the minute I was back in a war zone I could burn through half a pack in a day easily.

I looked up at the hill yawning above us—we weren't even halfway. The burning sensation was like a soldering iron searing through my lungs. I couldn't breathe.

"I can't go any farther," I whimpered. "I need to breathe. Please don't leave me."

"I'm not going anywhere," he assured me. "We'll stop here for a moment."

We attempted to take cover behind an olive tree, which was of course absurd, given that an olive tree's circumference is about the same as that of my leg. More bullets hissed and sighed overhead.

The blood was thumping in my head. I was no longer aware of anything other than that we were in a bad situation and we needed to get out of it. We continued running, dashing from one tree to the next. I could now see Nasser standing at the top of the hill, obviously out of breath. He looked distraught. What now? Where to? How do we get out of here?

Suddenly, Abu Ibrahim arrived on his motorcycle.

"Get on it," Ben shouted. I looked at him helplessly, incapable of making a decision by myself, reluctant to leave him.

"NOW," he shouted.

I hopped on the motorbike. My long *abaya* meant I had to sit side-saddle, so I clasped my arms around Abu Ibrahim to hold on. It was the only time I ever touched him. We roared off and the only thing I could hear was the wind thudding between my headscarf and my ears and the bullets still cracking through the sky. A tank opened up its machine gun in the distance—*datatatatatatat*. I slumped behind Abu Ibrahim's broad shoulders and watched in a dream state as the bike flew over bumps and tore along the road. We are moving too quickly to get shot, I thought; we might be flying.

There's a moment after you finish breathing out before you breathe in again when your lungs are empty, and if you focus on it you feel a singular type of calm. The only thing you can hear is your heartbeat and it's beautiful and still precisely because it is fleeting. That's how I felt on the back of the bike. Like I was watching from underwater, waiting to come back up and take a hungry gulp of air but suspended in that moment. Calm. Unafraid. Detached.

The bike smacked into the wall by the house where we were staying, jolting me back to reality. I bounced off, and Abu Ibrahim screeched back to the olive grove to collect the others. Once I was off the bike and breathing in the cold air, the burning in my chest returned. I rapped on the old metal door.

Abu Ibrahim's wife immediately bundled me upstairs. I kicked off my muddy shoes and she and the other women peeled off my socks and hung them up to dry. Using the last remnants of my strength, I lifted off my *abaya* and removed my body armor before collapsing onto a mattress on the floor. The women made a fuss over me, putting cushions under my head and pouring me glasses of sweet dark tea. They peppered me with questions.

"Why were you in the battle? What happened?"

"Are they still fighting? You're crazy to go out with the men!"

"Why is there so much gunfire? Was anyone hurt? Did you see Abu Ibrahim?"

"We were getting scared—there's so much gunfire."

I desperately wanted them to stop talking so that I could concentrate on the burning in my chest instead of trying to formulate answers in Arabic. I briefly wondered if I might throw up.

"The fighting was bad. One man was hurt very badly," I mustered. "Not Abu Ibrahim. Another. I've never seen him before."

"Who was it? Did anyone else die? What is happening now? Why were you out there? We were worried."

I gasped for air, no longer sure if the burning was from the cigarettes and exertion or whether I was in the grip of some kind of panic attack. I had never felt this exhausted in my life. Little Bilal observed me shyly from the other side of the room. I smiled faintly at him.

There was another knock on the door downstairs. Gunfire could still be heard hammering through the winter air. Abu Ibrahim's wife went downstairs. I heard the door open and voices talking. And then a wail. The other women leaped up. I pulled myself up to a sitting position. She staggered into the room, trembling, her face contorted.

"*Azzu mat, Azzu mat*," she cried in disbelief. "Azzu is dead, Azzu is dead."

The whole room was suddenly consumed by a terrifying wail.

It took me a moment to understand what she was saying. This was tall, skinny Azzu with the bushy moustache she was talking about. The same Azzu who had taken us around Idlib the day before, standing protectively next to me as we walked through a market and telling me in a quiet voice about who controlled which parts of the city. The same Azzu whose wife had just poured me some tea and who was now sobbing hysterically on the floor.

She began rocking back and forth, moaning and sobbing and spitting out a stream of curses against Bashar al-Assad. One of the women hugged her tightly and began whispering over and over again.

"*Inna lillahi wa inna ilayhi raji'un.*" We belong to God and to Him we shall return.

I looked over at Abu Ibrahim's mother.

"*Ya Allah, ya Allah, ya Allah, ibni, ibni,*" she shrieked (Oh God, oh

God, oh God, my son, my son). I watched in shock as she began tearing out clumps of her hair before swooning. The other women jumped to catch her and pulled her hands away from her head.

"*Khalas, khalas*," Abu Ibrahim's wife pleaded with her, weeping (Enough, enough).

The room was stifling with the heat of their grief. I could feel it spilling over me and pooling inside me, rising like a flood, threatening to overwhelm me.

I felt I should excuse myself to give them some privacy, but there was nowhere to go.

In previous war zones I'd covered, journalists stayed together in a hotel. The dangers were still present, but the periodic distance gave you room to breathe and reboot. In Syria, there was no such space.

And maybe that made me better at my job. To be immersed in someone else's suffering, to take it in without flinching, without turning away.

The women seemed oblivious to my presence, weeping and writhing around me. Bilal sat in the corner watching the whole scene, blinking with disbelief. I wanted to take him in my arms and carry him far away.

Suddenly, I heard one of the fighters shouting my name from outside. I ran down to the door. He told me they were to take me to the hospital to meet up with Ben. The thought of going anywhere was enough to exhaust me, but I needed to get out of the room that was hot with the tears and wailing of these grieving women. And we needed to keep working. I grabbed my *abaya* and a pair of rubber sandals that were lying around and we set off.

There was only one hospital in town that the rebels could use. All the others in the city were run by the government. Activists and fighters who had the misfortune of being taken to a government hospital usually ended up tortured or dead. Or they simply disappeared like so many in Syria. Swallowed up into dark prisons, never to be seen again.

This hospital was a third-floor walk-up. As soon as I entered, it was clear that it was more of a clinic than a hospital, and a poorly equipped one at that. Several bloody, lifeless bodies lay sprawled out on stretchers by the entrance. An overworked nurse darted around the room barking orders at people. I recognized Azzu at once. His face was gray, his lips colorless under his bushy moustache. The Buffalo stood next to him, wailing—"the honor of the Arabs is dead."

I looked at him blankly. The smell of blood was overwhelming—pungent, metallic, meaty.

"*Allah yerhamo*," I mustered. May he rest in peace.

Ben was moving around the room with his camera, getting shots. He spotted me and came over.

"You OK?" he asked.

"I'm fine," I lied. "What's next?"

"We need to start feeding ASAP. I called [our bureau chief] Andy and told him to grease the runway and get an editor ready for our material so we can make the show tonight. Let's get back to Abu Ibrahim's so you can start writing."

Despite the overwhelming emotions of the day, we had to work. I had no idea how I was going to quiet my mind and write a script that was coherent and did justice to what we had seen, but in some ways it was a relief to have something to focus on. Covering war is a bit like being a trauma surgeon in the ER, though of course we are not saving lives. But when things get bloody, you have to take a deep breath and immerse yourself completely in your job, switching off any human response to the horror of what's happening. The rest of the evening was spent in a daze of writing and cutting and feeding.

Azzu's body was brought into the workshop next door and the women were allowed in briefly to pay their respects. Ben gave me the camera to go and shoot. It was a devastating scene, with Azzu's wife sobbing hysterically and hugging his lifeless body until the men came back in and had to pry her off him. The women were ululating wildly as is customary in the Arab world when something wonderful or terrible happens, their grief piercing the night air. A Jordanian friend would later tell me the women do it when martyrs die to celebrate the fact that they are going to paradise. Somehow, being behind the camera made it easier: I wasn't looking directly at them anymore, there was a barrier between us now, a distance.

Sometime after midnight, the script was finally written and tracked and all the video was in. After some deliberation about security, we decided to try to attempt a live shot with the BGAN. By some miracle, the signal was strong enough for us to transmit live to New York. I stood in the alleyway where we were staying, preparing myself. For once, I didn't feel too nervous. I badly wanted to tell the story of these people. The sound of mourners reading the Quran over Azzu's body could be heard in the background.

The *CBS Evening News* anchor, Scott Pelley, started out by asking how many people had been killed.

"Four people were killed in the fighting today, Scott. And it's important to remember that this is a small city. Everyone living on this street was either a relative of or knew or grew up with one of the men who died."

By now, the alleyway was full of Abu Ibrahim's neighbors, standing in their doorways, watching quietly as I told America what I had seen.

"It's simply no match, Scott," I said. "They're fighting with Kalashnikovs, they have no military training, they are not particularly physically fit, they are up against a pretty sophisticated army that has artillery, that has tanks, and of course the greatest fear here on the ground is that soon the Syrian army will begin to use its airpower as well."

The whole episode had been a salutary reminder that this was a very one-sided conflict. The rebels lacked training, equipment, discipline, and leadership.

At the end of the live shot, someone in the control room spoke into my earpiece. "Amazing segment" were the only words I could hear. No American journalist had yet managed to report live from inside a rebel-held area. We took advantage of the working BGAN signal to check our emails for the first time in days. Messages were flooding in from bosses and colleagues. Among them was a note from the celebrated war correspondent Marie Colvin. She and Ben had become friends covering the revolution in Egypt.

"Saw your piece," the note read. "Great job, guys. Am trying to get to Homs."

I made him read it out to me twice. Marie was a legend in our field. I had first seen her in Gaza in 2006. She had been sitting in the hotel lobby smoking and talking on the phone. With her distinctive eye patch (concealing the eye she had lost covering the Sri Lankan civil war) and throaty voice, she was impossible to miss. I had been reading her dispatches for the Sunday *Times* for years but was completely intimidated and too shy to approach her. And now she had told Ben that she liked our work.

I felt too revved up to sleep, so I dug out the emergency Valium I carried with me, split it in two, and swallowed one half.

Ben watched me, smirking.

"Well, it's not like we can have a beer." I shrugged.

We spoke for a while about what a mess the offensive had been—the lack of planning and preparation and the lack of communication. Four men had died and nothing had been achieved. The rebels had heart—but heart alone wasn't going to win this war. And hearts quickly shrivel and harden in the face of death and destruction.

It was getting late. Ben got up to go to the other side of the room, where he and Nasser slept behind a curtain.

"This is going to sound ridiculous, but do you mind just sitting with me until I'm ready to fall asleep?" I asked.

"Sure thing," he said, pulling the chair up to the end of my bed.

"You saved my life today," I told him, involuntarily welling up. "I'm so grateful."

"I didn't save your life," he laughed.

"You did," I insisted. "I couldn't have got up that hill without you."

"Don't underestimate yourself. You're no babe in the woods. You remind me of that chick from *Game of Thrones*—Khaleesi, mother of dragons."

I managed a half-delirious laugh.

As I was nodding off, I heard him quietly get up and go to bed.

The next morning, I woke up early and climbed up to the roof to call Philipp on the satellite phone.

"Oh, darling, well done you."

The sound of his voice had an immediate calming effect. He had seen my piece from the night before and was proud but also worried.

"Don't get complacent, darling."

"I won't," I promised him.

When I came back down, I was surprised to find a tray heaped with delicious food that the women had brought us. There was fresh *labneh* (yogurt) and olives and juicy red tomatoes and warm boiled eggs, as well as a delicious hot grain cereal cooked with cinnamon. Olive oil and *za'atar* (a mixture of thyme, oregano, and marjoram) and flat bread completed the meal. It was almost inconceivable to me that, in the midst of their grieving, these women would take the time to prepare such a feast for their foreign guests.

Abu Ibrahim and Muhanned and his brother Bassel were already sitting with Ben and Nasser. The air was heavy with the death and defeat of the day before. Even Muhanned had nothing to say. He sat and smoked, rubbing his temples and shaking his head. I quietly watched Abu Ibrahim as he sat silently tearing his piece of flat bread into smaller and smaller pieces. Eventually, he put one bit in his mouth. He looked down at the ground as he struggled to chew on the small morsel, unable to swallow, until finally he gave up and sobbed softly. The sight of his agony was unbearable to me. I wanted to fling my arms around him and hold him and tell him how sorry I was. Instead, I sat silently, hot tears rolling down my cheeks.

After breakfast, it was time for noon prayers, and then Azzu's funeral, in keeping with Islamic custom that the dead be buried within a day. Abu Ibrahim, the Buffalo, and their father were helped by several other men as they hoisted the open coffin onto their shoulders and began the slow, solemn march to the burial ground, their faces crushed by the weight of their loss.

As we walked, other funeral processions could be heard in the distance. They all congregated in a square in the center of town. Ben and I ran up to a roof to get a good vantage point. One of the dead was a young boy, not more than ten years old. I looked down at his smooth, placid face as he was carried away by the crowds beneath me. He looked like he was sleeping.

"Heaven holds a special place for the martyrs," the crowd chanted.

But what exactly were these people dying for? They wanted to overthrow the regime and yet they had little sense of what would come next. Who would take over? What would their new country look like? At protests, men and women would chant "we need freedom, we need freedom," but what did they want to do with that freedom?

How could this hodgepodge of small, local fighting groups and activists merge into a coherent body with a proper chain of command and a clear vision of what they wanted? There was no real unified sense of purpose beyond a shared desire to see Bashar al-Assad and his brutal regime overthrown. The uprising was incredibly vulnerable.

With no meaningful assistance being offered by the international community, especially the West, this revolt could easily be hijacked by anyone with a simple but compelling narrative and the discipline to enforce it. The regime was well aware of this weakness and set out to exploit it as a variety of rebel groups, which often spent as much time attacking each other as they did the Syrian army, gradually won more territory. In a move as cunning as it was cynical, Assad had ordered the release of dozens of prominent Islamists from prison, betting they would ruthlessly subsume more-moderate factions supported by the Gulf states, Turkey, and to a lesser extent the West.

The revolution threatened to be co-opted by religious and, more importantly, sectarian fanaticism, as Sunni jihadi groups sensed an opportunity. That suited Assad perfectly. Alawites and other minorities would look to the regime for protection, and Assad would declare to the world that he was a bulwark against international terrorism.

About a month after we left Idlib, I asked then–secretary of state Hillary Clinton about just this issue, after a conference in Istanbul on how to support the Syrian opposition. I had been given seven minutes of her time.

"Are you not concerned that if no support comes from the outside, that this could really devolve into a very bloody, ugly insurgency, and that if we aren't the ones that provide that help, other nonstate actors like extremist groups such as al Qaeda might be the ones to fill that void?"

Her answer was fluent but evasive.

"Well, I think that's why you heard today that a group of nations will be providing assistance for the fighters, and that is a decision that is being welcomed by the Syrian National Council [the umbrella body representing moderate opposition groups].

"The United States will be doing other kinds of assistance. Other countries will as well. So we have evolved from trying to get our arms around what is an incredibly complex issue with a just nascent opposition that has now become much more solidified with a lot of doubts inside Syria itself from people who were either afraid of the Assad regime or afraid of what might come after to a much clearer picture, where we are now, I think, proceeding on a path that is going to have some positive returns."

I had the sense that she knew full well that the Obama administration's policy of saying that Assad must go, while doing little to bring that about through material support to the rebels, was doomed to fail. President Lyndon Johnson had famously said, "Never tell a man to go to hell unless you're sure you can send him there." And yet the Americans had very publicly told Assad to go to hell without any plan for how to make it happen. Clinton was savvy enough to know that such a failure would have real consequences, not just in terms of civilian casualties but in terms of global security.

I wanted to ask her whether the West had created a moral hazard by intervening in Libya, raising the expectations of thousands of courageous Syrians who were marching toward a hail of bullets every day. I wanted to tell her that providing the exiled opposition (which had precious little connection with many of the groups doing the fighting) with some office space and supplying them with pens and paper wasn't going to address the challenge of ousting Assad. I wanted to tell her that expecting the Saudis and other Arab nations to lead the charge in providing assistance for the fighters was wishful thinking. I wanted to tell her that her words were hollow and empty, that they didn't help people on the ground. But we only had seven minutes.

After a week in Idlib, Ben and I decided it was time to leave. Since our live report, it was obvious to the regime that we were in Idlib and we didn't want to push our luck. Journalists like us would make an obvious target, and I was keenly aware that our presence posed an even greater threat to our brave and generous hosts.

I said goodbye to the women upstairs. They posed for photos with me and then smothered me with kisses and showered me with gifts: necklaces, perfume, a bracelet.

"I can't take these," I said, embarrassed by their generosity. I had never experienced such hospitality. The fact that it came from people who had so little made it all the more humbling.

"You must," they insisted, pressing the gifts into my hand, "to remember us."

Downstairs, Abu Ibrahim stood by the door with his four sons as Ben shut the boot of the car. Ben shook his hand and hugged him.

"I can't thank you enough," he said as he got into the car. "I have left our generator for you."

I kissed and hugged all the boys, one by one, then stopped at Abu Ibrahim and stretched out my hand.

He smiled and bowed his head, holding his hand up to his heart. I understood that the gesture of refusing to shake my hand was not intended to offend but rather as a mark of respect.

"It's very hard for me to express my gratitude in Arabic," I said, my voice trembling.

Tears sprang to my eyes. I had so much more to say but a lump had formed in my throat and I couldn't speak.

He nodded, understandingly.

"Thank you SO much," I managed, wiping away my tears.

I got into the car and closed the door, waving at them through the window as we drove off. Once they were out of sight, I let myself cry for a while.

"I'm sorry," I explained to Ben. "He's just such a decent man."

"He is," Ben agreed.

The plan had been to cross back into Turkey with the same smuggler who had brought us in. But that smuggler was apparently elsewhere in Syria, so we were now with a different man, who took us to a safe house near the border where we sat in silence and waited. The relentless rain of the past week had rendered large parts of the border impassable.

As night fell, the smuggler informed us that we would need to go to a different part of the border to cross. We got back in the car and drove for forty minutes to another house, where a couple lived. I sat with the wife and she made some dinner as we chatted. As the hours passed, I felt more and more nervous. The week had been full of risks and dangers; now there was just one left before we would be safe and free. But because it was the last one, it felt so daunting.

Eventually, the smuggler came into the room and said it was time to go. The woman ran to her room and came back with a small booklet. It was a *surah*, or chapter, from the Quran, *Surah* Ya Sin. It asks God for concealment from the enemy and is often recited to seek His protection.

"Please take this," she said. "May Allah protect you."

I thanked her warmly and kissed her goodbye, stuffing the *surah* into my backpack. I have carried it with me on my travels ever since.

The smuggler drove us about fifteen minutes to yet another safe house right on the border before handing us over to another man. "He will help you cross," he said gruffly, before driving off.

We sat on the floor in silence, waiting.

"When do you think we might be able to cross?" I asked the man, growing increasingly worried that the night was slipping by.

"Soon, *insha'allah*," he said. "Are you in a hurry?" he added, laughing.

Finally, the man said that it was time to cross. We were carrying all our equipment on our backs, with Ben shouldering the heaviest load. The earth was too muddy to drive through, which meant that we would have to walk quite a bit longer.

"Are you OK?" I whispered to Ben as we hid behind an olive tree in the dark.

"I'm fine," he replied.

The smuggler turned around. "Shhhh." He held up his hand to his lips.

In the darkness, I could make out the shadow of another man in a long dark coat, coming toward us. The smuggler motioned to us that we should follow him. We staggered behind him as he walked briskly through the no-man's-land. He seemed to be zigzagging all over the place.

"This guy has no fucking clue what he's doing," Ben hissed angrily under his breath.

Suddenly headlights lit up the ground beside us. We all threw ourselves onto the ground. We lay silently, waiting for the vehicle to pass.

A few minutes after the car had disappeared, we got up again and continued following the man in the coat. He was walking quickly now, obviously frightened that we'd so nearly been detected. Ben and I struggled to keep up. The ground was completely saturated with water and the mud sucked at our feet as we trudged through it.

"Fuck," Ben suddenly said. His foot was stuck in the mud. He pulled and pulled until it popped right out of his boot. He fished the boot out with his hands. The smuggler had continued walking and was almost out of sight.

"You go ahead," Ben said to me as he struggled to put it back on.

"Nonsense," I whispered. "Make sure to do the laces tightly so it doesn't come off again in the mud."

We pushed on, trying to run to catch up with the smuggler. At points the relentless rains had created impromptu rivulets that we had to jump across. We came upon one that was larger, almost like a stream, that required quite a leap to cross. Ben put down his backpack and said that I should cross first. He would then throw the pack over before crossing himself. I hiked up my *abaya* and took a running jump. But as I landed, my ankle slipped on the mud and I heard a sickening crunch as it twisted underneath me.

"Ouch, fuck, fuck, fuck," I whispered, writhing in pain in the mud, clutching my throbbing ankle.

Ben threw the pack over and jumped across to help me. Once on my side, he put the pack back on, took the bags that I was carrying, too, and then helped me up.

Together we hobbled across the remainder of the border. The smuggler was long gone but we could see a farmhouse in the distance near a village, and we walked and stumbled toward it. As we got closer, we called the number of the smuggler who had left us and told him what had happened.

"Wait where you are," he instructed us.

Twenty minutes later, a car came to pick us up and took us to an empty house. The smuggler in the coat was waiting inside.

"You're an asshole," Ben shouted at him. "You fucking left us."

The guy didn't understand English, though he realized that Ben was not pleased. He muttered something in Arabic about wanting to get paid.

"I'm not giving you a cent."

"Calm down," I told Ben. "It's not worth arguing with these guys. They're criminals. Let's just pay them and get out of here."

My clothes were wet and covered with mud and the throbbing in my ankle was getting more and more painful. Ben relented and organized for a car to pick us up before grudgingly handing over some money to the smugglers.

An hour later, we walked into the hotel lobby. It was three in the morning and we must have looked quite a sight—me limping in my bedraggled *abaya*, Ben carrying all our bags on his back, both of us completely covered in mud. The hotel receptionist's jaw dropped before he recovered and smiled politely.

"Welcome back, sir, madame."

Back in my room, I stripped off my dirty clothes and hopped gingerly into the shower. It was the first time I had been alone in a room for a week. I closed my eyes and drank up the solitude as the hot water pounded down on my skin.

Before going to sleep, Ben and I had a celebratory beer in his room. He looked at my foot, which was now purple and swollen.

"We're gonna have to get that looked at tomorrow before your live shot for *Face the Nation*."

I groaned, suddenly exhausted.

"Is the regime gonna go after Idlib next?" I asked, changing the subject.

"I think so." Ben nodded grimly, taking a sip of his beer.

We sat in silence for a bit before going to bed.

AFTER TURKEY, we went back to London for a break. But within two weeks, Ben and I were heading back to the region, first to Beirut to report on the ongoing crackdown on Homs, and then to see if there was a way to cross safely into Syria from Lebanon.

I met Ben in the departure lounge, where he was drinking a Bloody Mary.

"Did you listen to Marie on *Anderson Cooper* last night?" I asked him.

Marie Colvin had managed to make it into Baba Amr, the opposition enclave in Homs that was being pounded in a massive regime offensive, the bloodiest of the conflict to date. The operation appeared to be reaching some sort of crescendo with a deluge of shells raining down on the area. In addition to her powerful pieces for the Sunday *Times*, Marie had spent much of the night on the phone with various television outlets, describing the abject horror of what was happening. Her reports, which detailed watching a baby die from shrapnel wounds, were incredibly brave and hugely damaging to the regime.

"I was watching," he said. "I tried to get her on *Evening News* afterwards but it didn't work out, so we are going to try again tonight."

A voice came on over the loudspeaker announcing that our flight was boarding.

As we filed into the plane, I looked down at my phone. A series of urgent emails had just come in.

"Can I offer you some champagne?" the flight attendant said sweetly as she leaned over us.

"Ben, two journalists have been killed in Homs."

"Goddammit," he said, his jaw clenched.

He pulled his phone out and called the London desk to try to get some more information.

"Hey, what are you hearing about these two journalists?"

He nodded, then sighed.

"OK, thanks. I gotta go."

His face was ashen as he looked over at me.

"Marie's dead."

Nine

Austin first reached out to me on Twitter.

"@clarissaward Drop me a line?"

I looked at his profile. Austin Tice—freelance journalist currently inside Syria, former U.S. Marine Corps officer, studying at Georgetown Law. As I scrolled through his timeline, it was clear to me that he had been doing some interesting work in some seriously dangerous places in Syria. He had spent two months traveling through much of the country, from the Turkish border to the city of Rastan in the middle of Syria. Now he was in Yabroud, just an hour from the capital, Damascus, filing regularly for the McClatchy newspaper group and the *Washington Post*. He was handsome—tall and muscular with olive skin and dark eyes. I was sufficiently intrigued to follow him back.

I was also bored. It was July 2012 and Ben and I had spent the better part of a week sitting in a hotel in Antakya, Turkey, waiting for the go-ahead from the CBS management to travel into Syria.

The regime of Bashar al-Assad really appeared to be on the ropes.

A few days earlier, a huge bomb had exploded in a building in Damascus where Assad's national security staff was meeting. Among the dead were the Syrian defense minister and Assef Shawkat, Assad's brother-in-law and deputy defense minister. The word was that Bashar's brutal younger brother, Maher, had been seriously injured. There were feverish rumors about who had been responsible: the opposition or insiders convinced that Assad was leading the regime to its doom. The attack had sent shock waves through regime supporters.

And now everyone was talking about Aleppo, where the rebels were rumored to be planning a big offensive. Throughout the first year of the uprising, Aleppo, the economic engine of Syria and the country's most populous city, had been largely unaffected by the growing popular opposition to Assad. There were small pockets of protests here and there, but for the most part residents stood on the sidelines and waited to see what would happen. It was as if they knew how terrible the consequences would be if their city was to become the litmus test of the revolution. If Aleppo fell, the logic went, it would certainly spell the end for Assad, and therefore the regime would do anything to prevent that.

We had organized to spend a week inside rebel-held territory with a group of young volunteers who spent their days driving an ambulance to the front lines to treat the wounded. They called themselves the Medical Battalion, though they had little medical experience. One of them was a vet, another a nurse, just one was studying to be a doctor. Still, in rebel-held Syria, an "almost" doctor was better than no doctor at all.

While the rebels had taken a lot more territory since our previous visit in February, the land they controlled was still a scattered archipelago, and one frequently had to move through regime areas to get from one rebel stronghold to another.

As with all trips into Syria, organizing the logistics and security took longer than expected and required a deep well of patience. The bosses in

New York and London needed to be satisfied that all the details were in place. But communications in rebel-held areas were often spotty, and the Syrian opposition's approach to organizational detail was more fluid than that of CBS management.

"Where will we be staying?"

"At my brother's house, *insha'allah*."

"Where is your brother's house?"

"It's in a very safe area, you will be comfortable there."

"Sounds great but where exactly?"

"It's near the border, very easy to reach from Turkey."

"That's great but does the village have a name?"

Then the power would go and they would disappear offline before popping up on Skype a few days later. Of course, once you managed to get all the relevant information and do your due diligence and put together your security proposal and get the green light, you would cross into Syria and invariably find there had been a change of plan.

"We stay at my other cousin's house in different village. But very safe."

Antakya in Turkey is not an easy place to kill time. With the exception of a small, lovely pocket in the old town that hosts a great (but invariably empty) museum of beautiful old mosaics, it is a drab-looking place. There's one road to and from the airport, dotted with a few supermarkets and car dealerships and a handful of sad, gray hotels. We were staying in one such hotel—the Anemon—which was far enough from the center of town that there was nothing to do or see within walking distance. My room had two single beds, a small TV (with only Turkish channels), and a room-service menu that I knew by heart because I had eaten everything on it ten times. Of course, on the way out of Syria, the Anemon seemed like the height of luxury. There was a shower! There was beer! There were no bombs!

But for now I had nothing to do but kill time, and so Austin and I began shooting emails back and forth. It was immediately clear that he was not typical. How many guys decide to spend their summer break from law school traveling through a war zone alone as a journalist, with no previous journalism experience? And how many of those were successfully filing for the *Washington Post* within a few weeks? While he had served in Iraq and Afghanistan as a marine, Austin had never been to Syria before and he spoke no Arabic.

During the course of some light Facebook stalking, I came across an impassioned post of his, responding to his friends who voiced concern about his safety.

> I don't have a death wish—I have a life wish. So I'm living,
> in a place, at a time and with a people where life means more
> than anywhere I've ever been—because every single day
> people here lay down their own for the sake of others.
> Coming here to Syria is the greatest thing I've ever done,
> and it's the greatest feeling of my life.

The post was full of youthful zeal and more than a little hubris, but one phrase leaped out at me: the idea that in Syria "life means more than anywhere I've ever been." I related completely; things just seemed to matter more in Syria, there was a sense of purpose and meaning to existence that I hadn't seen elsewhere. Colors were more vivid, experiences more raw, life reverberated with a sense of profundity. Even the landscape, the olive groves in Idlib, shimmering green and silver, felt transcendently beautiful. It was a stark contrast from how I felt back home in London—gray and dull like the weather, uninspired and detached.

Austin was refreshingly candid. At one moment, he would talk about his journalistic pursuits in soaring terms: the aspiration to give a voice to the voiceless, the passion for the pursuit of truth. And the next, he would concede much more pragmatic motivations, such as his love of adventure, short attention span, and the fact that he would rather eat garbage than sit in an office all day.

In one of our exchanges, he asked me about our work. "What's the juice for you?"

"The juice for me," I replied, "is to truly experience the lives of all different kinds of people in an array of intense situations which can occasionally be quite profound."

We talked about my concern that the Syrian uprising was losing its original spirit, one I had seen so vividly in Damascus, because it had become so bloody.

"Nothing in the world is pure," he said. "If you yearn for that, you'll always be disappointed. I'm satisfied to catch glimpses of brilliance in the rubble."

"Rubble's not the only place to find those glimpses," I replied.

"Nah, you're right. But the contrast makes it brighter."

It was a relief to talk openly with someone about Syria. I didn't feel comfortable talking this way with my colleagues—it was raw, too personal. I was pretty sure that some of them could relate, but such things were usually buried beneath a layer of bravado and gallows humor, the vulnerability only occasionally rising to the surface during drinking sessions.

And as supportive as he was, Philipp and I couldn't really talk about Syria, either. It was too abstract for him, too removed from his frame of reference. My correspondence with Austin provided a much-needed emotional outlet.

At about two in the morning, I wrote that we should both get some sleep. I drifted off with a warm feeling, the excitement of having formed a connection, of having made a friend who understood and shared a love of Syria.

The next day, I was sitting with Ben eating French fries and mayonnaise while he smoked Camels and vented about CBS management, who were peppering him with questions about our trip and putting pressure on him to bring a security guard in with us.

"How do they not understand that bringing in some super-white SAS [British special forces] moron who wears Oakleys and is covered in fucking tattoos does not make us any safer?"

I laughed. Ben was always outraged with "management" and he was usually right. One of the legacies of the war in Iraq had been the integration of private security into our teams when we were covering conflicts. It allowed news organizations to reduce their insurance costs and perhaps a part of their accountability at the same time. To our bosses, these security guys were trained medics who knew how to navigate war zones and who were aware of tactics and munitions, which therefore allowed them to sleep at night. Often, they really were an invaluable extra pair of eyes and ears (not to mention an extra set of hands), but the reality was that in many places they were viewed as spies and mercenaries.

"I hear you," I said, swirling another fry in mayonnaise, "but you have to admit that having some military expertise must make war zones easier to navigate."

He arched an eyebrow and looked at me.

"Like, I have been chatting to this freelance journalist who is traveling in Syria right now. He's a former marine captain and I think that must give him a huge advantage. He's been to some of the most dangerous spots that no other journalists have reached."

Ben sighed and stubbed out his cigarette.

"Listen, Khaleesi," he said, "you're gonna come across a lot of kids in Syria who don't have much experience and take a lot of risks, and they're a liability."

I felt a prick of irritation. It was true that the Arab Spring had opened the floodgates to inexperienced freelance journalists. After all, anyone could go on Expedia and book a ticket to Cairo or Antakya. Often they didn't have conflict experience or body armor or even basic medical training, let alone proper insurance. But many news outlets were willing to turn a blind eye and buy their work without giving them real support, as long as they continued to get amazing material from the front lines. In Iraq, it had been much tougher. You needed an armored car and multiple permits to move around anywhere and you relied heavily on the US military for access. Still, Ben's words sounded harsh to me.

After a week, we finally had the go-ahead to travel into Syria. This time we crossed the border with the help of a smuggler known as Zaza, who had smuggled hashish and diesel before the uprising began and now made a tidy sum moving people, mostly journalists and jihadis. He was a slip of a man with a big bushy beard and the sleepy air of someone who was permanently stoned.

The crossing itself was smooth, and we arrived early in the morning at a safe house just across the border.

"Sleep for a few hours and then we will come and get you," Zaza told us. I scanned the room for a place to crash. It was filthy and completely empty except for a couple of foam mattresses on the floor that looked as though they had seen better days. The sun was already bearing down and the air inside was stuffy.

Two Spanish journalists, Javier and Ricardo, had joined us on the crossing. Javier spoke English, but Ricardo's wasn't great and my Spanish was rusty, so we began chatting in French. Javier, it turned out, lived in Beirut, where I had been based for years. Ricardo was from Barcelona and, in a strange coincidence, had become friendly with Austin during a trip he had taken to Homs. They were heading to Aleppo for the rumored rebel offensive. I briefly wondered if we should be heading there, too.

After a few hours of fitful dozing in the stifling heat of the safe house, Zaza came back with some water for us. It was Ramadan, and I always felt guilty when people who were fasting had to source food and drink for us and then watch us consume it. But our own water had run out so I guzzled it gratefully, making sure to hold the bottle away from my mouth as I poured it in—as many Syrians did when they shared a glass or bottle of water, following the example of the Prophet Mohammed.

At noon, Abdullah, the young media activist who was to be our guide, finally arrived. I had been introduced to him through another activist on Twitter and he had then provided contact with Zaza. He would give us a place to stay until we linked up with the Medical Battalion. Ricardo and Javier and I exchanged email addresses and said our goodbyes. At just twenty-three, Abdullah already had the eyes of someone who had seen too much war. One of his brothers, he told us, had already been killed fighting. A year later, another one of his brothers would be killed. As we drove along, I noticed how his fingers drummed nervously against the steering wheel. He never cracked a smile, which was unusual for Syrians I knew. Either he was just jonesing for coffee and a cigarette due to his Ramadan fast, or he was suffering from post-traumatic stress disorder. I recognized the flat voice, the distant gaze, the detached demeanor from my trips to Gaza and Iraq.

We spent the next week with a group of young volunteers who criss-crossed northern Syria offering emergency medical care on the front lines. The days were long and scorching, with hours spent in the car punctuated by short stops to drop off some first-aid equipment and pray. I would sit behind the men and watch as they stood in a line next to one another, hands folded across their chests, heads tilted down to the ground. A gentle, skinny young nurse with a wide smile always led the prayer. He was known for his beautiful voice, and listening to his *tajweed* (recitation of the Quran) gave me goose bumps. His name was Wasim Hussino but the guys had nicknamed him Bulbul, which is the name of a common songbird in the Middle East.

One night we were trying to get to a poor, mountainous area called Jabal al Zawiya, and we came to a stretch of road that was controlled by the regime. Two tanks were parked a couple hundred yards away from us. The men stopped the car to discuss options. The only choice was to try to drive past the tanks as quickly as possible before they had a chance to fire on us. I was in the middle in the back seat sandwiched between Bulbul and my cameraman. Hearing their plan, I began to panic.

"What's happening?" I asked Bulbul.

"Just pray," he replied. These were quite possibly the last two words I wanted to hear before doing something stupidly dangerous. I grabbed the hand of my cameraman, and Bulbul began praying loudly. The driver turned off the car's headlights, pressed down on the accelerator, and the car lurched forward, practically flying across the stretch of road, with Bulbul's voice getting stronger and stronger.

"And we have put before them a barrier and behind them a barrier and covered them, so they do not see," he recited a verse from the book of *Surah* Ya Sin in the Quran, the same chapter given to me by the woman in Idlib.

I closed my eyes tightly and tried to hold on to his words. The car finally slowed down and the guys whooped with relief. We had made it safely across. Perhaps the soldiers had been napping or eating. Bulbul smiled at me as if to say, see, I told you so, and we both laughed.

Once in Jabal al Zawiya, we followed the men as they distributed first-aid kits to fighters and families near the front lines. Bulbul would go through each kit and methodically explain what each item was for and how it should be used. As I watched him demonstrate how to dress a gushing wound for the tenth time that evening, I marveled at his gentle patience. Undoubtedly, most of what he said would be forgotten by the next morning, but he remained cheerful and resilient.

Whenever there was a wireless connection, I would jump onto my phone and message with Austin and swap stories about our day.

"There's a very specific smell that comes from too many dudes spending too much time in too small of a room," he wrote to me one evening.

I smiled. It was a relief to be able to let go of the intensity of the day and joke around with someone who was experiencing something similar.

Austin was staying with a Free Syrian Army unit in a town called al Tal, not far from Damascus, and was getting a little stir crazy with the slow pace of progress during Ramadan. He was increasingly desperate to get to the capital. After years of working in the Middle East, I was used to the pace. Ramadan meant no one woke before 11 a.m., and everyone was a little bleary-eyed until the sun dipped below the horizon and the fast could be broken.

"Please don't do anything stupidly brave," I warned him. "Cliché, barf, trite, boring, I know, but we lost Anthony Shadid and Marie Colvin within a week of me leaving Idlib in February and it made so many sick with sadness, so no shenanigans please." Shadid, one of the greatest Middle East correspondents ever, had died in Idlib at just forty-three after suffering a severe asthma attack.

After a week with the Medical Battalion, it was time to leave. I had requested time off and was headed to my parents' house in France to meet up with Philipp and some of my best friends whom we'd invited to stay. Philipp and I spoke every day when I was on assignment, even if it was just a few minutes on a satellite phone. The conversations were usually brief because our worlds were so far apart in those moments. I felt guilty about putting him through the anxiety of being in such a dangerous place and I knew that I needed to get back to him and bridge some of the distance that inevitably grew between us during these assignments.

I was conflicted about leaving. The rebel offensive in Aleppo was just kicking off. What if Aleppo fell? What if the regime falls? I often felt this way at the end of a trip to Syria. On the one hand, sweaty and exhausted and dirty and desperate for a mental break. On the other hand, consumed by separation anxiety.

"Take your vacation," Ben told me. "A good soldier sleeps when he can. We'll come back soon."

We said our goodbyes to Bulbul and the others, and I felt the familiar pang that came with wanting to be able to give them a big hug and tell them how remarkable I thought they were. But custom and my limited Arabic skills only permitted me to hold my hand to my heart and thank them effusively.

Six months later, one of the Medical Battalion would send me a message on Skype to tell me that Bulbul had been killed when a bomb hit the ambulance he was driving. He was twenty-eight years old.

ARRIVING IN FRANCE was like being transported to another universe. I sat in a daze watching my friends as they drank rosé and laughed together and caught up on one another's news. The great Christiane Amanpour once told me that the only way to survive covering conflict is to have a full life awaiting you at home, with great friends whom you can do "normal" things with, like go to the movies or see an exhibition or go dancing and have a giggle. It was excellent advice and I was blessed to have wonderful girlfriends.

In addition to Chiara, there was Victoria, one of that rare breed of woman who is seriously smart and beautiful, as well as being incredibly cool and a ton of fun. Victoria and I had grown up together since we were toddlers and she was the closest thing I could imagine to having a sister. We had overlapped at ABC for a couple of years and even managed to successfully pitch a trip to Sweden to do stories about H&M and Absolut vodka, arguing that we would save money by sharing a hotel room. And then there was Alanna, one of my best friends from boarding school. Oxford-educated, she worked in branding but constantly questioned if she was doing the right job. She is one of the wisest and most sensitive souls I know, outrageously funny and generous and, like so many of the best women I know, riddled with self-doubt and anxiety.

France was basically heaven—the rolling green valley, the vineyard, the cherry trees, the heady smell of lavender in the warm air, the goats' cheese and fresh baguettes, my loving friends and family and dogs. But my mind was elsewhere.

"How was Syria, Claz? It must have been bloody intense," Alanna asked.

"Yeah, tell us about it," Victoria added.

"Oh, it was fine," I answered vaguely.

"Why don't you talk about it? We haven't heard anything from you."

The last thing I wanted to do was talk about Syria. I wouldn't be able to explain it properly and maybe they wouldn't get it and then I would feel depressed. I batted at the air dismissively.

"It's a mess. All very depressing, really."

I picked up my phone to check if Austin had replied to my last message. I hadn't heard from him all day and it was making me nervous.

Philipp looked at me with concern.

"Darling, why don't you try putting your phone down for a bit?"

I knew he was right. I knew I was wired and jumpy and not taking advantage of the opportunity to really relax and unwind. And I knew that it was hurting him that I was shutting him out. But I couldn't let go, I couldn't detach. That phone was my only connection to Syria.

That evening, Austin finally emailed me. I jumped up from the table in the middle of dinner and disappeared to message with him. After more than a week in al Tal with no action, Austin told me he had decided to take matters into his own hands.

"I tried to walk to Damascus last night, made it about halfway before the FSA caught up with me / caught me / however you want to put it. They were not thrilled, I didn't really care . . . I'm kind of pissed at my weenie handlers who kept me drinking chai all day instead of going to the battle."

I was shocked by his recklessness.

"How the hell did you think you were going to walk to Damascus alone? The insanity of it is frightening."

For the month that we had been communicating, I had held Austin to a different standard. He was a former marine. He could do things ordinary journalists couldn't do, I told myself. He could get to places we couldn't reach. But I was no longer convinced. It was clear that he was becoming desensitized to the risks he was taking. Danger that would have been unfathomable a couple of months ago no longer raised an eyebrow.

A week later, Austin made it to the Damascus suburb of Daraya. By now, I was beside myself with worry. I told him it was time for him to get the hell out of there, that he needed a break.

Eventually, he agreed. Rather than traveling back north to Turkey, he said he would try to cross into Lebanon so he could meet a girl from Georgetown called Amy, whom he had started dating just before he left and whom he was crazy about. I was just relieved he was going to leave.

The rest of my vacation flew by. I spent most days on my phone, chatting with Austin and making plans with Ben. We had pitched a story about Aleppo to *60 Minutes* and they had given it the green light. It would be my first-ever piece for the venerable newsmagazine show and I was both excited and petrified. I had only spent a little time at the *60 Minutes* offices, which were on the other side of the street from the news division's offices, but it was a deeply intimidating atmosphere with everyone competing against each other. People didn't often smile at each other in the hallways. One younger producer joked to me that he once decided he was sick of the frostiness and so decided to greet Lesley Stahl with a big smile and a "good morning." She apparently had jumped before replying "thank you" and running off, as if the producer were a lunatic stalker off the street.

My *60 Minutes* shoot didn't start until September, so the news desk asked me to go to Lebanon for a week to cover any Syria news. I would likely overlap with Austin when he arrived to meet Amy.

On August 11th, I sent Austin an email wishing him a happy birthday. He replied with a short message. The regime was jamming the satellite connection so he barely had any internet access, but he said he was working on a killer story for the *Washington Post*.

The next day I sent him a message as I headed to the airport to catch my flight to Beirut.

"If I cross when I have plans to, we'll be throwing back cocktails pretty soon," he replied. "Of course, plans never really work out here. But in this case, I'm gonna wish extra special hard they do."

I never heard from Austin again.

For the first couple of days I tried not to worry. We had a story to shoot and I needed to keep it together. I told myself that he probably just didn't have internet access, that it could take a couple of days to cross that border anyway. But I couldn't eat. I checked my phone every two minutes, hoping for a message.

By day three I was panicking. I reached out to Nancy Youssef, the Middle East bureau chief for McClatchy whom I knew had been in touch regularly with Austin. I had never met her or spoken to her before, but she called me back immediately. She told me that McClatchy hadn't heard from him and that they were worried, too. She was getting on a plane to Beirut from Cairo. I reached out to Ricardo, the Spanish photographer whom I had met on the border who knew Austin, too—he hadn't heard anything. I sent messages to every activist I had met in Damascus. I also wrote to a Syrian called Mahmoud who had traveled with Austin in Idlib province and was a good friend of his. Mahmoud was something of a loose cannon—he liked to work with journalists but he had no idea what he was doing and he appeared to be an arms dealer on the side. Still, he had great contacts with all the rebel groups, including those around Damascus.

That afternoon, Mahmoud sent me a message on Skype.

"Austin has been captured by the regime."

I felt winded.

"That's impossible, Mahmoud. Are you sure? How do you know? Is it 100 percent confirmed?"

He went offline. I leaned over the nearby sink trying to keep my balance.

"Please God, let Mahmoud be wrong, please God, please let him be wrong, please God, please."

The next week passed in a blur. I didn't eat. I didn't sleep. I picked up Austin's friend, Amy, from the airport in Beirut. I told her the bad news and gave her a hug as she wept. She and Nancy checked into the hotel I was staying at and we stayed up all night talking to activists and rebel groups in Syria, trying to get more information about where Austin might be. During the day, we combed through photographs and videos of massacres and bombings, looking for Austin. Most of the corpses were mangled beyond recognition, but Austin had a tattoo on both his right and left arm and also one on his back that could be used to identify his body.

One evening, as I was preparing for a live shot, Nancy called me.

"A producer at Al Jazeera is saying that Austin is dead."

I slumped to the floor and sobbed. For a while I just lay there wailing. Usually, I found that crying calmed and comforted me, like I was dealing with something or processing it and that would help me find peace and let go of it. But this crying felt different. It felt like falling into a bottomless pit. There was no end to it, nothing safe to hold on to.

I had never met Austin in person, but I truly felt like I knew him. During the course of our intense correspondence, we had shared so much about our lives. I believed there was a real connection. Our friendship was somehow inextricably linked to this deep sense of attachment to Syria, to the pain and promise and the meaning that life had there. The idea that he was dead filled me with horror, not just because he was my friend, but because it felt like a grim marker of a shift in Syria. The war was entering a new chapter that was going to be even darker and bloodier than anything I had seen before.

Later that night, Al Jazeera told us that the producer had been wrong, that it was not Austin who had died. I cursed all those in the industry (and there are many of them) who pass on the latest speculation and rumor without thought for the hurt and anxiety they cause. My sense of relief was quickly overshadowed by the sickening uncertainty of having no idea where he was, who he was with, what they were doing to him. . . .

My colleagues and bosses in London largely left me alone, though I knew what they were saying behind my back. It was the same thing my mother said to me on the phone.

"Clarissa, you have to get a grip. You never even met this guy."

Her comment made me furious. My mother was my greatest supporter (and my most candid critic), and we were extremely close. But she struggled to be gentle, especially when I was in a bad way, because it upset her so much to see me like that. She was a complete control freak, and as such, she wanted to be able to make everything OK, and it frustrated her when she could not. Her default mode was invariably tough love, which was hard to take in my vulnerable state.

In addition to feeling sick with anxiety, I felt tremendous guilt. Partly,

I believed I had let Austin down. Why hadn't I been firmer with him? Had I assumed he was immune to risk just because he was a marine? And partly because I was now a burden on Philipp and my parents and friends and colleagues.

The guilt was combined with a bitter anger. How could Austin be so bloody stupid? How could he be so selfish? Nancy and Amy and I would joke that we were going to take turns shouting at him when he finally turned up in Beirut.

He never did turn up.

BEN HAD ALREADY BEEN IN ANTAKYA FOR WEEKS, working on setting up our *60 Minutes* story. The piece was to have two main elements.

One part would look at the destruction of Aleppo as the regime brutally pounded parts of the city controlled by the rebels. Government forces were now using their dominance of the skies to hit the rebels. They had started manufacturing crudely fashioned bombs out of barrels stuffed with explosives and nails and shrapnel, called barrel bombs. They dumped these crude but terrifying and very destructive weapons from the backs of helicopters over civilian neighborhoods. Some weeks earlier, there had been reports of fixed-wing aircraft being used for bombings, too. The regime was suddenly on the back foot as the rebels gained momentum and it could not afford to lose Aleppo. Its overarching military strategy appeared to be that if the Syrian armed forces killed enough people, the rebels would eventually crack or be deserted by the civilian population. It was cynical and cruel and effective.

The second part of the story would look at the proliferation of jihadi groups among the rebels. Just as I had expected after my trip to Idlib seven months earlier, well-organized and ruthless extremists had exploited the power vacuum and were gaining more and more power. Some vowed allegiance to al Qaeda; they dreamed of making Syria an Islamic state. And in the not-too-distant future another group would emerge to eclipse al Qaeda in its medieval cruelty.

The deployment of the regime's air power and the use of barrel bombs made traveling in rebel-held Syria exponentially more dangerous. We were staying at a safe house in the northwestern Aleppo suburb of Hraytan. As it got dark, the shelling would intensify, thudding away late into the night. It was impossible to sleep, at least for me, because of the noise, because of the fear, because of the sense of helplessness. There's a randomness to artillery fire that wreaks havoc with your brain. Usually, you have no way of guessing where exactly it's going to fall, no way of anticipating the best place to hide. And after all, it's artillery fire—shells big enough to destroy the house where you are sheltering. So you sit very still and try to calm your mind and just wait it out. Finally, at about 2 a.m., the shelling would subside and we would fall asleep for a few hours, exhausted. Then at dawn the fighter jets started. I could hear them wheeling overhead, screeching through the morning air. I knew that statistically we would be very unlucky to take a direct hit, but that logic provided limited comfort. That bomb was going to drop somewhere and sometime soon. The threat itself was a psychological weapon almost as potent as the bomb's destructive power.

I remember one Syrian woman telling me that if you can hear the jets, you're OK. If you're about to get killed you don't hear anything. I don't know if there's any truth to that, but in that moment it didn't provide much comfort, either. I just wanted the bomb to drop soon so that it would be over either way and I would either be dead or go back to sleep.

I looked around the room where our crew was all sleeping. Ayman Youssef al Haji, our new driver, met my eyes. It was my first time working with Ayman but I already liked him. He was tall, with kind eyes and a calming demeanor. His banged-up old Ford never got above 50 miles per hour, but he was attentive and observant and his presence put me at ease. Now, with the jets overhead, he smiled at me from across the room and sort of shrugged, as if to say, "*Allahu a'lam*"—God knows. Some of the group seemed to sleep through it. Others perhaps pretended to be asleep. After all, what was there to say? There was nothing really to discuss. I often sense that men prefer not to talk about fear because it makes it real. And to a certain extent I understand that—it doesn't seem to make a difference or help matters much.

The previous night, when the shelling had been heavy, the men all sat together. Between our crew and our hosts there were probably fifteen of us in the room. The atmosphere was tense and thick with cigarette smoke. Everyone was acutely aware of the shelling but no one talked about it. Instead, they bickered and made dark jokes about geopolitics. Only when we tried to set up the portable satellite, on the roof, did the fear reveal itself.

"Don't turn that on," our host said. "The regime can track the signal and target us."

Ben tried to explain patiently. "This is a BGAN and the signal cannot be triangulated. It would be impossible."

"No, no," the host insisted, "they have new Russian software and they can see satellite signals."

Ben rubbed his eyes and sucked deeply on his Camel cigarette, trying to summon whatever patience he had left.

"We have done a lot of research on this and I would explain the technology of it to you if we had more time, but trust me when I assure you that this signal cannot be seen by the regime."

Our host relented and Ben went up to the roof to turn the device on. When he came back down, the shelling intensified. It was closer to the house and our host turned on him in panic.

"Please, you have to turn it off, they are targeting us now."

Ben gritted his teeth.

"How many times do I have to explain to you that it is technologically impossible for them to see our signal? The fact that there's shelling has nothing to do with our BGAN."

Our host was unconvinced. Another shell landed nearby, causing the house to tremble. Finally, I piped up.

"Ben, maybe just turn it off just in case," I pleaded. I knew Ben was right, I knew it was irrational to link the BGAN to the shelling. I knew that fear was overpowering rationality. But in that moment, I had little use for rationality—and placating our host mattered.

He looked at me with irritation.

"Please," I said. "I'm sure you're right but it's freaking everyone out so just turn it off."

He stubbed out his cigarette and stomped out of the room back up to the roof, shaking his head and muttering all the way.

I decided to go into the other room and sit with the women for a while. It is one of the great privileges of being a Western woman working in conservative Muslim societies that I am allowed to pass freely between the two spaces, between the two genders. I remember someone joking in Afghanistan that female war correspondents were to be treated as honorary men. But we were also able to enter the intimate and private space forbidden to our male colleagues. Wherever I have gone, I have found women to be a fountain of information. They know what's going on in the village, what the power dynamic is. Broadly speaking, they are less likely to lie than men and much more likely to feed you.

The atmosphere in the women's room was completely different. Here the fear was palpable. No one attempted to repress or avoid it, so there was far less tension. One woman was rocking back and forth in the fetal position clutching a pillow.

Another woman called Nada looked at me with her tired, bloodshot eyes. "She does this when the shelling starts," she muttered.

"Do you ever get used to it?" I asked them.

"No, you can't get used to it. Some days, I can't leave the house. Even when you are no longer afraid of death, it just destroys your nerves."

Another shell landed nearby and we all jumped, as if to prove her point. A girl in her teens began reciting from the chapter of Ya Sin in the Quran.

"I know this *surah*," I told her. "You recite it for protection—right?"

She nodded. "Do you have something like this in your book?"

I thought of the Bible. I knew a lot of the stories but I didn't know them by heart in the way Muslims learn to recite the Quran.

"We sing hymns, which is kind of similar, I guess."

"Sing a hymn for us, please," she asked.

I laughed, suddenly feeling shy.

"Please," she pressed.

"Um, OK," I conceded. I began to sing "Jerusalem," a hymn that we sang regularly at my boarding school. It is full of grandeur, history, and soaring lines and is also the most patriotic song in any Church of England hymnbook.

"And did those feet, in ancient time, walk upon England's mountains green?" My voice was hesitant and a bit flat. I coughed and corrected the key and kept going.

"And was the holy Lamb of God on England's pleasant pastures seen?" As I sang on, it occurred to me how absurd William Blake's lyrics sounded in this context. I was sitting in Syria, with shells landing all around us, singing about building Jerusalem in Great Britain. But the women didn't understand the lyrics anyway and they appeared to be enjoying it.

I pushed on to the third verse:

Bring me my bow of burning gold
Bring me my arrows of desire

Bring me my spear! oh clouds unfold!
Bring me my chariot of fire

I was getting into it now, the defiant spirit of the hymn seemed to lift my anxiety and it really is such a great song. I belted out

I shall not cease from mental fight
Nor shall my sword sleep in my hand
Till we have built Jerusalem
In England's green and pleasant land.

As I finished, the women burst into applause. "It's beautiful," Nada said.

"Thank you," I said, feeling totally silly and elated at the same time. The shelling finally seemed to be quieting down and I went back next door to get ready for bed.

"What were you auditioning for *American Idol* over there?" Ben joked.

"I was singing 'Jerusalem' for them," I explained.

"Yeah, I heard," he said. "I think the regime heard, too."

We laughed and got into our sleeping bags. I fell asleep quickly.

But at dawn the jets came back and I lay awake in the soft gray light, waiting for the explosion. I wondered what Austin was doing, where he was right at that moment, whether he could hear the same fighter jets as they took off around Damascus.

Moments later, there was a loud explosion. The jets had targeted a hospital a few streets away. We rushed out to see the aftermath. The bomb had just missed the hospital, hitting a nearby house instead. The owner was killed. His wife and children, by some miracle, were injured but survived. I walked through the smoking wreckage and did a piece to camera. Hospitals, clinics, markets, courthouses, schools—these were the preferred targets of the Assad regime. These were the common spaces where civilians congregated. Attacking them delivered a stark warning to those living in rebel-controlled areas. There is no possibility of normal life for you. Nothing is sacred here. We will destroy your towns, we will eviscerate your homes, we will bury your children under mounds of rubble.

We were due to go to the front lines in the old city of Aleppo, a jagged sequence of warrens created by tunneling through the walls of one house to the next. By 9 a.m. we were ready to leave. Our escorts, however, were not. One hour passed, two hours, and still we waited. There's an old saying when you spend time with the US military that you are always being told to "hurry up and wait." In Syria, they don't tell you to hurry up so much, but there is an awful lot of waiting around. I have always found the waiting part excruciating—not because I am impatient (though I most certainly am) but because it's during those long stretches with nothing to do that your imagination plays havoc with you. It's too easy for your mind to create vivid scenarios of horror and death.

By the time our ride finally arrived in the early afternoon, I had worked myself into quite a state. The only time I had ventured out of the house all day, to stretch my legs in the garden, a shell had landed a few hundred yards away. The shock of the blast had made me jump in the air and I ran back inside. Ben was smoking a cigarette in the kitchen.

"Shit—you OK?" he asked.

"I don't know if I can do this," I confessed, tears welling up in my eyes. "It sounds pathetic but I'm just really scared."

"It's not pathetic at all, Khaleesi. Admitting you're scared is actually a very brave thing to do. And it is dangerous. Now, if you're uncomfortable we can call this whole thing off right now."

I thought of all the work that had gone into the story already. Frankly, the bombardment was relentless anyway. As far as safe houses went, this didn't feel very safe.

"Fuck it, let's go," I told Ben.

It took over an hour to reach the outskirts of the city because there was only one way to get into the rebel-held part of the city via a circuitous route. The streets were peppered with the skeletons of bombed-out buses and flattened cars. Building after building was pockmarked with shrapnel. The sound of artillery thudded in the distance, like some deathly accompaniment.

We met up with Colonel Abdul Jabbar al Oqaidi, who had defected from the Syrian army six months earlier and was now in charge of rebel forces in Aleppo. He wanted to show us that life was still continuing as normal in rebel-held areas, and so he took us to one of the few functioning markets.

"This is a liberated area," he told me confidently as we strode past a stall full of tomatoes.

A shell landed nearby as if to challenge his assertion. How could anyone live here? I tried to focus on the interview, but moments later another shell crashed into the neighborhood—this one closer. I looked around, feeling panic rising in my gut. Was no one else frightened? Colonel Oqaidi's men were talking furiously into their radios. The impact of another shell—*boom*. I could feel the vibrations in the ground.

"We need to move," one of our escorts said.

We bundled into our car and followed behind Colonel Oqaidi's convoy, racing deeper into the heart of the old city. The once-charming warren of ancient streets and alleys was deserted. Large parts had been reduced to rubble.

At one point the convoy stopped so that Oqaidi could get out and inspect his men on the front lines. But there were regime snipers in the area, and as soon as they spotted us they opened fire. I could hear the familiar ping and whiz of flying bullets but couldn't tell exactly where they were coming from.

"Get down, get down," Ben shouted. I tried to obey, straining to put my head down on my lap, but my bulky body armor inhibited my movement and I was only able to lean forward at a 45-degree angle.

"Fuck, fuck, fuck. When can we get out of here?" I asked as the car sped off for a more secure area.

"We need to get some B-roll of Oqaidi and his men," Ben said. "You don't need to get out of the car, though, just sit with Ayman and hang tight."

The car stopped at another guard post on the front line and Ben and the cameraman got out to go shoot. I moved to the front seat. Ayman smiled at me warmly.

"*Tamam?*" he asked. OK?

"*Ya'ani,*" I replied. Sort of. We laughed.

The sun was going down and the shelling was intensifying again. A drab ghostly light hung over the decrepit empty buildings. There was an eerie silence interrupted only by the periodic *thwump* of shells landing.

This is what hell looks like, I thought. The rebels' mantra was "death over humiliation." But at this cost? I remembered hearing a story about an old man who shouted to some rebels as they walked past his house in Aleppo: "What was so bad about humiliation?"

I hated waiting. I hated sitting still while my whole being was screaming to get out of there.

Ayman saw me nervously fidgeting with my pen.

"Why are you here, Clareesa?" he asked sympathetically.

"Ha," I replied, mirthlessly, "that's a good question, Ayman. I'm not sure I know the answer."

Another shell exploded. I flinched and looked for a cloud of smoke to see how far away it was.

"Don't be scared, Clareesa. It's still far from here."

I nodded weakly; distance was relative. I was scared out of my mind and Ayman could see it. It was the first time we had worked together, but Ayman noticed things and paid attention to the difference between what someone said and how they acted.

He reached into his pocket and pulled out a chocolate bar.

"Here," he said, "have some."

I smiled and thanked him, taking the chocolate. I was too nervous to eat anything, but his quiet kindness had a calming effect on me and I took a bite.

"*Ti govorish po russki?*" he asked me. Do you speak Russian?

"*Da, kanyeshna*, of course I do. How come you speak Russian?"

Ayman told me that he had lived in Russia and worked there in the garment industry for some years in the late '90s. Bashar al-Assad's father, Hafez, had had close ties with the Soviet Union during and after the Cold War, and many Syrians had gone to study and live in Russia. When the uprising began, Russia had thrown its support squarely behind the regime, and Ayman was now careful never to speak Russian in public.

We spent the next half hour chatting, mixing Russian and Arabic to express ourselves and understand each other. I learned that Ayman had eight children, four of them daughters. He lived in a town near Aleppo called Tal Rifa'at, and his biggest fear was that he would soon have to marry off his eldest daughter, just fifteen years old, because he could not afford to feed them all. In rebel-held areas, there was almost no work other than fighting, and most families were struggling to make ends meet. Working with Western journalists provided a rare and much-needed opportunity to make some cash.

By the time Ben and the cameraman got back to the car, it was dark. The shelling was still intense, but once we were on the road I felt more secure. We drove to a large villa on the outskirts of Aleppo where we interviewed Colonel Oqaidi. The shelling had finally died down. Afterwards, we sat outside in the balmy night air and drank fresh pomegranate juice. I felt suddenly calm and profoundly grateful. Grateful for the mild breeze, for the cool, tart juice, for Ayman's kindness—small mercies amid the intensity of the day. I closed my eyes for a moment and thought of Austin.

"Wherever you are, know that I am thinking of you. Don't lose hope. Things will be OK."

The second part of our piece posed risks of an altogether different nature: trying to discover how far extremist jihadi groups were penetrating the rebellion (much as Assad hoped they were) and how they were behaving. We had obtained video that showed men belonging to a jihadist group carrying out some kind of trial, convicting four Syrian soldiers of waging war "against the people" and then summarily executing them. We wanted to meet the rebel leader—Ahmed al Abaid—whose men were apparently the ones responsible. But how could we prove it? And what would his reaction be if we did?

Ben had spent days coaching me on the interview beforehand.

"*60 Minutes* is all about the interview," he explained. "Nothing else really matters."

The most important thing, he said, was to listen. And follow up. Don't just move on to the next question on your list. React. Respond. Engage. Challenge.

"Don't look down at your questions. That's my job and I will let you know what you still need to ask at the end. Be in the moment, listen to what he's saying. Draw him out and then challenge him."

I had spent days watching *60 Minutes* interviews. Morley Safer. Steve Kroft. Bob Simon. Ed Bradley. Mike Wallace. Lesley Stahl. Each of them had their own inimitable style. It was a joy to study them. Whether it was Wallace confronting Ayatollah Khomeini by telling him that the Egyptian president called him a lunatic, or Steve Kroft door-stepping Greg

Mortenson after exposing the *Three Cups of Tea* author for making false claims about his charity, the interview was a performance, a dance. Whether it was adversarial or not, there was chemistry, there was energy.

Ahmed al Abaid was not at all what I had expected from a jihadist emir. I had anticipated fiery diatribes about creating an Islamic state governed under Shari'a (Islamic law), whereby the hand of the thief would be cut off and the adulterer stoned to death. Instead, I encountered a very savvy and soft-spoken man who smiled and laughed eerily throughout the interview. He said that he was fighting for a free Syria, though he acknowledged that Islamic law should be implemented. I had the sense during the interview that he was only just tolerating my presence, but he never raised his voice and he never betrayed any obvious sign of irritation. He wasn't giving anything away and I could feel myself panicking at how flat his answers were.

I asked him about how his men treated their prisoners.

"We got a judicial system here and everybody is happy with it. Sometimes, when we release prisoners, they refuse to leave," he said, grinning.

"Yeah, right," I thought to myself. He denied that his men had executed anyone in their custody. I felt deflated. Not that I had expected him to admit to extrajudicial executions—it was too easy just to say that they weren't his men in the video—but I knew that the interview was lacking.

After we had finished, his aide gave us a thumb drive with some videos of the group fighting on the front lines and other material to use in our piece. Ben scrolled through it later that night.

"Khaleesi, get in here, you gotta take a look at this," he suddenly shouted.

I rushed in and stood over his computer. He began to play the video. Four government soldiers stood in a room while a voice off camera declared that they had been found guilty of "waging war against the people." It was exactly the same as the video we had obtained, only it stopped at the point of conviction and did not go on to show the executions of the soldiers. Al Abaid's aide had said all the material on the thumb drive was video of their group, so we could now prove that they were responsible for the executions.

"We have to go back and confront him with this," Ben said excitedly.

"OK," I agreed hesitantly. "But how are we going to do it without getting ourselves killed?"

"That's what we need to think about," Ben said.

We spent the next day working out a plan to take to the bosses at *60 Minutes*. We would tell Abaid that we had forgotten to ask a couple of important questions and that we needed to come back for just twenty minutes to finish up. Normally, a *60 Minutes* interview takes at least an hour and a half to set up and requires dozens of lights and reflectors. This time, we would set up quickly and use only natural light. We would have the video cued up on two phones—one with the short version given to us by his aide, one with the full version, including the executions. We would show him both, ask him to comment, and then we would pack up our gear, trying not to look as though we were leaving in a rush. Ayman would have the car engine running and we would book it out of there to the border. Abaid lived in a town called Azaz, right by the Turkish border, so it was only a fifteen-minute drive to get out to safety. But a fifteen-minute drive escaping angry jihadis would probably feel a good deal longer.

The bosses signed off, somewhat to our surprise, and Abaid agreed to let us come back, so the following day we returned to Azaz. As we set up for the interview, I went over the plan again and again in my head. We needed to get in and get out fast. Haithem, our Egyptian producer, would translate my questions but not Abaid's answers. The idea was to save time, and my Arabic was good enough to follow the gist of what he was saying anyway.

My hands trembled as I handed Abaid the first video.

"Can you tell me what that video is showing?"

"Well, those were government soldiers. In the fighting during the battle, we kind of arrested them."

"And what sentence were they given?" I asked.

Abaid began to look suspicious. "That's something that the judges know more about than I do."

"Because we have another version of the video," I went on. "It's a longer version and it ends quite differently."

He watched the video, his face darkening as the gunshots rang out. I could see how furious he was, yet he managed to restrain himself, handing the phone back to me.

"You know about these executions?" I asked hesitantly.

"No, I was not aware," he said grimly.

"But it is your men who are carrying out this execution?" I pressed.

His jaw clenched. He was in a corner and there was no good way out of it.

"I really don't know what can I say," he stammered. "I no speak," he added in English.

I looked up at Ben pleadingly as if to say, is that enough? Can we go now? He nodded at me. I thanked Abaid for his time. He stood up and walked toward the door, then paused and turned back to us, before thinking better of it and walking out.

"OK," Ben said, "we have five minutes to pack up and get everything in the car."

We practically ran out of Abaid's house. Driving toward the border, we kept looking behind us to see if we were being followed by his men. Once we had crossed, the car erupted into cheers. Ben called New York to let them know that we were safe.

"Well done, Khaleesi, that took real guts," he told me. "You looked that man in the eye and called him a liar. That's not an easy thing to do."

We flew back to New York to put the piece together—a process that at *60 Minutes* was as exciting as it was terrifying. I quickly became friendly with the late Bob Simon, who was as well known for his barbed one-liners as he was for his beautiful writing and incredible war reporting. We would sit in his office and he would playfully trash the other correspondents while peppering me with questions about Syria and offering advice on how to navigate the storied hallways of 60. Our chats made the whole experience feel less stressful and intimidating.

One year later, Bob would console me after I missed the Egyptian military's bloody dismantling of the Muslim Brotherhood protest site, Raba'a al Adawiya, in Cairo. I had spent most of the summer in the scorching city covering the army's crackdown on the movement, waking up at six in the morning to drive to the site of the latest bloodshed, walking through rooms packed with bloody bodies. After waiting more than a month for the anticipated crackdown, I flew back to the US to collect an honorary doctorate that I was being awarded by Middlebury College. The day I landed in New York, the attack on Raba'a began. Bob's response was priceless.

Clarissa:

I can offer no words of consolation. It happened to me several times and I still wake up in the middle of the night haunted by the memories.

To "share," as is said these days:

—I was pulled out of Beijing, kicking and screaming, three days before the massacre at Tiananmen square. The assholes in NY said something about "downsizing the bureau."

—I was taking a drive in the English countryside on Yom Kippur, 1973. I couldn't get to Israel for four days. Guess it serves me right. I shouldn't have been driving on Yom Kippur.

—I was doing a stupid story in Denmark when the Israelis pulled off Entebbe.

—Due to family matters, I left Beirut the day before Sabra and Shatila.

—And top this: I turned down an opportunity to interview the Archbishop of Krakow a few months before he was elected pope.

So I feel your pain. But I did get my share of stories—and I still haven't made it into *Vanity Fair*.

sympathetically,
Bob

The *60 Minutes* process had culminated in my first screening with Jeff Fager. These screenings were legendary. The pressure was intense. There were about ten people in the room watching, but only Jeff's opinion mattered. If he liked the piece, you were set. If he didn't, you were screwed. It was well known that Fager could be mercurial, but at the end of the day people accepted it because he had an extraordinary gift for making television.

"Really great stuff, guys," he said, as the lights came up. "This is going to be a fantastic piece."

My elation didn't last long. The next day I had a call from Amy, Austin's girlfriend. I was standing in a towel in my hotel room, about to shower.

"A video of Austin has appeared online," she said weakly. "It's awful. I just wanted to warn you."

I felt overwhelmed by nausea. Amy had given me no hint of what to expect before hanging up.

My laptop sat open on the desk. I stared at it for a while, trying to work up the courage to go and look at the video. How many YouTube videos had I watched before of hostages and executions in Syria and Iraq? How different it was when the hostage was your friend, the friend you'd never met.

I sat down at the computer, found the video, took a deep breath, and pressed play.

It showed a group of men who, at first glance, looked like jihadis leading Austin up a hill. He was blindfolded and still wearing his own clothes. I recognized the green shirt, now torn at the sleeve, that he had told me was a Christmas present from an old girlfriend of his. The relationship hadn't worked out, he said, but he loved that shirt.

He knelt on the ground and began clumsily reciting the prayer that Muslims say before death: *"La illahah illallah"*—There is no God but God. He stumbled over the Arabic words.

"Oh Jesus, oh Jesus," he whimpered breathlessly in English, and then, *"Ya Allah,"* almost collapsing onto one of his captors. Then the video cut out.

My whole body was convulsed with horror. I dug my nails into the palms of my hands and stifled the urge to scream at the top of my lungs until there was nothing left. Then I watched the video again. And again. I watched the 47-second clip four more times and then closed my laptop, vowing never to look at it again.

There were plenty of odd things about the video. The men wore sparkling-clean Afghan-style outfits that I had never seen in Syria. There was no flowery diatribe from a masked gunman about the evils of the Zionist entity or the perfidy of America. There were no demands to release prisoners or pay a ransom. This "jihadi" group didn't even appear to have a name. And why would they force Austin, a non-Muslim, to recite the prayer that Muslims say before death? Analysts would later agree that the video did not appear to be produced by a genuine jihadi group. More likely, it was the regime, or a group loyal to it, that had taken Austin, and the video was a crudely staged attempt to deflect blame elsewhere.

Over the coming years, I would become close to Austin's parents, Marc and Debra, and a team of his friends and colleagues who worked tirelessly to try to bring him home. More than seven years on, little is known about where Austin is and who exactly is holding him. The US government has said as late as November 2018 that it believes he is alive and continues to push for his release. On my stronger days, I believe that he will survive and eventually be freed, and that one day we will finally get to meet and throw back those cocktails together.

Ten

I f you keep on poking and cornering a wild dog that wants nothing but his freedom, *wallahi* [I swear to God] he will bite you and he will bite you hard."

It was September 2014. I was sitting on the floor of a small room behind a shop in northern Syria. Opposite me was Israfil, one of thousands of young men who had left the comfort of their homes in the West to come to Syria and fight jihad against the Assad regime. His passport was Dutch but nationality held no meaning for him any longer. He was defending the *ummah*, his fellow Muslims, and following in the footsteps of the *sahaba*, the companions of the Prophet. Everything he did he believed to be imbued with deep, religious significance.

He was dressed in military fatigues, his long dark hair pulled back with a bandana, an ammunition belt draped around his neck. He had brought a sword with him that he propped up proudly by his side.

"Make sure you can see it in the shot," he had instructed as I set up the interview.

I was nervous for plenty of reasons. Among some jihadi groups, Westerners were becoming an attractive target for abduction. I had only been allowed to bring my now-trusted driver, Ayman, on the short trip from the Turkish border. There was no producer, no cameraman—just me fiddling with two cameras and wireless microphones. My producer, Randall, was waiting for me on the Turkish side.

It had taken me months to organize this interview, including persuading my bosses that the plan for my security was watertight. I had just one hour to do it and get back to the border crossing with Turkey before it closed. I willed myself to stay calm as I tested the microphones for the tenth time.

As Israfil spoke, he became more animated and incensed. He loved being in front of the camera, enjoyed the effect that his chilling words would have on people watching.

"We don't want you, we want our own laws, we don't want your rules," he spat. "We want Islamic law, it's the only solution."

Israfil firmly believed that he and his "brothers" were working to create some kind of utopian society in Syria and that the West would strive to prevent that from happening because it feared the strength of the Muslims.

He talked without emotion about the country he had grown up in.

"The food, electricity, warm water," he said. "These are the things that I miss—but the West? Ah, hypocrisy. It's filled with hypocrisy."

By the end of the interview he could barely sit still.

"This fight never ends. Never ends. This is our religion. This is our faith. This is what we believe in."

Pressed for time, Ayman and I drove back to the border with him. As we bumped along the rutted, dusty roads, Israfil appeared to become even more agitated. His knee bounced nervously as he surveyed the scores of tents flanking the road that housed hundreds of thousands of displaced Syrians.

"I would fight anybody," he bellowed, gesturing grandly out the window. "Even if it was my own father that was bombing these people, I would fight him and kill him myself."

He turned from the front seat to look at me, his eyes flashing. My heart was pounding but I tried very hard to hold the camera still.

"Do you feel that this is your home?" I asked him.

"Yes, of course," he said. "We left everything behind when we migrated here. Everything. Everything—our families, our friends, basically our future."

He was invoking the Islamic concept of *hijra*—migrating as Prophet Mohammed and the first converts to Islam had done when they fled their Quraysh oppressors in Mecca to start a new community in Medina.

I looked down at my watch. The border was closing in ten minutes. As soon as we arrived, I jumped out of the car and Ayman and I ran to link up with a smuggler who would get us across. He shoved us into the back seat of a car waiting in a long line of vehicles. I was wearing a *niqab*, the full veil that covers the face. Ayman and I had agreed to pretend that we were husband and wife and I was to let Ayman do all the talking. It was stifling in the car and I was starting to sweat under the heavy, black fabric. I looked at my watch again, then looked at Ayman. We had been waiting nearly half an hour and the line of cars wasn't moving at all.

Finally, the smuggler came back.

"They've shut the border to vehicles," he told us.

"We have to cross," Ayman said firmly. "My wife is very sick."

The smuggler thought for a moment.

"You will have to walk."

We got out of the car and walked toward the first checkpoint manned by a rebel group. I kept my mouth shut and my eyes focused on the ground. Border crossings were notoriously dangerous because all the different groups had spies and lookouts there: the jihadis, the moderates, the criminals. All keeping an eye on who and what was coming in and out of the country.

Ayman showed his ID card to the rebel fighter standing at the checkpoint. The man looked at me briefly, then looked back at Ayman's ID before ushering us through. At the next checkpoint there was an X-ray machine that we had to put our bags through. I thought of the cameras and microphones. If they were discovered, it would be clear that I was a journalist. I watched as my bag went through and saw the young man looking at the imaging screen. He glanced up and motioned to us to come over.

"What's in here?" he asked Ayman.

"Please, take a look," Ayman replied casually.

He started to sift through the chocolates and cheap clothing that I had stuffed on top of the bag to make it look less suspicious. Quickly satisfied, he pushed the bag back over to us. I smiled under my *niqab*—we were nearly safe. We walked another few hundred yards, and then the smuggler managed to wedge us onto an overcrowded bus that ferried Syrian refugees back and forth across no-man's-land. There was absolutely no room on the bus and nothing to hold on to, and as it started moving I collapsed onto a family standing next to me. I apologized, but we were all so relieved to be out of Syria that we just looked at each other and laughed.

Once on the Turkish side we both relaxed; Ayman lit a cigarette.

He looked at me for a while before speaking.

"He scared me," he said, talking about Israfil. "You know, these guys ruined everything."

Like most Syrians, Ayman had been slow to realize that the uprising against Assad had been hijacked. He had turned a blind eye to the extremists. After all, they were fighting a common enemy and the jihadi groups had qualities the more moderate groups did not: discipline, a clear chain of command, and a steady stream of cash—mostly from private donors in the Gulf. Saudi Arabia and Qatar were both supporting the armed opposition but they had different political visions for the future of Syria, with the Qataris supporting the Muslim Brotherhood and the Saudis supporting a Salafist group, while declaring the Brotherhood and political Islam as anathema. As a result, they were working at cross purposes, creating a rift between the different rebel forces on the ground. Meanwhile, some of their citizens were taking matters into their own hands and privately funding jihadi groups. They would turn up in Antakya with plastic bags full of money to bestow upon the group with the coolest-looking YouTube videos.

Ayman wanted to believe that the Syrian opposition could use the jihadis to help them defeat Assad and then get rid of them.

I once asked a Syrian-American doctor how Assad's opponents could have been so naive in the face of the jihadist expansion.

"Imagine you're drowning, that you're about to die, and you're desperately looking for anyone to help you, but there's nobody there," he said. "But then you see someone holding out their hand. Maybe you don't like the look of that person, but it's your only chance to survive. So you take their hand."

An old man who was listening nodded as the doctor spoke.

"Yes, my son has a big beard now, too," he said. "But when he sees a pretty girl he still dances." He jumped up and struck a dancing pose and we all laughed. Like Ayman, he saw the influence of the jihadis as superficial, a passing foreign trend that wouldn't change the fundamental nature of the Syrian people. Syrians, after all, while conservative in many parts of the country, had never been extreme. For hundreds of years, the country had in fact been a cosmopolitan melting pot, a center for commerce and trade and literature and learning, where Sunnis and Shi'as and Christians and Alawites had lived—for the most part—in peaceful coexistence.

The old man did not know that hundreds of thousands more people would die in Syria's civil war, that they would be bombed and starved and gassed and tortured. He could not have foreseen the trauma and desperation induced by the brutality of the regime, which would remorselessly bring the nation to its knees, chipping away at the humanity of its people and forcing more than half of them from their homes. Those who had the means or education would try to restart their lives in new countries. Those who stayed behind had nothing left but God. Many ended up pushed into the arms of the extremists.

Israfil had provided my first real glimpse into the militant Islamist groups then flourishing in Syria, embracing al Qaeda's ideology. It was a world that had previously been inaccessible to me, shrouded in secrecy, a world where Arabic was the lingua franca and where talking to female, Western journalists was unthinkable. But with the war in Syria, there had been an explosion of Western jihadi activity on social media—young men who were excited to brag to their friends back home and to inspire new recruits.

I had first spotted Israfil on Twitter and sent him a message. He replied in perfect English, suggesting that we communicate on Kik, a messaging app primarily used by teenagers chatting about Justin Bieber. Kik was not encrypted, but it didn't require a phone number to sign up, so it was popular with Western jihadis. I also started chatting to fighters from the UK, Denmark, and Australia. Jihad was now virtual and accessible to all.

Israfil had chosen his name—after the angel whom Muslims believe will blow the trumpet to herald Judgment Day—when he arrived in Syria. Back in Holland, he was Salih Yilmaz. He'd been born in Brunei in 1987 to Turkish parents. His father had died when Yilmaz was twelve years old, and the family moved to Holland, where they had relatives. Holland was home to a substantial Turkish population, the result of mass immigration in the 1960s and 1970s when the country invited in Turkish guest workers.

When Yilmaz was a teenager, his first love abruptly ended their relationship, breaking his heart and sending him into a downward spiral of depression.

"I will never love a woman that way again," he texted me one night.

Smoking pot and partying had partially numbed the pain, but he needed a sense of purpose. He had dreamed of becoming a soldier ever since he was a little boy, excited by military hardware and instinctively drawn to the discipline and simplicity of the lifestyle. There were good guys and bad guys; he was with the good guys, and the rest was just doing what you were told.

And so he joined the Dutch army. He married a fellow soldier, a pretty Dutch girl who converted to Islam. It wasn't the same kind of dizzying passion he had felt for his first love, but it was comfortable and safe. He decided to try out for special forces but was rejected two years in a row.

"They told me I was too skinny," he said.

The rejection propelled Yilmaz into another depression. He dropped out of the military and began playing video games obsessively for hours on end. He rarely left the house, and his relationship with his wife began to suffer.

One day, as he was close to a new record on Call of Duty, his doorbell rang. A couple of Jehovah's Witnesses stood at the door, a copy of *The Watchtower* in their hands. He invited them in.

"I was so impressed that these people gave all their time to their religion, that their whole life revolved around it."

Yilmaz's family was devout but at the time he was barely practicing. Inspired by the devotion of the missionaries who had visited him, he began getting back into his faith. It offered a glimpse of purity and grace amid the depravity all around him in Holland—the sex, the drugs, the crime.

At the same time, the war in Syria was beginning. Yilmaz spent hours online watching YouTube videos of massacres, of women wailing over the bodies of their dead children. His fellow Muslims were being slaughtered by a godless regime, with the full backing of Iran and Russia, and the rest of the world was doing nothing about it.

For sure, Western governments were saying that "Assad must go," but the Obama administration was cautious, tentative, guided by the president's mantra: "Don't do stupid shit." The situation in Syria was too complex, the opposition too fractured, the lessons of nation-building in Iraq still too raw, they argued.

Like many Muslims across the world watching the carnage unfold, Yilmaz was consumed by a toxic mixture of despair and rage. The impotence of the international community confirmed his belief that no one cared about the blood of Muslims being spilled, that the rulers of the Muslim world were just corrupt lackeys of the West, and that the only people who could make a difference were devout young Muslims such as himself.

So, in October 2012, he decided to do something about it. He divorced his wife, left Holland without telling his family, and traveled to Syria, where he offered his services as a military trainer to different rebel groups.

Where most Western jihadis took steps to conceal their identity on social media, covering their faces and using noms de guerre, or *kunyas*, Israfil reveled in cultivating a public persona. He was online almost every day, posting videos of himself fighting on the front lines or playing with cats and answering questions from his followers. Tall and lithe with dark, almond eyes and straight white teeth, he became exceptionally popular with women as well as men.

Online, jihadi life in Syria looked almost glamorous—"five-star jihad," one British fighter famously called it. The days were spent fighting, defending the oppressed, and doing charity work in the service of God, all set to the soaring soundtrack of Islamic a cappella, known as *nasheed*. It was heady stuff.

Israfil frequently rhapsodized about the deep bonds of brotherhood among the fighters. He posted photographs of them standing together, their faces deliberately blurred (except for his own), pointing one index finger to the sky to symbolize the Muslim proclamation of faith—*la il-lahah illallah*, there is no god but God. It reminded me of street gangs in the US throwing up their gang signs. At home in the West you were a nobody, he seemed to say, but here you can be a hero.

Talking online to Israfil and other jihadis like him required learning a new vocabulary. They called themselves *muhajireen*, those who had migrated, and their Syrian hosts were the *ansar*, or supporters (after the Muslims of Medina who supported the Prophet and his Meccan followers when they came to Medina to set up the fledgling Muslim community). This world was *dunya*, vastly inferior to the *akhirah*, or hereafter. You referred to male Muslims as *akhi*, my brother, and females as *ukhti*, my sister.

"I can't wait to be in *Jannah* [paradise]," Israfil wrote to me one night. "Just walking around this beautiful garden and eating delicious fruit."

"Is that how you imagine Paradise?" I asked.

"It's described quite clearly in the Quran."

"Yes, but do you not think it's possible that sometimes words or images are used in the Quran to describe things that are indescribable? To make transcendent ideas and experiences more tangible to humans?"

He waited some time before replying.

"If the Quran says that Paradise is a beautiful garden with delicious fruit in it, then that's what Paradise is."

ISRAFIL WAS A "FREELANCE" JIHADI, moving between groups as they mutated, dissolved, and merged. But by the autumn of 2014, the landscape was changing. An Iraqi cleric—Abu Bakr al-Baghdadi—had climbed the pulpit in Mosul's eight-hundred-year-old Great Mosque a few months previously and declared himself caliph of an Islamic state that already covered large swaths of Syria and Iraq. His group had driven whole divisions of Iraqi troops out of Mosul, Tikrit, Fallujah, and much of the Sunni part of Iraq. It had been halted less than thirty miles from Baghdad. The group was called the Islamic State of Iraq and Syria, or ISIS, and its motto was *baqiya wa tatamaddad*—remaining and expanding.

The arrival of ISIS and the declaration of its grand ambition was a shock to Muslims and non-Muslims alike. Osama bin Laden had never dared call himself a caliph, and the whole idea of establishing a caliphate required many historical conditions that most Muslim scholars said had not been met by Baghdadi and his group.

But this moment had been long in the making. ISIS had sprung to life during the US occupation of Iraq, in a US military prison known as Camp Bucca. The Americans were rounding up former Ba'ath Party members, anyone associated with Saddam Hussein's regime, and random Iraqi men of military age, as well as fighters with the Sunni jihadist insurgency that was attacking American forces. And they were putting them together in Bucca; Baghdadi was detained there for ten months. On paper, Baathists and jihadists did not make for obvious bedfellows; the former were secular Arab nationalists, more well known for corruption and drinking whisky than for any zealotry for Islam. But imprisoned for weeks and months together, bonds were formed and networks established. They were Sunni Muslims and Arabs united by a common enemy, the Americans. The Baathists knew how to run a state and the jihadis knew how to fight—an unusual combination that would make them a formidable force. So they decided to join forces, forming al Qaeda in Iraq.

Al Qaeda in Iraq reached its zenith in 2006, before the US "surge" and concerted efforts to buy off Sunni tribes began to sap its strength. By 2010, with its main leaders killed or imprisoned, the group—by then known as the Islamic State in Iraq—had withered. That was when Baghdadi became its leader and began to plot the group's resurgence.

By the end of 2011, President Obama had fulfilled his electoral campaign promise to pull all US troops out of Iraq, and the Syrian uprising had taken a military and sectarian turn. It provided the perfect opportunity for the group to expand. Life in rebel-held areas of Syria had become increasingly chaotic, with different groups vying for power. There was no law and order, no security. By 2013, ISIS, as it now called itself, was seizing on the vacuum, imposing its radical interpretation of Islamic Shari'a law with unmitigated ferocity. Its brutality had a powerful effect: thousands of Syrians were frightened into submission and other rebel factions were outmaneuvered or simply eliminated.

There was no one to stop them. The rebels were focused on fighting the regime and could not afford to open a new front. The West—and especially the United States—had all but turned its back on Syria. After years of military misadventures in the Middle East, Americans had become allergic to intervention.

In August 2013, Assad's forces had used chemical weapons in the Damascus suburb of Ghouta, as the regime sought brutally to stomp out pockets of rebellion. The world witnessed images not seen in decades, as fourteen hundred people gasped for life, many of them children.

President Obama had declared that the use of chemical weapons would be a "red line" in Syria and trigger American intervention. But instead of retaliating, the Obama White House forged a deal with the Russians to dismantle Assad's chemical arsenal. The red line had been crossed, but there was no real price to pay. The message was clear—Syria was officially a war of no consequences. Whether you were a murderous regime or a brutal jihadi group, you could act with impunity. It was a low moment in US foreign policy, and the chemical attacks by the regime on a helpless population continued.

Ben Rhodes was one of President Obama's top foreign policy advisers, though he had come to the job with little foreign policy experience. He was also my boss David's brother, and I had met him socially on several occasions. At a party hosted by *The New Yorker* in 2012, we drank whisky together and talked about Syria. He wanted to do more, he said, but even then I had a sense that the White House viewed the conflict as an abstract intellectual exercise rather than an agonizing, humanitarian crisis of epic proportions.

My issue with Rhodes and his cohort was not that they were against intervention in Syria—there were plenty of smart reasons to oppose it— but that their Syria policy didn't come from a place of conviction or principle. It was something they had stumbled blindly into and then tried to make it look inspired, as opposed to improvised. It was the type of policy that a bunch of risk consultants would have come up with: muddled, incremental, unimaginative, risk-averse, and above all inhumane. To call it a policy at all seemed an overstatement.

While taxation and selling oil provided the lion's share of ISIS's revenue, the terrorist state was also developing a lucrative sideline in kidnapping. Western journalists and aid workers would become favorite targets as the group expanded its reach in Syria.

After Austin was captured, I worked with another intrepid freelancer, Jim Foley, to try to figure out who was holding Austin and to pressure various governments into lobbying for his release. I was impressed by Jim's tenacity and by his generosity of spirit and we became friends. It didn't matter if he was working on the front lines or if he was on a rare break at home with his family; he always took the time to make calls, to offer his insights on developments.

Jim and I exchanged emails up until he was abducted by ISIS on Thanksgiving Day, 2012. Ten months later, Ricardo and Javier, the Spanish journalists whom I had met in the safe house on the border, were also kidnapped by ISIS. The following month, an American friend of mine, Peter Kassig, was captured as he tried to deliver medical supplies to the city of Deir Ezzour in the eastern part of the country.

There would be others, too: Steve Sotloff and Kayla Mueller from the US; Daniel Rye from Denmark; Nicolas Henin from France; John Cantlie, Alan Henning, and David Haines from the UK; Haruna Yukawa and Kenji Goto from Japan. The continental Europeans were more fortunate. Their governments facilitated the paying of ransoms and most of them were eventually released. Javier and Ricardo returned to their families after six months in captivity. But the British and US governments had stringent policies against paying ransoms. Parents of at least two American hostages have said that they were threatened with prosecution if they caved in to ISIS demands. As a result, they paid the ultimate price.*

In August 2014, after nearly two years in captivity and no word on his fate, Jim was executed by a British fighter with ISIS in the most vile and horrifying manner. Video of it was shared across the world. In a deadly calm London accent, the masked executioner said it was a response to the US bombing campaign against ISIS in Iraq, which started after the group took control of Mosul, and the world woke up to the seriousness of the threat they presented.

I was lying in bed in a hotel room in South Africa on a *60 Minutes* shoot about a lion whisperer when I heard the news of Jim's execution. I only managed to watch the first few seconds of the video before throwing my phone to the floor. I buried my head in the pillow and screamed as hard as I could over and over again. I felt a strong urge to cut myself, not to hurt myself but as if somehow letting the blood out would release the poisonous rage that consumed my body.

---

* In February 2019, the British government stated that they believed John Cantlie to be alive ("John Cantlie, a British Journalist Held Hostage by ISIS, Is Believed to Be Still Alive," *New York Times*, Feb. 5, 2019).

The next day I messaged Israfil.

"How the fuck could anyone do anything so disgusting, so fucking evil?! What the fuck is wrong with you people?"

"I am not ISIS. I am not responsible for their actions."

"So, do you agree it was wrong to kill Jim?"

"I am not a judge, I can't say."

His ambivalence enraged me even more.

"Where's your humanity?" I spat.

I thought of a photograph he had shared with me of him as an eighteen-year-old, holding his baby niece and smiling at the camera. He was wearing a necklace and a T-shirt that said BROOKLYN on it. He looked handsome and friendly and normal. What happened to that guy—where did he go?

In that moment, I decided I had to meet him. He was not a member of ISIS, but he was certainly an extremist and could provide some insight into this cancerous evil that appeared to be spreading by the day. I had some sense of the varying reasons why so many young Western men were traveling to Syria to fight: adventure, camaraderie, the escape from dead-end lives in grimy corners of Europe, the chance to make a mark, the promise of redemption. But at what point did some of them become brutal murderers and psychopaths—and why? Had Israfil already crossed that line? What could his story teach people about the roots and process of radicalization?

For the most part, ISIS kept its distance from other jihadist groups. Its tactics were so brutal that even al Qaeda had denounced them. But in other parts of the country, the jihadis became so enmeshed in society that the lines became blurred. Ayman had a cousin who fought with Jabhat al Nusra, the prominent al Qaeda affiliate in northern Syria, and a brother who fought with the nominally secular FSA (at this stage more well known for corruption and ineffectiveness than as champions of democratic values).

Families like this were becoming more common in Syria. There were so many different groups with different backers. Some were violent jihadis, others were Islamists in the vein of the Egyptian Muslim Brotherhood. Still others were fighting with moderate groups. At the end of the day, many of them still prayed and drank tea together.

The Russians and the Syrian regime pointed to temporary alliances between jihadi and more moderate groups as evidence that all the opposition were terrorists. It was an excuse to bomb everyone and everywhere. I soon came to realize that words like terrorist didn't make much sense in Syria. After nearly a decade of reporting in the Middle East, I knew that Islamism was a pretty big tent and that Islamists came in many different varieties. To denounce all of them as terrorists may have been a convenient oversimplification but it was also a patent falsehood. Moreover, it ignored the reality on the ground, that the Assad regime, bombing hospitals and schools, was seen as the worst terrorist of all. But Assad's goal was to reduce a complex situation to black and white—a binary choice between the regime, the "legitimate" government of Syria, and the forces of Islamist terror.

IN THE SPRING OF 2013, I saw how the Syrian rebellion was mutating during a second trip to Jabal al Zawiya, the poor, mountainous area of Idlib province that I had visited previously with the Medical Battalion. It was the base of operations for the Syrian Martyrs' Brigade, one of the few so-called moderate rebel groups that was still around. The US had decided to support a handful of such groups because they were not Islamists and because it understood so little about the complexion of the civil war. In reality, many of these groups were corrupt opportunists, engaging in rampant criminal activity and often selling their US-donated equipment to other more militant groups.

We stayed in a small village called Freekah in the house of the group's "media liaison." Mohammed was twenty-three years old with dark hair, bright green eyes, and a constant smile on his boyish face. He had been studying English literature when the uprising began. In another life, he would have gone on to become an English teacher or work in the tourism industry. But now he wore camouflage and carried an AK-47 and hosted visiting journalists. He was delighted to discover that I had also studied literature in college, and in the evenings he would pull his English books down from the shelf: Johnson, Keats, Shelley. He would read out loud to me, periodically looking up excitedly to gauge my reaction.

"It's beautiful, no?"

Mohammed lived with his mother and uncle and two sisters in a very small and simple house. The family was very poor. At mealtimes, they would serve us bread, which they made in an oven in the garden, along with olives and canned luncheon meat, or occasionally an egg. We were a big crew of five people and so I would only eat a small amount before pretending to be full, anxious that we didn't take all their food.

One day, we drove to the town of Ma'arat al-Nu'man, which had been a frequent target of the regime, sitting on an important highway. One third of the town had been obliterated already. The fighter jets wheeled overhead, and I felt that familiar sickening pit in my stomach as I tried to focus on doing a piece to camera.

"Don't worry, don't worry," Mohammed told me, grinning.

I had never met someone so good-natured.

As the screeching of the jets continued, I grew increasingly anxious. The cameraman, a German perfectionist with a fantastic eye called Thorsten Hoefle, was laboring over a shot of an old man sitting on a plastic chair in the deserted street, surrounded by rubble. It was a beautiful shot—the old man looked somehow regal, sitting proudly amid the destruction, surveying what was left of his town. He appeared not to notice the jets anymore. So often in television, a single image can convey more about a story than words. This image spoke of dignity, of pride and strength, but it also showed the sense of loss, of emptiness and vulnerability.

Finally, Thorsten was satisfied and we packed up our gear and drove off. I could still hear the jets and I wondered where they were going to strike. Minutes later, there was a massive boom. Mohammed got on his radio and started speaking to some of the local rebels.

"They just bomb the street where we were filming," he said.

I thought immediately of the old man on his plastic chair. Was he dead? Had he perhaps gone inside to get a drink of water moments before-hand and miraculously survived? We would never know.

As we drove back into Freekah, we found a state of complete chaos. Six bombs had landed on the village. Two women and a little girl were dead. One of the bombs had hit the house next door to where we were staying, killing the woman who lived there. Her daughter stood outside what was left of her home, screaming and cursing Bashar al-Assad as neighbors tried frantically to dig her mother out.

Suddenly, jets could be heard overhead again, throwing everyone into a complete panic. People were running in different directions, shrieking. As I ran with the crew, I realized that there was no point in running. There was nowhere to run to. Nowhere was safe in Syria. At a certain point you just had to accept that you were powerless. I understood why so many Syrians felt they had nothing left but to fall to their knees and pray to God.

One man rushed over to our cameraman, holding up a parachute that he had fished from the rubble. The regime often attached mines to para-chutes to slow down their fall to the ground. These were crude, unguided ordnance, designed simply to terrify.

And they had the intended effect. That night Mohammed's sister was hysterical. She had been in the house when the bombs were dropped. The blast had blown out all the windows and sent furniture flying across the room. Now she lay on the ground rocking back and forth, wailing "*tayyara, tayyara*" (plane, plane) over and over again. I took out my emergency Valium from my bag and gave it to her, holding her head on my lap as she finally calmed down and fell asleep while Mohammed watched from the corner of the room.

After we left Freekah, Mohammed and I continued to stay in touch. We talked regularly on Skype. When he got married, he introduced me to his wife. She had a shy smile and giggled when I told her what a lucky woman she was. Nine months later, the couple had a beautiful little boy whom they showed off proudly through the grainy screen.

Privately, Mohammed confided to me that he was broke. The rebel group he had been with had stopped paying his wages months ago. He didn't have enough to feed his family even, let alone to repair the damage to the house. His mother had heart problems, but going to Turkey was not an option because it was too expensive. As we talked, I noticed a bitterness had crept into his voice. Why did America do nothing to save the Syrian people, he asked angrily, while the Russians and Iranians were helping the regime to kill them?

Soon after, Freekah was hit again. Mercifully, Mohammed's house was not hit, but several members of his extended family were killed, as well as friends and neighbors. When I called him on Skype the next day, his eyes were red and he barely spoke.

"I am sorry, Clareesa. I am so tired."

I told him not to worry, that we could chat another time. But we never did. I sent him a message on his birthday. Nothing. I asked for a photograph of his son. Nothing. I asked him to please write back to me so that I would know he was OK. Still no reply.

One day, months later, I finally heard back from Mohammed.

"I am OK," he wrote.

"*Alhamdulillah*," I replied. Praise God. "Where have you been?"

"I am in Raqqa," he wrote simply.

"What are you doing there?" I asked incredulously.

Raqqa was the headquarters of ISIS's self-proclaimed caliphate in Syria and a dangerous place to visit if you weren't one of them.

He didn't respond.

"You don't belong with those Da'esh guys," I went on, using the Arabic acronym for ISIS.

There was a long pause before he answered.

"You don't know Mohammed so good anymore."

A FEW MONTHS AFTER MY INTERVIEW WITH ISRAFIL, he suddenly went offline. When I finally heard from him, his tone was different—terse and bordering on rude.

I reached out to some contacts with jihadi groups in Syria who knew Israfil and discovered that he had left Idlib province to join ISIS. Once he arrived in Raqqa, ISIS sent him to a camp for new recruits to ensure that they were loyal. The days consisted of military training and hours of indoctrination. There were rumors of recruits being forced to carry out executions to prove that they were not covert members of Western security services.

I continued to talk to Israfil occasionally because it was important for my work to have a contact in ISIS, but it became increasingly difficult and distressing as his mind-set became more sinister. On one occasion, he sent me a photo of severed heads that the group had displayed on spikes in the center of town.

"Why the hell would you send me this?" I asked, traumatized by the image.

"It's just so crazy," he replied dreamily.

I once argued with him after a bombing in Kuwait that targeted a

Shi'a mosque, killing twenty-seven. He would not accept that there was anything wrong with killing these worshippers. They were not civilians, he argued, they were *rafida*, a derogatory term for Shi'as, meaning rejectors.

Shi'as could not be considered Muslims, he said, because they disparaged the Prophet's favorite wife, Aisha. (Shi'as generally have a negative view of Aisha for her role in the Battle of the Camel against the Prophet's son-in-law, Ali, whom they consider to be his rightful successor.)

"We can't allow these people to insult the mother of the believers," he said, using the honorific given to all of the Prophet's wives.

In December 2014, the plane of a Jordanian air force pilot had been shot out of the sky by ISIS as he conducted a bombing raid against the group. The pilot survived and was captured. It was clear that he would be executed, but ISIS still managed to shock the world by releasing the video of burning him alive inside a cage, a display of savagery in clear violation of the Islamic *hadith* that states: "Nobody punishes with fire except the Lord of the Fire [Allah]."

Israfil was not bothered by the barbarism of the execution, nor by its apparent contravention of Islamic principles regarding treatment of prisoners, saying that ISIS had found legal precedent for such a punishment. The group was extremely proficient at cherry-picking obscure references from the vast corpus of Islamic texts to justify the most grotesque acts. And there were plenty of young recruits with little education who were happy to take what they said at face value.

Never mind the fact that all but one of the Quran's 114 chapters begin with, *"Bismillah ar-rahman ar-raheem"* (In the name of God, the most merciful, the most compassionate). ISIS had taken this merciful and compassionate God and turned him into a bloodthirsty and oppressive monster.

I soon realized that there was no real point in having these discussions with Israfil. Any person with ideas that did not perfectly co-incide with his was a *kafir*, or infidel. Any Muslim who didn't agree with ISIS's conduct and goals was no longer a Muslim. And any non-Muslim should repent and be converted or be wiped off the face of the earth. He had managed to reduce the richness and depth and tolerance of Islam to a Manichean ideology. Everything was black or white, good or evil, you're either with us or against us. They were the perfect enemy for Assad.

One day, I asked Israfil if he had ever executed anyone.

"I am not going to answer that," he replied, "but let's just say that if a man was found guilty of *riddah* [apostasy] I would not hesitate to take his head off his shoulders."

He said it matter-of-factly, as if the taking of a human life was no big deal. I felt dizzy. Israfil had always been a fundamentalist but now he was a bona fide psychopath.

Moments later, he was bragging to me that he managed to get sushi in Raqqa. I interrupted him.

"Wait, sorry—how can you say you would cut someone's head off like it's not a big deal?"

"Clarissa, this is Allah's law. There is only one true Shari'a—do you not understand that?"

By then, I had read a lot about Islam. I started out by reading various *seerah*, biographies of the Prophet. I bought volumes of *hadith*—compilations of sayings and deeds attributed to the Prophet—and multiple translations of the Quran. I struggled with the Quran. It was dense and mysterious and repetitive and opaque and so alien to anything I had read before. But reading Quranic exegesis by contemporary scholars made it much more accessible. From there, I delved into the writings of some of the prominent classical Islamic jurists—from Ibn Taymiyyah (a favorite of the jihadi groups) to Al Ghazali and Ibn Arabi.

The more I read, the more I realized how vast and multivalent Islamic theology was. There was not just "one true Shari'a" at all. The main four *madhabs,* schools of Islamic jurisprudence, for Sunnis, often had different rulings regarding the same issue on whether and how any punishment should be implemented.

"Islam is not a monolith, Israfil. Read a few *tafsir* [exegesis] of any *surah* in the Quran and you will find multiple interpretations of the same verses. That's why there are multiple *madhabs.*"

"There is only one Shari'a," he repeated.

I felt exasperated by his ignorance and thought of frustration shared by the millions of Muslims who had been screaming at groups like ISIS for decades. Their attempts at reasoning hadn't made any difference and neither would mine.

In *Eichmann in Jerusalem,* Hannah Arendt wrote about the postwar trial of Adolf Eichmann, one of the most notorious war criminals in Nazi Germany.

"What he said was always the same, expressed in the same words. The longer one listened to him, the more obvious it became that his inability to speak was closely connected with an inability to think, namely, to think from the standpoint of somebody else. No communication was possible with him, not because he lied but because he was surrounded by the most reliable of all safeguards against the words and the presence of others, and hence against reality as such."

ISIS had created a language and a way of thinking based on circular logic that blocked off the need for reason, for empathy, for self-doubt. In this way, even bland bureaucrats were capable of perpetuating grotesque horrors.

After the conversation about executions, my communications with Israfil petered out. Occasionally, his wife, Zahra, would message me. She was a nineteen-year-old girl from Azerbaijan who had fallen in love with him online and traveled to Syria to marry him, leaving her heartbroken family behind. Several months after the couple moved to ISIS territory, their baby, Jibrail, was born. Soon after, she sent me a message. Israfil was away fighting, as he often was these days, leaving her alone with the baby and scared out of her mind. By now the US was leading a massive bombing campaign against ISIS that was hammering Raqqa day and night. She admitted to me that Israfil had become physically abusive toward her, then begged me not to say a word to anyone.

"It's so bad here," she told me.

One day, I heard from a source that Israfil had been killed. I sent a message to Zahra. She wouldn't confirm but she seemed hysterical.

"I want to get out of here," she told me. "How can I?"

I felt a twinge of sympathy for her. In our conversations, she had always struck me as naive but sweet.

"I can't help you, Zahra," I replied.

Eleven

For the longest time, I didn't want to talk to anyone about Syria. My experiences there were something sacred to me. Words didn't do justice to them. There were so many small acts of kindness by sincere people that would never make it onto the evening news. These were the things that moved me to the core, that compelled me to keep coming back even as I was sinking deeper into a depression.

At first, I didn't realize that's what it was. In the movies, people go to war and see horrible things and then they come home and have nightmares about it and cry a lot and the narrative makes sense. In real life, it's not like that. Or at least it wasn't for me. I would come home, nerves jangling, revved up and high on a mixture of exhaustion and euphoria after a successful trip.

Philipp would come to hug me and my whole body would stiffen.

"You're being weird again," he would say.

"I know, just give me some time."

At home, I felt like a caged animal, unsure of what to do with myself and unable to relate to those around me. The quiet and the calm only amplified the dull emptiness and the niggling rage. As the poet Dorothy Parker wrote:

> I have a need of wilder, crueler waves;
> They sicken of the calm, who knew the storm.

Sadness would have been a blessing in a sense, a sign that I was sane, that I was processing things in a healthy and normal way. Numbness was harder to contend with. I knew that if I stopped moving, I would never be able to get up again. So I just kept moving, kept working, kept pretending.

In the supercharged atmosphere of 2014, with the rise of ISIS, the war in Ukraine, and the ever-worsening situation in Syria, there was no danger of being marooned in the bureau. But there was every risk of burning out amid one high-pressure trip after another.

Covering Ukraine was arduous and exhausting, but it was Syria that continued to take the emotional toll on me. I grew thinner and thinner, though I continued to eat normally.

One day, I was in New York working on a *60 Minutes* piece when the CBS medical correspondent, Dr. Jonathan LaPook, pulled me aside as I walked down the hallway.

"Clarissa," he said gently, "I'm a little worried by how thin you are. Is everything OK?"

He put his hand on my shoulder, and the kindness of his touch shifted something inside me. Tears started streaming down my face.

"I'm so sorry," I said with embarrassment, swallowing to stifle a sob. "I don't know why I am crying. I guess I've just been under a lot of stress."

He pulled me in for a long hug and I wept gratefully into his chest. What was happening to me? Why was I even crying?

"Are you eating?" he asked as I pulled away to wipe my nose.

"I am, I really am," I answered truthfully, "but I can't seem to put on any weight."

He nodded thoughtfully.

"Have you talked to anyone?"

I laughed. After Austin had disappeared, I had taken CBS up on the offer of going to talk to someone. I had never been to see a therapist before, and I was almost excited by the prospect of trying to come to grips with what I was going through. I arrived at the therapist's office and sat down. He began going through a list of questions.

"How much do you sleep a night?"

"It depends if I am on a breaking news story or not."

"Are you often tired?"

"Sure, sometimes," I said.

"Do you have suicidal thoughts?"

"What? No, of course not. Wait, what is this?"

"Just let me get through the questions, please."

At the end of the list, he seemed pleased, scribbling something down on his pad.

"So, in my opinion, you are absolutely well enough to continue working," he said.

"Of course I am," I replied. "But aren't I supposed to be talking about my feelings and stuff?"

He explained that he was an occupational therapist and that his job was to assess for CBS whether or not I was OK. I felt angry and embarrassed. Later on, I told Ben Plesser about it.

"They're assholes, Khaleesi. And they don't care about you, they care about whether you're a liability."

I promised him that if I ever went to see a therapist again, I would do it privately.

Of course, the irony was that I had never been more successful. After my first solo trip to Damascus, I had been awarded a Peabody, the most prestigious award in television news. Next came the duPont-Columbia University award. The following year, Ben and I won two Emmys for our Syria coverage (I spent the night sobbing because I had forgotten to thank the editor in my acceptance speech). I was asked to contribute four *60 Minutes* pieces a season. *Vanity Fair* had done a spread on me. I should have been on top of the world.

But at home I was a mess. I was depressed and full of anxiety. It felt like being immersed in a deep fog that wouldn't clear. I was barely managing to go through the motions and even that was a Herculean effort. I didn't want to be me anymore. During an argument with my mother one day, I flew down the stairs toward her in a violent rage. I stumbled before reaching the bottom and fell down the stairs, landing in a heap and twisting my ankle painfully. I lay there on the ground sobbing and howling like an animal—how cathartic it felt just to wail. My mother stood looking down at me, hands on her hips.

"I don't think this is about your ankle," she said glibly.

Philipp bore the brunt of it. He would come home to find me crying in bed.

"I'm worried about you, darling," he said once, reaching over to rub my arm. I could see in his eyes that my behavior was hurting him, that it was scaring him even. But I wasn't strong enough to pretend anymore.

"Just leave me alone," I said, turning away.

He walked toward the door, stopping before he left.

"I love you very much," he said.

I deliberately didn't reply. Not because I didn't love him, nothing could be further from the truth, but because that love was buried under layers of calcified shit that I wasn't ready to deal with.

Syria was the first conflict where I had really given of myself in ways that were unsustainable. I was too attached to the story and yet I knew that the quality of my work depended on that intimacy. The more I gave and the closer I got, the better my work was. And the better my work was, the more I felt a weight of responsibility to really do something "for" Syria.

Intellectually, I knew that I couldn't do a damn thing to change the situation in Syria anyway, no matter how many risks I was willing to take. And yet I could not shake this oppressive feeling that I was failing, that I wasn't doing enough, that I was letting people down. It sat like a dumbbell on my chest all the time. I knew I desperately needed some distance from the story, but I was racked with guilt about walking away.

ON DECEMBER 28, 2015, I was in Palm Beach, Florida, at my parents' house, where I was staying for the holidays. We were drinking kir royales in the sitting room when I looked down at my phone to see a message from a colleague that our beloved friend and driver, Ayman, was dead.

"I am so sorry to have to tell you this sad news."

I felt as though the air had been kicked out of me. I stood up and wordlessly walked into my bedroom, closing the door behind me. I read the message another three times, blinking stupidly at the screen of my phone, before asking for more information.

Ayman had been killed three days earlier, while visiting an injured friend in a hospital in Azaz, near the Turkish border. An air strike had hit the hospital. By then, hospitals were being targeted on a regular basis. The Russians had started flying sorties in support of the regime a few months earlier and the strikes were a lot more accurate and a lot more devastating.

I imagined him sitting by the hospital bed of his friend, his warm, deep-set brown eyes smiling. I pictured his hands gesturing as he talked.

They were lovely hands, smooth and strong and brown with long, lean fingers and clean, pink nails. I remembered watching them as he sewed a hidden-camera button onto a shirt for me. We were in Turkey working on a *60 Minutes* piece about the crush of Syrians braving a treacherous sea to reach Europe. I had been trying unsuccessfully to sew the button for ten minutes before he got impatient watching me and took the shirt and began quickly and easily sewing it on.

"*Mashallah* [wow], Ayman, who knew you were such a good seamstress," I joked.

"I wasn't kidding when I told you I worked in the garment industry," he replied.

We had both laughed.

I remembered him bringing all of us ice cream during a particularly stressful shoot on our trip to Aleppo, his tall frame bounding toward us, three crispy cones balanced in each hand, red-and-white sugary ice cream melting all over him, grinning as he handed them out. I remembered him breaking off that piece of chocolate for me in the car when I was scared on the front line. Small acts of kindness. I thought of all our chats. Ayman smoking a cigarette, nodding thoughtfully as he listened. Ayman talking about his daughters. Ayman reminiscing about his time in Russia as he drove his painfully slow old car.

I sat on my bed and tried to imagine what Ayman looked like now, another body dug out of the rubble—bones broken, face a dull blue-gray, swollen and contorted, frozen, brittle, eyes open and lifeless, hair white with dust.

His family told me that it was a Russian air strike that had killed him.

I felt a surge of rage. I had interviewed the Russian foreign minister, Sergei Lavrov, a couple of years earlier to confront him about Russia's support of the regime. At the time Russia was not yet using its own aircraft in Syria, but it was stepping up its supplies of weapons and ammunition to

Assad. I spent a lot of time preparing for the interview and had documents listing the weapons that the Russians were providing to the Syrian army.

Lavrov could be a pugnacious and intimidating interviewee, but I was completely thrown when he refused to look at me. Lavrov seemed to have found a spot on my right knee that he focused on with laser-like precision.

Not only that, he didn't stop for breath. I began to panic. If I didn't interrupt him, I would not get to ask another question, I wouldn't get to hammer him with the evidence I held of Russian complicity in the war.

I took a breath, looked directly at Lavrov, and interrupted. And I did it again and again for the remainder of the interview. He never appeared rattled, and by the end of our fifteen minutes I felt exhausted but satisfied that I had at least put up a fight.

"*Bolshoi vam spasibo, gospodin Ministr Sergei Viktorovich*," I said, thanking him formally in Russian, though the interview had been in English.

He took off his microphone, smiling, and replied to me in English.

"You know, you sounded quite pathetic." It was the first time he looked me in the eye.

Did the foreign minister of Russia seriously just call me pathetic? I asked myself.

"Oh, no, I hope not," I said lamely as I shook his hand.

After he left, my Russian producer, Sveta, looked mortified.

"In Russian, *patetichni* has different meaning than in English. It means more like emotional," she said, almost in apology.

I arched an eyebrow. "Sveta, I know what *patetichni* means, and you and I both know that Lavrov speaks perfect English. He said it to fuck with me."

If I couldn't get accountability from the men in power, I would try to get it by showing the truth of what was happening on the ground. Two months after Ayman's death, I went back to Syria to do a story on Russia's aerial bombardment and particularly on its targeting of hospitals. It was extremely dangerous; few Western journalists had gone into rebel-held parts of Syria in over a year. But it was the only way I knew to respond to Ayman's death. It was the only means I had of exerting any control over my life.

It was an exhausting and intense but successful trip. At the end of it, a Syrian man who had been looking after us shoved a bag into my hands. It was filled with chocolates and a letter. Once we were safely back in London, I opened up the letter.

"Please tell the world the truth about Syria," it read.

I burst into tears. It was such a simple and sincere request. The world had failed Syria so egregiously, so callously, and yet these pockets of hope—that good would somehow win out—persisted.

Near the end of 2016, as Russian bombs were raining down on Aleppo and the eastern part of the city was about to fall to the regime, I felt a familiar flash of rage and despair. I wrote an email to Ben Rhodes, now Obama's point man on the Syrian conflict.

I read it over before hitting Send.

Dear Ben,

Hope you are sleeping well as Aleppo burns. Thank goodness we have the Russians to sort it all out!

Best,
Clarissa

He never replied.

Twelve

I n September 2015, my contract with CBS was up, and I had a decision to make.

As wonderful as my time at CBS had been, it was becoming trickier to balance covering the news and working for *60 Minutes*, navigating between the competing demands of Jeff Fager and David Rhodes. News had a habit of breaking just as I was shooting a piece for *60 Minutes* or buried in an edit that would often take weeks rather than days. I would then be faced with an uncomfortable choice—leave the *60 Minutes* piece, with the cost and disruption that entailed, or miss out on a big story.

Jeff Zucker came calling. JZ, as he was known, was a man of extraordinary energy and editorial insight who had taken the helm at CNN in 2013. He had given the place a new purpose; Ted Turner's creation was on the march again, making money, investing in programs and correspondents, breaking news. It had reach and access. TV screens and laptops in government offices around the world were tuned to CNN; it was part of the conversation, the famous red logo omnipresent in hotels, airports, gyms, and bars.

JZ had a straightforward manner; there was no bullshit. He also had a plan and went through what he envisioned me doing at the network. I would have the opportunity to make hour-long documentaries, as well as reporting and anchoring. I was flattered but I was also genuinely excited, not least because CNN had the space and the desire to tell the stories that had taken up so much of my professional life.

When I had first dreamed of becoming a correspondent, in those months after 9/11, I had always imagined reporting for CNN. My first internship in Moscow had been with the network. CNN had the advantage of having two networks, one seen in the US and one seen around the world, in more than 200 countries and territories. So much of my life had been spent living overseas, covering international stories; it had become frustrating not to have any global exposure. How many times had I sat in a bureaucrat's office in the Arab world explaining what CBS was?

Eventually I called David Rhodes to break the news. I was leaving.

"Which offer are you taking?" he asked. His voice sounded pinched.

"I'm going to CNN," I told him.

"Thank God," he said, relieved that I hadn't gone to CBS's great rival, NBC. His two words assured me I was making the right decision.

Three years later, CBS network head Les Moonves, Jeff Fager, and Charlie Rose would all be out at CBS, amid allegations of sexual misconduct, leaving the network floundering.

My first big story for CNN was the Paris attacks of November 2015. The pace of the network was unlike anything I had experienced. At one point we had seventy staff in Paris; almost every show was being anchored from the Place de la République rather than a New York studio. The demand was insatiable—for profiles of victims, interviews with survivors, the response of hospitals, lines on the investigation and the backgrounds of the perpetrators. At CBS, we had relied heavily on the Associated Press or Reuters for news lines. At CNN, we did our own research, developed sources, and bugged French officials for lines at almost every hour of the day.

It was a baptism by fire, an introduction to the network that never sleeps. And the pressure was all the greater because I'd been told: "JZ wants you front and center on this."

It was also a tremendously exciting opportunity. While I'd become immersed in trying to understand the world of Salafi jihadism—what made young men become Islamist terrorists—there hadn't been space to share that at CBS. At CNN, there was time to explore these issues in depth, to refresh continually your firsthand knowledge of the big stories.

As one of the last international journalists to get into rebel-held Aleppo, I found myself the object of attention from an unlikely quarter: the United Nations Security Council. The US ambassador to the UN, Samantha Power, invited me and two Syrian-American doctors, as knowledgeable observers of the situation, to speak at an informal session about the siege of Aleppo.

Former secretary of state Madeleine Albright often said that CNN was the sixteenth member of the Security Council. But, in reality, it was an entirely different platform on which to speak, and an entirely different audience to address. Still, on this day in August 2016, it was true for at least 12 minutes as I spoke behind a nameplate that simply read: CNN.

I had made a few notes that morning, and literally walked over to the UN from my hotel with a couple of sheets of paper. In retrospect, I think my preparation was a bit casual, but at least it allowed me to speak with spontaneous passion.

I told the assembled dignitaries about my first visit to Aleppo in 2012, how I had sat in a room listening to the jets soaring overhead and looked across at Ayman, who would tragically become one of the conflict's countless victims, who had simply shrugged and said: "Only God knows."

I recalled my emotions at that time, four years previously. "This is what hell feels like," I said, "and there's no way it can get any worse than this. But it did."

Again I imagined Ayman, lying lifeless in the smoking rubble of what used to be a hospital. I looked over at the Russian delegate. He was staring at me murderously. I spoke of the regime's calculus: "Bomb them, starve them out, until they finally leave."

And I spoke of the destruction of trust that would long outlast the physical damage inflicted on Syria.

I had been in war zones for more than ten years, I told the council, but "I have never seen anything on the scale of Aleppo."

I'd been surprised by how emotional I had felt in front of this collection of diplomats more used to wrangling about dry resolutions than listening to what it's really like out there. It was somewhat cathartic. But my words, like the tens of thousands spoken and written in outrage or indignation over the course of the Syrian conflict, would change nothing. In the end—four months after I spoke—it was brute force that won the day in Aleppo.

THE MOVE TO CNN was not the only significant change in my life. For over a year, I had been seeing a wonderful therapist. Mark Brayne had been a journalist with the BBC before becoming a therapist, and he understood the ways in which covering conflict could sink deep into your bones and grind you down. He also understood that war reporting attracts certain types of people, that we are often incredibly hard on ourselves and that much of that behavior is learned in childhood.

He used a technique called EMDR (eye movement desensitization and reprocessing). Essentially, he would ask me to revisit a traumatic memory and then tap my knees softly (left right, left right) as I talked about it and why it upset me so much. The next step was to provide comfort to the version of myself in that memory, to make peace with it, to forgive, to the point where it no longer caused anguish. I sobbed through most of the first few sessions.

Over time, I learned how to be gentle with myself. Mark explained that while it's hard for us to change our patterns, we can get better at recognizing what triggers them and prepare accordingly. I slowly felt the grip of anxiety loosen.

I had also started to pray. It kept me sane and humble. It helped me understand that I couldn't control everything in my life. It enabled me to be mindful and thankful, to accept the darkness and embrace the light, to try to be kind and make good decisions. I marveled that I had survived in this job so many years without a spiritual anchor.

Throughout all of it, Philipp had stood by me, loyal and loving. One day, after eight years together, he decided that he wanted to get married and really settle down in one place. I didn't need to be asked twice. Much of our relationship had been long distance. After I moved to Beijing, he had moved to Geneva, then when I had come to London, he had gone to Singapore. The fact that we continued to love each other and make it work, after so many years so far apart, left no doubt in my mind that we were meant to be together.

It was a beautiful but unfussy wedding. My mother naturally organized the entire thing (though I was allowed to choose which flowers I wanted in my bouquet). I found my dress less than a week before the event, and we booked an appointment with the registrar at Chelsea Old Town Hall before doing a big lunch for about forty guests at our Notting Hill home. I found the whole thing incredibly moving and cried joyfully throughout much of the day.

Seven months later, I was expecting our baby. Philipp and I were over the moon.

I didn't want to tempt fate by broadcasting news of my pregnancy to everyone in CNN's London bureau. It was too early to be confident that the pregnancy would advance, and I was just a little apprehensive about how it might change their perceptions of me. But it did make an assignment to travel to Greenland for a documentary on climate change just a little tricky.

Our CNN quartet traveled to the very apex of the Greenland ice sheet—a research center called Summit Station. A balmy summer night might mean minus 10 degrees centigrade if you were lucky, not exactly s'mores weather.

When the guide told us we would be sleeping in tents, I laughed out loud. But he was serious, and the next thing I knew I was cradling a special Arctic sleeping bag and getting ready for a night under canvas on top of the world, literally if not metaphorically.

Besides the poleaxing cold and the altitude, I had to cope with a common side effect of pregnancy: the frequent and urgent need to urinate. Our Arctic survival kit included two bottles. One was marked water; the other was for peeing. While hardly appealing, it beat the thought of leaving the warmth of a sleeping bag and trudging to an outhouse across the snow.

On my first night there, I realized at about 2 a.m. that I had to go. After a few minutes of mentally preparing myself for how cold it was going to be, I unzipped my sleeping bag and got up. The air was like freezing needles against my body. I hastily took the bottle to the corner of the tent, pulled down my pajama bottoms and began peeing. Without going into too much detail, let me tell you that peeing into a bottle in the dark as a woman is an art form, one I didn't master immediately. One of my socks was soaked by the end and I had to peel it off before closing the bottle and zipping myself into the sleeping bag as quickly as possible, rubbing my hands feverishly against my arms and legs to try to warm them up.

I managed to nod off for a couple of hours or so before I woke up needing to pee again. I had been rationing my water intake to avoid this scenario but to no avail.

I opened the sleeping bag, swearing at the cold as I went to empty the bottle. Unfortunately, the contents of the bottle had frozen solid. I tried warming it up under my armpit to melt it. By now, I was shivering uncontrollably. I unzipped the tent to peek out and see how far away the outhouse was. A gust of freezing air hit me; no way was I stepping into that. I zipped the tent back up and hastily looked around for another receptacle before grabbing the bottle with WATER written on it. Let's just hope I don't get thirsty, I thought.

The condensation from my breath was freezing on the scarf I had wrapped around my head and I could feel the icy crystals pricking into my skin. I flopped back into my sleeping bag and began trying to warm myself up. I was exhausted (a common side effect of pregnancy, especially in your first trimester) but couldn't sleep (a common side effect of being at a high altitude). My mind was racing. I didn't want pregnancy to change the way I worked or lived and yet it was already clear that there were big changes happening in my body.

"Dear God, please let my baby be OK," I whispered into the frigid air. "Please don't let the cold or the altitude hurt him—or her."

I felt a flutter of panic in my chest thinking about how my colleagues would react when they eventually found out I was pregnant. I remembered all too well how cavalier I had been when discovering that other women working in combat zones were expecting. "I guess I won't be seeing her around anymore," I'd say.

I had always viewed becoming a mother as perhaps the least extraordinary thing a woman can do. Which is not to say that I didn't want to have children, because I knew that I did. But I was wary of the consequences, of becoming obsessive about diet and back problems, and then endless conversations about strollers, teething, and the right kindergarten. It just seemed so dull. I was determined to be different, to take pregnancy and childbirth in my stride.

I was fortunate not to be plagued by terrible morning sickness. There were waves of nausea, but those were quickly dealt with by consuming one of the enormous cheese sandwiches I carried in my pockets. The other crew members put it down to my extraordinary appetite, which had already become the subject of some mirth at CNN.

As if to punish myself, and for reasons I don't quite understand to this day, I went directly from the ice sheet to St. Martin in the Caribbean to cover the aftermath of Hurricane Irma. I was determined not to slow down. We ate canned food and washed in bottles of seawater. After I had been there three days, Philipp sent me an article saying that St. Martin had mosquitoes with Zika virus, which can be very dangerous for pregnant women.

"It's a bit late now," I replied.

From the Caribbean, I lobbied the bosses at CNN to travel to the border between Bangladesh and Myanmar. More than half a million Rohingya Muslims had fled Myanmar after a brutal crackdown in which the Burmese military and paramilitary forces set their villages alight and raped and murdered countless Rohingya. Yet it wasn't getting as much media attention as I felt it deserved. It was perhaps too remote, too difficult to explain.

My bosses were a little surprised that at five months pregnant I wanted to undertake such a taxing assignment. But they didn't object—so long as I had all the proper vaccines and was comfortable that the trip could be done sensibly.

It was as if I were trying to cram in as much reporting as possible before the final trimester of my pregnancy literally took me *hors de combat*. There was a constant niggling fear in the back of my mind that if I slowed down, I would become irrelevant, that I would miss out on big stories, that people would forget about me. It's an affliction common with television correspondents who often joke that "you're only as good as your last live shot."

I walked into a London travel clinic.

"Hi, I'm traveling to the border between Bangladesh and Myanmar," I explained. "I'm not sure what shots I need, but I'm pregnant."

The nurse looked at me blankly. "You're going where?"

I explained that I was a journalist going to cover the Rohingya crisis. She nodded before telling me that she didn't have the expertise to help me. I would need to see a specialist. I felt there was a touch of judgment in her eyes and tone.

Two days later, I was sitting in the Hospital for Tropical Diseases talking to a consultant about my travel plans.

"I realize I probably sound like a lunatic," I apologized. "What sane pregnant woman pushes to go to the middle of nowhere in Bangladesh?"

"It's all right," he assured me. "I've had lots of aid workers and journalists like you in here."

He explained that malaria was the only thing I really needed to worry about. It could easily kill a pregnant woman and her unborn baby. And there was only one anti-malarial prescription that was safe for pregnant women. It was called Lariam and had the unfortunate side effects—for some people—of inducing hallucinations, depression, and vivid nightmares. I was fortunate that these never visited me.

The first thing that struck me about Bangladesh was its untouched beauty. We were staying in Cox's Bazar, a coastal city, its name a legacy of its colonial past. There were vast, empty beaches fringed by palm trees and bright emerald-green rice paddies that looked as if they hadn't changed in hundreds of years. The air was warm and humid and smelled of the sea.

We began in the sprawling, squalid camp that had sprung up along the border to house the hundreds of thousands of refugees. You could walk for two hours and still not reach the middle of it. A handful of clinics and schools run by aid workers did not even begin to meet the scale of the need.

Talking to the women in the camp was horrific. Every tent, it seemed, held stories of agony, shame, and death. One mother described the moment that her two-year-old son was ripped from her arms by soldiers and thrown into a fire as she lay on the floor, semiconscious. Another young woman, Rashida, told us that she and four other Rohingya women were dragged into a hut and raped by soldiers who then stabbed them. She survived by pretending to be dead.

"It would be good if I had died," she whispered to the translator, "because if I died then I wouldn't have to remember all these things."

Her hands picked frantically at a thread on the edge of her yellow scarf. She spoke in a monotone, eyes glazed, describing every detail mechanically as if trying to recount what had happened without reliving the moment. The heat and humidity in the tent were stifling.

After the interview, we gave some money to our fixer and asked him to buy the woman a sewing machine. Strictly speaking, you're not supposed to give money or charity to interview subjects because it can look as though you're paying someone to tell their story and that can potentially affect what they tell you. In this case, I didn't care. She had already given the interview with no incentive other than getting her story out in the world, and I couldn't now walk away from that tent without doing something to help in a tangible way.

The United Nations had described the eviction of the Rohingya as a "textbook example of ethnic cleansing." Others spoke of genocide. What made it more shocking was that it had been carried out under the watch of a Nobel Peace Prize laureate, Myanmar's civilian leader, Aung San Suu

Kyi. For years, Suu Kyi had been the darling of the West, lauded as a brave freedom fighter whose incredible personal sacrifices eventually brought democracy to her country. And yet now she remained impassive, refusing to condemn the barbaric massacres, the burning of villages, the rapes. She refused even to call the Rohingya by their name, opting instead for "Bengali," the epithet favored by the Burmese because it enforced the idea that the Rohingya were foreign.

There were plenty of bold words from world leaders. But there was no accountability, nor any "safe and voluntary return." There was a great deal of standing idly by, amid well-rehearsed but ultimately hollow condemnation. It felt so much like Syria. The ideals that liberal democracies liked to parrot were honored in the breach.

After two days in the camp, collecting stories about cruelty almost impossible to comprehend, we began to look for new arrivals. We would wake up at the time of *fajr*, the dawn prayer, and begin driving up and down the coast, looking for Rohingya, many of whom were arriving on boats at night. It was monotonous, staring at the coastline, bleary-eyed, scouring the beaches for groups of figures. The van lurched and bumped over the rutted roads, sending my lower back into spasms as I held my growing belly.

And then, seemingly out of nowhere, they appeared. They stood on the side of the road, a group of about fifteen men, women, and children, huddled in the cool morning air. As we stopped the car and began walking toward them, they watched us with unblinking eyes. The quiet beauty of the image was arresting, painterly. The women's pink and yellow headscarves fluttered in the breeze, their features softened by the pink light of the rising sun.

They told us that they had been traveling for two days. They had no food, no money, nothing but the clothing on their backs. Their village had been torched by Burmese paramilitaries and so they had decided to follow the hundreds of thousands of Rohingya who had already fled to Bangladesh.

One of the women was heavily pregnant, though she still looked emaciated. I walked up to her and involuntarily touched her bump.

"I am pregnant, too," I said.

She nodded without smiling. She was seven months pregnant, she told me. I thought briefly of my carefully choreographed birth plan and maternity leave. Where would this woman give birth? I wondered. Who would look after her? It never got any easier to understand or accept the randomness of privilege in this world.

To complete our story, we needed footage of Rohingya actually arriving in Bangladesh. Our fixer, Emrul, suggested we traveled to the mouth of the Naf River, which separates Myanmar from Bangladesh. We had heard that the majority of new arrivals were now coming this way, floating across on hastily improvised rafts.

We stood on the beach, where a group of Bangladeshi border guards had assembled. A few Rohingya families who had arrived earlier sat on the sand resting and drinking water given to them by the locals after their exhausting journey. Some photographers hovered.

I walked toward the water and looked out. At first, they looked like specks in the distance, blobs of color bobbing on the water. But as they got closer, you could see a tangle of human forms huddled on rafts, paddling furiously to cross the water.

The rafts were crudely made from jerry cans and plastic bottles, held together with bamboo. Squinting into the hot noon sun, I saw that one man had improvised an oar, using a stick with a pan tied to the end.

Our cameraman, Scottie, was preparing his shot for when they washed up on the shore. But as they got closer, the border guards began furiously blowing their whistles and waving the rafts down the shore.

"What are they doing?" I asked Emrul.

"They don't want them to land here, they want to send them farther down the river toward an official camp."

I looked in panic at Scottie. If we didn't manage to talk to these people who were risking their lives to make this crossing, then we would be missing the most important element of the story. A few of the photographers were now wading into the water to get a better shot.

"Give me the fluffy," I said (referring to the handheld microphone that looks like a large fluffy stick). "We have to go in."

"Are you sure?" he said, motioning toward my bump.

"Yes, let's go."

We started to wade out into the river. The water was cold and the sand was soft, causing my shoes to sink. Scottie was having trouble trying to balance the camera while navigating the suction of the sand.

"Just keep moving your feet," I said.

I looked down at the water, which was up to midthigh by now. It looked reasonably clear. Hopefully, there were no larvae or leeches in it. I was pretty sure that wading in river water in Bangladesh was not recommended for heavily pregnant women. But I pushed on toward the raft.

"*Assalamu 'alaikum*," I called out to them (the traditional Muslim greeting, literally meaning peace be upon you).

"*Wa 'alaikum assalam*," a few on the raft replied.

Standing next to them, I was now shocked to see that at least half the passengers were small children and even babies.

"Do you know how to swim?" I asked. Blank, unflinching eyes stared back. Emrul translated for them. A collective shake of the head. "No one does," a woman said.

They told me that they had been on the water since dawn, a good six hours. The distance wasn't far, but their flimsy raft and improvised paddles had made progress slow. They had no food with them, just some drinking water that they shared, along with whatever household goods could be salvaged from their homes.

"Aren't you worried for your children?" I asked, at a loss for anything more intelligent to ask.

"Of course, we are worried," the woman said. "Look at her, she's got two babies on her lap and they keep slipping off the raft."

She told me her name was Zohra Begum. She said that she had fled after her village was burned down by Myanmar's military. She had no idea if her husband was alive.

The raft was moving more quickly now, and Scottie and I could no longer keep up. I watched as Zohra and the others glided past us.

As we waded back toward the shore, I felt suddenly exhausted and cold. My soaked clothes clung to my body, causing me to shiver. Was anyone going to care about this story, I wondered. Did people have any empathy left? Yet another corner of the world was witnessing unspeakable cruelty.

As we walked down the beach to our van, we happened upon a group of Rohingya who had managed to evade the Bangladeshi coast guard and make it to the shore. They sat in a circle on the sand, resting. Some local Rohingya had brought them food.

I asked the group if they had a message for America, and immediately regretted the trite nature of the question. They looked at me with empty, exhausted eyes that seemed to say this isn't about geopolitics, this is about survival.

One woman wearily attempted an answer.

"There is no peace in Myanmar, and so we left to save our lives and our children's lives," she said. "We came here, and we are at your mercy."

Mercy, it seemed, was in short supply. It made one wonder why anyone chose to have a child at all, to bring a baby into a world where ugliness persisted even once people knew about it.

BY THE TIME I GOT BACK TO LONDON, my neat round bump was not so little anymore. I was six months gone, and according to the scans, the baby was healthy and normal. I was bursting with love and excitement and yet full of trepidation about how my life was about to change. I had recurring dreams that I had the baby and then left him in a taxi.

I still couldn't deal with all the "self-help" books brought by well-intentioned friends. They had twee titles like *Belly Laughs* and *Three in a Bed*. I did try to read some of them, but after a few pages my eyes would glaze over and I would return to whatever novel I was reading.

One day, Philipp and I decided to bite the bullet and go buy some stuff for the nursery. Neither of us were good "baby" shoppers, partly because we felt so inept in the presence of so many couples who had studied assiduously. As they moved with assurance among cribs and strollers, we felt hopelessly inadequate, almost embarrassed.

We headed hesitantly toward the strollers.

"What brand did your friends recommend?" he grunted, his head already aching at the dizzying amount of merchandise on display.

"The Bugaboo," I said, looking down at the price tag of one. Eight hundred pounds. I nearly jumped. At college, my friends had bought cars for less.

"But what's the difference between them?" he asked. "There's like a dozen of them."

"How the hell should I know?" I hissed.

The store was stifling hot. My scarf was practically strangling me.

What if I was becoming boring and bourgeois? What if, after twelve years jumping out of helicopters in war zones across the world and witnessing history and learning languages and meeting people from all different walks of life, I was now just another privileged, pregnant white lady with a big ass looking at overpriced strollers in a generic department store, wearing an ugly brown coat because it's the only thing that would zip up?

I closed my eyes and willed the voice in my head to stop. I didn't want to hear any more. I knew it was about to tell me that I'd never shift that last ten pounds of "baby fat" and that my breasts would shrivel into raisins after breastfeeding. It would say that my brain would turn to mush, that I would become one of those people who babbles endlessly about how wonderful, intelligent, and healthy their baby is.

I thought about a blog post a friend had sent me: *The Birth of a Baby Is Also the Birth of You*. What did that even mean? What about the old me? What happens to her? Does she die?

"Let's just get this one," I said, pointing to a navy blue Cameleon Classic.

"Fine," Philipp said.

After leaving the store, we went to a nice restaurant for lunch and I felt shabby in my ugly coat. I was clearly being difficult, and Philipp called me out on it. I burst into floods of unexpected tears. He looked shocked and uncomprehending and also deeply mortified by my emotional outburst in a public place.

"You have no idea what I'm going through," I sobbed, pretending to look down at the menu. He didn't argue with me.

It was probably my fear of the mundane, mixed with apprehension about my capacity for motherhood, that pushed me to make one more big trip before even my indulgent bosses drew the line. It wouldn't look good for CNN if one of their senior correspondents was abducted or hurt weeks before she was due to give birth.

For months I had wanted to go back to Yemen, where a civil war had brought the country to the brink of famine, and from where I'd last reported during the summer of 2015. It was almost impossible to get there because Saudi Arabia and the United Arab Emirates had imposed a near-total blockade on the country. Their stated objective was to try to oust Iran-backed Houthi rebels who had taken control of the capital and much of the northwest of the country. But even after more than two and a half years of the blockade, the Houthis still held sway in large parts of Yemen—and people in the country were starving to death.

The war in Yemen was the pet project of Saudi Arabia's newly minted crown prince, Mohammed bin Salman, an ambitious and inexperienced thirty-two-year-old with the full backing of the US. Thousands of civilians had been killed, many by American bombs that were being sold to the Saudis at great profit—and yet few in the world appeared to be paying any attention.

The conflict had been called the forgotten war, because the Saudis had control over Yemen's airspace and were able to prevent journalists from entering the country. It was an advantage they were determined to exploit, and one that made me livid. In 2017, I had tried to reason with the Saudi general who was the spokesman for the coalition, but he had dismissed me rudely. I followed up with a story on the severe malnutrition of Yemen's children that was titled "The images Saudi Arabia doesn't want you to see." I sent him the link to our story on WhatsApp and he blocked me.

One of CNN's best London-based producers, Salma Abdelaziz, had been working for weeks on ways to get into Yemen. A young Egyptian-American, she had been in Syria with me and I trusted her implicitly. She was bright, tenacious, and incredibly calm in stressful situations. Eventually she found a way to get to the largest city in southern Yemen, the port of Aden. It was controlled by UAE forces, but there were many different factions in the city and she had managed to befriend someone with connections at the airport who would help grease the wheels for us.

It was a fantastic opportunity to tell a story that was largely being ignored in the media. I told Philipp that I wanted to go, and he frowned. It was dangerous, he argued; there was a war going on, there was disease, the hospitals were terrible. I had all my arguments ready. That's exactly why I have to go, I said. We weren't going anywhere near the front line; I had gone back to the tropical diseases clinic and they had given me strong antibiotics in case I somehow got cholera (the doctor hadn't seemed surprised to see me again).

Eventually, Philipp sighed and said OK.

"But remember, this isn't just about you anymore."

I nodded emphatically, without really processing what he was saying.

The journey to Aden was long and arduous. We had to fly via Amman, and we had to clear all our gear through Jordanian customs (a two-hour process) and then wheel it through to another check-in. As the team hoisted the boxes onto the conveyor belt, the Royal Jordanian Airlines manager came over to us.

"Excuse me, madame," he said nervously, "how pregnant are you?"

I looked down at my large bump and answered him honestly. "Six months. But I have a letter from my doctor."

He looked relieved and took the letter.

"Thank you," he said after reading it over, "and please be very careful in Aden."

He clearly thought I was insane. Even our CNN security consultant, Adam, who was traveling with us, had admitted to being apprehensive about me doing this trip. I told him about my visit to the Hospital for Tropical Diseases and we mapped out what medical facilities there were in Aden.

The flight from Amman to Aden was three and a half hours long but in the middle of the night. The Yemenia plane was at least thirty years old, filthy and packed. We were the only foreigners on board. My bump practically grazed the seat in front of me. Sleep was clearly out of the question.

In principle, the purpose of the Saudi blockade in Yemen was to stop Iranian weapons and supplies from reaching the Houthis. But it was a sledgehammer to crack a nut—and had drastically reduced imports of desperately needed food, medicine, and fuel. What little managed to get through was being heavily taxed along the way as it passed through territory controlled by different warring factions.

The UN had said in the week before our visit that more than eight million people were on the brink of famine. Outbreaks of cholera and diphtheria preyed on a weakened population.

We had rented a villa in the diplomatic area, and a truck full of armed guards accompanied us everywhere. Kidnappings and assassinations were a serious problem in Aden, with an embryonic ISIS franchise compounding the insecurity. Western journalists were an obvious target. The city was nominally under the control of the Saudi-led coalition, but the streets were controlled by a patchwork of militias. Some were loyal to the coalition, others closer to ISIS or al Qaeda. Then there was a Southern secessionist movement that was growing in influence. All were heavily armed and vying for control of Aden's port and oil traffic.

The villa was shabby with intermittent running water, but it was relatively safe and there was one proper bed that the team graciously gave to me.

Our first mission was to visit al-Sadaqa Hospital, the main state-run hospital. Salaries hadn't been paid in months, and the building was filthy and dilapidated. An English-speaking doctor with exhausted red-rimmed eyes, Nahla Arishi, was assigned to show us around. I noticed how she winced with embarrassment as our cameras spotted her rinsing her hands with bottled water in the neonatal ward (there was no soap or running water to wash them properly).

In the intensive-care unit, she showed us three-year-old Khadir. He was suffering from a severe lung infection, but there was no ventilator to help him breathe. His eyes were closed, his chest heaving with the effort of taking in air. I peered into a small trash can at the bottom of his bed. It was full of emptied bags of blood and discarded needles. A fan was spinning limply in a futile effort to clear the warm, fetid air. Flies settled on Khadir's face and hands. His mother, Yamal, tried in vain to swat them away before slumping over his bed in defeat.

I quietly sat down next to her. He had been sick for weeks, she told me, but she had only brought him in three days earlier. The journey from their home in the province of Abyan had taken six hours, and with fuel now a scarce commodity, travel was prohibitively expensive.

"*Alhamdulillah*, praise God, he is doing much better," she said. I looked at his swollen eyes and labored breathing and nodded, unconvinced.

Khadir died the next day. He died because there was no ventilator to help him breathe, no proper medicine to help him fight the disease. He died because his mother couldn't afford to get to the hospital quickly. I felt a surge of anguish.

I had been experiencing anxiety attacks because my baby wasn't kicking as much as I was used to. My doctor had told me that the baby should be moving consistently. The internet in the villa was more sporadic than the water supply. I called Philipp in a panic and asked him to research what reduced movements meant.

"Placental abruption," he read out from a list

"PLACENTAL ABRUPTION??" I shouted hysterically.

"Darling, calm down. You're not having a placental abruption. You would have all sorts of other symptoms."

I closed my eyes and willed my imagination to slow down.

Philipp told me to go lie down on my left side and drink something sweet. Apparently, that was supposed to encourage the baby to move. I had no idea whether this was an old wives' tale or something he had just culled from the *British Medical Journal*.

I drank a Pepsi and lay on my sleeping bag.

"Where are you, my love?" I whispered. "Give me a kick so I know you're OK."

After some moments, I felt a squirm inside of me, then a gentle kick. I wept with relief and ached with love for this mysterious creature inside of me whom I had never met. It was my sacred duty to protect this little being. I suddenly fully understood what Philipp had meant. It wasn't about me anymore. I was a vessel. And it was a privilege. I felt humbled.

"Thank you, God. Thank you, God. I promise to honor this life inside of me."

The following morning, we left the villa early to visit the neighboring province of Lahij, which was hosting a large number of displaced people and had some of the worst malnutrition levels in the country.

In a small house in a dusty village, we came across five-year-old Ahmed Helmi, lying on a thin sheet on the concrete floor.

"It's the coolest place in the house," his mother, Soumaya, explained, looking down at the ground. "We do whatever we can to make him comfortable."

I looked down at his tiny, fragile body. There was little more to him than parched, papery skin stretched across brittle bones. Giant eyes—brown and unblinking—gazed up blankly from hollow sockets.

Soumaya explained that Ahmed had been suffering from severe malnutrition for four years. It had killed her second son just two months ago.

"He's really sick today. Since yesterday evening he can't eat anything.

I took him to a doctor in Aden and sometimes he starts getting better. But then he just gets diarrhea again and gets sick again."

There was no trace of emotion in her voice. I tried to contemplate how one copes with the prospect of losing a second child. She seemed to sense the question and looked me squarely in the eyes.

"Life is hard but you walk the path of God and God will look after you."

By now we were sitting on the ground with Ahmed lying in between us, drifting in and out of consciousness. Instinctively, I reached out and put my hand on his head and stroked his hair. It felt so soft and warm with life. He looked up at me briefly and I was suddenly seized by a wrenching sob.

Soumaya put her hand on my arm. I was ashamed that she was comforting me when her son was dying. But I couldn't stop weeping. A beautiful little boy was starving to death on a concrete floor, and thousands more like him would die in the next few months. But the world moved on, oblivious. It was pure agony.

"I'm so sorry," I apologized, wiping my tears away. "This is so embarrassing . . . he's just such a lovely little boy."

As we drove back to Aden, I couldn't let go of the sensation of Ahmed's warm, soft hair. Every time I thought about it, tears sprang to my eyes.

I had seen children suffer, some even die in war. And most of the time I had managed to hold it together, to keep a distance between myself and the story. There was a barrier. It wasn't one of indifference or cynicism; it was there so I could do my job.

But now, stroking my belly, I knew that things were different. Something had shifted. The barrier was gone. It was time to go home.

Epilogue

I lay blinking in the darkness of my hotel room, trying to get my bearings. My eyes were sore and dry from lack of sleep and the hot, dusty air belting out of the noisy heater above the bed. I had arrived in the city of Mazar-e Sharif, Afghanistan, 48 hours earlier. I looked at my phone and sighed: 4:30 a.m. We were scheduled to leave the hotel to meet our Taliban escorts at 9 a.m., meaning I had four and a half hours to obsess over every detail of a trip we'd spent months organizing.

I had always fixated on getting to places and people that others couldn't reach but, perhaps because I'd begun my career in the aftermath of 9/11, the Taliban had particularly fascinated me. I remember vividly watching hidden-camera footage from the late 1990s of Afghan women, in the all-covering, ubiquitous blue *burqa*, being beaten and executed in public. This was where the seemingly endless and futile war on terror had been born. And yet, seventeen years after the US invasion of Afghanistan, what did we really know about the Taliban today? Their world was shrouded in secrecy, inaccessible to outsiders, even as they were making huge territorial gains on the battlefield.

When Salma and I had first sat down to lunch in London with

Najibullah Quraishi, the Afghan filmmaker whom we hoped would take us into Taliban territory, he had laughed at our proposal.

"That's very difficult," he said, blotting his mouth gently with his napkin.

Naj had done many stories with the Taliban before. He was not a supporter of the group in any way, but he was fair and evenhanded, and they respected his professionalism. As we talked and ate, he kept the focus on the importance of security.

At the end of the meal, Salma asked if he was willing to work on the project with us. He paused for a while before replying.

"Let's try to see what can be done."

Four months later, after endless negotiations with the Taliban and CNN management, who proved significantly harder to persuade, we were finally ready to do the story. The Taliban had agreed to let us spend two days in their territory, just a couple of hours outside Mazar-e Sharif.

There were some ground rules: as women, we were warned that we had to respect Taliban customs. First, this meant Salma and I would eat and sleep separately from Naj and wear the *niqab*, the full facial veil, whenever we were out in public. Second, with peace talks between the US and the Taliban gathering momentum in Doha, we were told to stay away from deeply political questions. The leaders that we would be meeting with were local and were not authorized to comment on such sensitive topics. We were also told not to bring a tripod, presumably because, when carried over the shoulder, it could look like a weapon from the sky. Finally, we were told not to bring smartphones, just small, old-school Nokia cell phones with Afghan SIM cards.

The primary threats were kidnapping and air strikes. I felt confident that our invitation came from the highest levels of the Taliban's leadership. Naj had spoken directly to the group's spokesperson, known as Zabiullah Mujahid. With the peace talks going on, it would be crazy for the Taliban to do anything to us. Beyond that, I understood that the covenant of security, once an invitation had been granted, was something that even militant jihadist groups took seriously. But the latter threat was much harder to mitigate. The US had dramatically stepped up the number of strikes in the months before, as a means of leverage with the Taliban at the negotiating table.

We had made a deliberate decision not to tip off the military about our trip. On the one hand, doing so might have made it safer for us. But it also may well have endangered the people who were hosting us, and a trip like this only works if both parties come to it in good faith.

I rolled over in the bed and tried to push the fear out of my mind. Since the birth of my son, concern about my own personal safety had taken on a much deeper significance. I had often felt afraid in war zones, but this was something new, something different. Is there anything more terrifying than loving someone far more than you love yourself?

Ezra Albrecht Nikolas Nour, or Ezzie for short, had arrived on a snowy March morning in London almost a year before. It was so quiet on the way to the hospital, the sounds of the city muted by the heavy flakes. Philipp and I worried that the doctors and nurses wouldn't be able to get in to work.

Hours later, the midwife laid him on my chest and I wept delirious tears of joy. It was the greatest moment of my life.

In an instant, any anxiety I had felt before his birth disappeared. I was madly in love, but it was better than romantic love, I joked to friends, because I wasn't worried about whether he would text me back. I happily became that woman who stops to coo at babies in the supermarket and who could talk about the benefits of Monkey Music for hours on end.

If motherhood was warm and inviting, going back to work felt cold and vulnerable. It took me months to acclimatize. Not only because I missed my son—in many ways I was happy to be stimulated during the day and have adult conversations—but because I had to shift into a completely different emotional space.

During my maternity leave, I had been promoted to chief international correspondent at CNN. It was something I had worked toward my entire career. But it also meant that I needed to be more focused and driven than ever before. After four months at home with my son, of living organically and in the moment, of being open and loving and gentle and calm, I suddenly had to toughen up again.

I never questioned my decision to throw myself back into my work. I understood instinctively that this was what I was meant to do in life, that being true to myself would make me a better mother. But I ached when I was away from him for more than a few days, especially in sleep-deprived moments.

I sat up in the bed and opened my laptop and began writing an email.

> My Dearest Ezzie,
>
> Often, when I wake up at lonely hours in strange places,
> I try to imagine that I am in bed with you and Papi in the
> morning, drinking our coffee (or milk in your case) and
> playing together. If I scrunch up my eyes and concentrate
> really hard, I can actually smell you.

I wrote about how hard it was to leave him and the pride I hoped he'd one day feel toward my work.

When I stopped and looked at my phone, it was 6:30 a.m., time to get dressed and go over my packing one more time before meeting up with Salma and Naj.

Several hours later, I tied my *niqab* over my face and we set off, my stomach going berserk with the familiar tingle of nerves and excitement.

Mazar-e Sharif is often described as one of the safest cities in Afghanistan. The Taliban were forced to flee after a bitter battle in 2001, shortly after the US invasion. Now, though, they were just miles outside the city.

We got into the car and headed southwest, to a district called Chimtal. The Taliban had pushed in and taken over much of the district in September 2017. The Afghan government was still in control of the main road out of the city, but once you turned off the highway, you were quickly in Taliban territory.

After all these years of travel, it's rare that I get culture shock, but this was like taking a time machine and landing in a desolate landscape hundreds of years ago. There were very few cars, no proper roads. To get to the village where we were staying, we had to put the car onto a small hand-pulled ferry, manned by a boy who couldn't have been more than thirteen years old. It was mind-blowing to consider the billions of dollars that the US had poured into trying to build up Afghanistan's infrastructure, and yet so little of that had trickled down to areas like this one.

Our Taliban escorts waited for us on the other side of the river. Their appearance alone was somehow intimidating and dramatic. They wore large turbans wrapped partially around their faces and their eyes were lined with kohl. All of them carried AK-47s. Naj went up to them and greeted them one by one, leaning in and lightly touching their shoulders and then pulling back to touch their hands. It seemed much more intimate than a handshake.

"*Salaam 'alaikum,*" Salma said to them.

There was no response. The fighters did not even look at us. Naj had warned us that as women traveling with him, it would be deemed inappropriate, and even a slight to him, for the men to engage with us. But it was still surreal to suddenly feel completely invisible.

Part of the reason the Taliban was letting us into their territory was to show that they were in control and that they could provide basic services to people. But as we drove along, it quickly became apparent how vulnerable the militants still were.

Our Taliban escorts were on motorcycles ahead of and behind our two vehicles. Abruptly, the lead bike pulled over and motioned for us to stop. We pulled up alongside the bike, and Naj asked what was going on. The sound of *nasheed* (Islamic a cappella songs) and chatter on the large two-way radio the driver held blared from the motorbike. He looked at Naj and made a circle motion with his hand toward the sky.

"Planes," Naj said. My stomach dropped.

In the distance, we could see a chain of five helicopters flying. It was impossible to know whether they were Afghan or US forces. I looked at the white Taliban flag flapping above our escorts' motorcycle and remembered being told that they no longer flew the flag in villages because it inevitably led to air strikes. With our convoy, we were certainly a conspicuous target.

After a seemingly interminable wait, the Taliban fighters motioned for us to continue. We had no choice but to move on.

We drove for about half an hour to a medical clinic in the village of Pashma Qala. A worn plaque at the door showed it was originally a gift from the US in 2006.

Salma and I sat in the car as Naj shot video of people from the village streaming into the clinic. Suddenly, I saw a little girl come from behind the car and run into the road, just as a motorcycle was passing by. My whole body seized with fear—please God, let her not be hit. A bloodcurdling howl filled the air.

Salma's eyes were wide with horror. We got out of the car. A teenage boy had rushed up to the girl to see if she was OK. She continued to shriek but she was conscious and didn't appear to be bleeding. The man on the motorcycle that had hit her was a Taliban fighter. He stopped his bike and looked back. Slowly, he slung his gun over his shoulder and wandered toward the girl nonchalantly, then, seeing that she wasn't seriously hurt, he simply turned around and rode off.

None of the villagers standing by said anything. Perhaps they were afraid of the consequences. Our Taliban escorts stood by the gate of the clinic, observing the scene dispassionately.

The girl was carried inside, her frantic mother following behind. I felt a deep tug inside me and tears sprang to my eyes. Even when I was pregnant, I had noticed that my threshold for seeing children suffer had lowered drastically. Since Ezzie's birth, though, the urge to protect had become even more visceral and powerful. It was as if a channel inside of me had been opened up and I would never again be able to close it.

The doctor barely examined her before handing her mother some painkillers and moving on. Nobody seemed to be as shocked or horrified as we were. After years of fighting in this area, they had seen much worse and there were dozens more patients to tend to.

As the doctor went on to examine another woman and child, I asked him some questions. Who was in charge of the clinic? Who was responsible for the day-to-day management? He explained that the Taliban ran the day-to-day operations at the clinic but the government paid the salaries and provided medicine. This sort of ad hoc cooperation between the government and the Taliban was becoming more and more common in hospitals and schools in contested areas.

In the next room, we found two female employees, including a twenty-two-year-old midwife called Fazila. She wore a magenta-colored headscarf and had a wide mouth that curled up into a smile when I caught her eye. On the wall of her office, a family planning poster listed different types of contraception, including condoms and the pill. It was the last thing I expected to see in Taliban territory. Under the Taliban in the late 1990s, women were not able to get medical care from a male doctor, work most jobs, or even leave the house without a male guardian.

Fazila told us that the Taliban hadn't changed anything since it took over the clinic from the government eighteen months ago. She said women could still be treated by male doctors.

"The Taliban never interferes in our work as women," Fazila said. "They never block us from coming to the clinic. They don't interrupt us."

I looked into her eyes and wondered briefly if she was being told to say this for our cameras. But she seemed to be sincere and at ease. Clearly, the Taliban was trying to show it could take a more pragmatic and accommodating approach to governance.

For years, the group had been focused on fighting and taking territory with a singular ruthlessness. Recently, though, it had started taking an interest in ensuring that basic services were provided, like medical care and education. There was a growing understanding that they could not become more powerful without the support of the people, and particularly local elders.

I looked down at my watch. It was 4:20 p.m. We had given our word to CNN's security team who were overseeing our trip from Kabul that we would be at our accommodation for the night by 5 p.m. The Taliban switch off all cell-phone towers at night and we would have no way of communicating with the outside world.

As we started to head out of the clinic, we saw a group of women in the waiting area. One woman was cradling in her arms a disabled boy with big brown eyes. She looked up at us pleadingly.

"We don't have enough food to eat, we don't have medicines for our children," she said.

We asked whether life under the Taliban has changed from how it was in the late '90s. An older woman standing nearby shook her head emphatically.

"No. We are trapped in the middle and we can't do anything."

She went on to assail the Afghan government, who had been in charge of Chimtal until eighteen months earlier. Over the next twenty-four hours I would hear similar complaints. To many of the people in rural areas, it didn't appear to make a huge difference who was in charge. Their quality of life had not changed or improved. And after decades of war and hardship, they would turn to anyone who offered peace.

I wanted to stay longer and hear more but it was after four thirty. We had only thirty minutes more of cell-phone service, and the drive was at least as long as that. Naj was grabbing some more shots of the women.

"Naj, we have to go right now," Salma hurried him.

The drive back was tense. The sun was melting quickly into the horizon and air strikes were most common at night. Salma called our CNN security minder.

"I'm sorry, we are not there yet but we should be soon. Five minutes our driver says."

The line went dead.

"Shit," Salma cursed.

The cell-phone tower had gone for the night. Ten minutes later, we pulled up to the house where we would stay the night. Incredibly, our driver, who was using a different cell-phone network, still had a signal. Salma called the security minder again and spoke quickly.

"We are back at the house where we will stay the night and will call in the morning."

The line went dead again. But at least CNN knew we were safe and ensconced for the night.

In keeping with strict rules about gender segregation, we were to sleep in the main house with the women and children and Naj was to sleep in another building with two of our Taliban escorts.

Once inside, the women and girls clustered around and fussed over us, offering us food and making sure the small heater was pointed toward us, while peppering us with questions in Dari that we couldn't understand, then giggling when we would shrug apologetically. I reached into my bag for the candy bars I had brought as gifts and began handing them out.

One woman sat to my right staring at me intently. Every time I would look over to her, she would meet my eye and say something and start laughing and the others would join in. She was heavyset with mischievous eyes and I had the impression she was sort of the joker of the group.

Another woman sat breastfeeding her toddler son (Islam encourages breastfeeding until the child is two years of age). I beamed at her and held my hands over my heart and said in English, "I have a baby boy," trying to communicate that my body ached from missing Ezzie so much. Out of nowhere, the joker suddenly reached out and grabbed my right breast and we all began howling with laughter. It felt so good to laugh that hard, to let some of the tension of the day melt away. I still have no idea why she did it. I can only imagine she was pointing out how paltry my mammaries looked in comparison to the breastfeeding mother's ample bosom.

When it was time for bed, the women pulled out mattresses to sleep on. I saw one of the girls looking at me as I put on my moisturizer, so I took a dollop and rubbed it into her cheeks and then did the same with the other women. It was strangely intimate, kneeling before them, one by one, rubbing the rich cream into their skin, smiling into their eyes silently, unable to communicate verbally.

As Salma and I lay down on our mattresses, the wife of the host laid thick quilts over us. I snuggled gratefully under mine. There was such a coziness to the room. Lying surrounded by the warmth of the women's bodies, I quickly fell asleep.

The next morning we woke up early and the women gave us hard-boiled eggs and hot green tea with homemade bread and yogurt.

We packed up our gear and walked five minutes to visit the local madrassa, a religious school. Madrassas have a reputation for teaching a harsh, fundamentalist Islam. Under Taliban rule in the late 1990s, girls were excluded from educational institutions.

But we found dozens of children—boys and girls—poring over their Qurans, reciting verses as they rocked back and forth.

I knelt down to talk to a group of girls. Most of them were between eight and ten. They wore brightly colored headscarves and smiled shyly when they talked to me. Several of them said they could read. Taking a pen and paper that I handed them, they proudly demonstrated writing their own names, slowly in elaborate handwriting. One of the girls said she wanted to be a doctor when she grew up.

At the other end of the room, teacher Yar Mohammed walked along the row of pupils, his AK-47 over his shoulder. Periodically, he would crouch down to go over an *ayah* (verse of the Quran) with one of the kids. He agreed to sit down and talk to us, resting his AK-47 on the floor in front of him. He explained that he divided his time between the front lines and the classroom and said that the Taliban now encourages the education of girls.

"The Emirate has instructed education departments to allow education [for girls] of religious studies, modern studies, science, and math."

It didn't take long for this carefully crafted illusion of gender equality to be shattered. Mohammed added that once the girls hit puberty, they could no longer be educated in the same school as boys, because there might be contact between the sexes.

That means there need to be separate schools for the girls. So far, those don't exist. It's the same excuse that the Taliban used two decades ago to deprive millions of girls of education.

I looked over at the group of girls, diligently reading their Qurans, and thought of the words of an Islamic teacher, Abdullah, I'd met the previous day: "The people of Afghanistan want education for women but in an Islamic way, not an American way."

The sad reality was that female education was not a priority in poor, rural areas. And that went for government-controlled areas as well.

As we walked out of the madrassa, we found a group of men waiting for us. The Taliban governor for Chimtal district, Mawlavi Khaksar, had come to grant us an interview. The Taliban had started appointing "shadow" governors to compete with the Afghan government for influence and support.

Khaksar cut an intimidating figure. He wore a heavy black cloak. A pair of startling green eyes stared out at us from beneath a black turban that covered his face from his mouth down. He sat, flanked by four bodyguards, his AK-47 resting on his lap. One of the guards was hunched over a two-way radio, listening for security updates.

I remembered the instruction we had been given not to ask political questions. But this was too rare of an opportunity to pass up. I began asking him about the Taliban's indiscriminate attacks, the thousands of civilians who had been killed in suicide bombings. His eyes bore no trace of reaction as the question was translated to him.

"The ones who are responsible for civilian casualties are the ones who came with their aircrafts, artillery, B-52, and heavy weaponry," he said impassively.

There was no question that too many civilians had been killed in US and coalition air strikes. But the Taliban was certainly responsible for many more casualties, at least several thousand in the last few years alone.

I pushed again. "What about these suicide bombings at polling stations—these kill many civilians?"

His eyes narrowed for a moment.

"We deny this. This accusation is not acceptable to us."

I asked whether there could be peace in Afghanistan, but anytime the conversation veered into the overtly political, Khaksar told us to consult the Taliban's political spokesperson for comment.

It soon became clear that the Taliban's austere and insular interpretation of Islam had not changed.

"We implement the Shari'a, we follow Shari'a instruction . . . the Shari'a allows stoning to death," Khaksar said.

I wondered if he knew much about how nuanced Shari'a law is; if he realized that to sentence someone to death by stoning for *zina* (adultery and premarital sex), four people had to witness the act of penetration, and that if someone accused another person without proof, they were to be lashed for making a false accusation. Did he have any idea that many Islamic scholars across the world have viewed the *hudud* punishments as being intended as a deterrent more than anything else? That even in the premodern era, such punishments were rarely implemented unless the culprit repeatedly insisted on it? It struck me that, in some ways, the Taliban was not dissimilar from right-wing nationalists I had come across, insisting on returning to an idealized past that never really existed.

As we walked out of the house with Khaksar after our interview, the Taliban's military commander for the district arrived, and a dispute broke out about us. He appeared to be upset about our request to get a shot of the governor and me walking outside. He didn't want any member of the Taliban appearing on the street with a woman.

He asked if the governor could walk down the street with Naj instead.

Naj diplomatically explained that I was the presenter, not him. The men appeared to find this confusing.

"They should have brought a man," a companion of the commander grumbled.

Eventually, I became impatient and interrupted.

"If it's going to cause a headache, we will walk behind the governor. Let's just move on."

I had come across men in conservative societies who did not want to shake my hand. I had interviewed jihadis who didn't want to look me in the eye. But I had never had to walk behind a man before. Normally, I would have felt irritated or indignant and perhaps even grumbled about it. But the commander had a dazed and angry look on his face that made me nervous. I was focused on getting what we needed and getting out as soon as possible.

The commander took us to the outskirts of the village, where a mass of Taliban fighters had gathered along the side of the dirt road. They were carrying AK-47s and RPGs and waving the militant group's flag. It was an eerie scene because the fighters were silent. They stood staring at us with hollow eyes.

I looked at Salma and Naj with alarm. Gatherings like this were a major target for air strikes.

The commander appeared unfazed. He had been fighting since he was old enough to carry a gun.

"We are ready for any sacrifice. We are not scared of being hit," he told us. "This is our holy path, we continue our jihad."

I kept looking up at the skies, my ears straining for the sound of a drone.

"Why don't you go and stand near that wall," a man who was assisting Naj said to me. "It's better cover if there's a strike."

I felt a surge of panic and my chest tightened. Naj came running toward me from shooting video of the fighters.

"This is crazy," he said. "They are crazy."

We decided to shoot a quick piece to camera and then go. As I walked down the line of fighters, I was struck again by their dazed and empty eyes. Were they staring at us or through us? Did they really feel no fear?

Seventeen years of war with the US appeared to have done nothing to weaken their resolve or expand their fundamentalist ideology. Where could you find a more glaring example of the futility of conflict since Vietnam?

In all the war zones and front lines I had visited, I had confronted the same glaring reality: that enemies were rarely bombed into submission, that crushing force often hardened their values, rather than changing them, that even when a group was dismantled or destroyed, the seeds were sown for a new generation of hatred and violence.

I had seen so many cities leveled, so many people killed, and yet so little really changed.

That didn't mean that some wars weren't worth fighting. It just meant that the goals needed to be more specific and perhaps less idealistic, grounded in the reality of how parts of the world see us and not just the ideal of how we see ourselves.

I understood that in a sense I had failed in my quest to act as a translator between worlds. There were too many people who didn't want to hear the stories of others, who felt that listening was tantamount to weakness, who believed that humanizing "the other" was dangerous. Opening yourself to other perspectives certainly shattered illusions one had about simple narratives of good guys and bad guys, of black and white. And living in the gray was not easy.

As we drove out of Taliban territory, we passed a group of women squatting in a field in the distance, working on the land. An icy wind whipped across the bleak landscape. I imagined how cold their hands must be, how hard their lives must be.

I thought of the women whose room we had shared the night before, of their curiosity, their laughter and warmth. How many times I had been reminded that people are people, that there is a shared human experience, no matter how different our societies, that connects us.

Perhaps this is why I continue to feel such passion for my work, notwithstanding the frustrations and limitations. Certainly, it was the reason I started doing it after 9/11. As well as the need to inform and explain, there is a compulsion to humanize, to make real what is surreal and foreign, to remind the viewer that beyond the geopolitics of power and the brutality of war and the clashes of cultures, people are people.

I took off my *niqab* and leaned my head against the car window, basking in the glow of the sunlight and of such a successful trip.

Almost instantly, my mind went to home. I imagined the feeling of scooping up Ezzie and covering him in kisses, of his chubby little hands pulling my hair with delight. My heart soared with gratitude.

Acknowledgments

There are so many people across different continents to whom I am deeply indebted. It is impossible to thank everyone, but to name a few:

Thanks to my amazing parents and my Granny, Vivienne Ward, for inspiring me with her energy and enthusiasm and for always encouraging me to strive and to be curious. To my Auntie Mo and my cousin Simi and Uncle Nick and Auntie Vee for giving me so much love and so many happy memories as a child. To Teresa for your love and loyalty and for sticking with my family though thick and thin. To my brilliant Uncle Gerald for watching every piece I did and emailing me—rest in peace.

To my Wycombe Abbey partners in crime, thank you for making borstal fun, Alanna, Eddy, Bex, Dee.

To Mike Chinoy and Jill Dougherty for helping me get my first internship with CNN in Moscow.

To Matthew Alexander for keeping me from going insane on the overnights at Fox. To Steve Harrigan for being patient and generous with a very impatient overnight desk assistant. To Brian Knoblock for giving me my first shot in Baghdad. To Jonathan Hunt for being a great friend and mentor and making me do that clip reel. To all the Baghdad crew—you know who you are—our tight-knit community kept me sane during those crazy years.

To my agents, Carol Perry and Steve Herz, who took me on at the tender age of twenty-six and have been close friends and great supporters ever since.

To my incredible squad of Beirut girlfriends—Kate Brooks, Marcia Biggs, Myrna Atalla, Nada Hussein—we shared the best of times and worst of times. Thank you for listening to me weep over "Christophe" for months on end!

To Amy Entelis and Tori Smith for giving me my first job in network news. To Bruno Roeber and Angus Hines for showing me the ropes. To James Goldston for encouraging my quirky stories for *Nightline*. To Max Karmen and Tanya Stukalova for being such wise and wonderful souls and for helping a young rookie navigate the new Russia. To Volodya, rest in peace my dear friend.

To the wonderful team at CBS—Andy Clarke, Mark Phillips, Charlie D'Agata, Liz Palmer, Vicky Burston, Claire Day, Deb Thomson, Heather Abbott, Mark Ludlow, Brian Robbins. Thank you for the support and the laughs.

To those at *60 Minutes* who took a chance on me and made me feel at home—Jeff Fager, Bill Owens, Bob Simon, Graham Messick, Bob Shattuck, Harry Radliffe.

To Charlie Rose for being an early champion of my work. And to Bob Schieffer, Gayle King, Norah O'Donnell, and Scott Pelley for supporting and encouraging and inspiring me.

To Louise Callaghan and the editors at *The Sunday Times* for publishing my early writing on our work in Yemen.

To the amazing producers who have reared and steered me along the way—Randall Joyce, Ben Plesser, Agnes Reau, Erin Lyall, Beth Loyd, Salma Abdelaziz. And to the equally brilliant cameramen who have made this job a pleasure—Scott Munro, Thorsten Hoefle, and Scottie McWhinnie, to name just a few.

And to the scores of fixers and translators and engineers and drivers in the field and the army of technical and editorial staff in the newsroom.

Television news is a team sport and it would not be possible without you. I am so grateful.

To the incredible women who do this job who I am privileged to call mentors and friends—Arwa Damon, Lynsey Addario, Liz Sly, Martha Raddatz, Liz Palmer. Thank you for providing inspiration and support. And special thanks to Lynsey for being such a generous friend and sharing your experience of the delicate dance of juggling motherhood, work, and writing a book.

To Abu Ibrahim and his beautiful family and Razan and Hussein and Bulbul and the countless other activists and fighters in Syria who have lived through hell and risked everything to get their story told. I am humbled by your bravery and deeply pained by your sacrifice. Thank you for every small act of kindness.

To Austin Tice, I continue to pray for you to come home every day. To Debi and Marc Tice, some of the strongest and most loving parents I know. To Nancy Youssef, a fantastic reporter with a huge heart and a dear friend who has worked so hard to help Austin. To everyone who has tried to help bring Austin home.

To the journalists and aid workers we lost in Syria—Anthony Shadid, Mary Colvin, Ayman Youssef al Haji, Jim Foley, Steven Sotloff, Pete Kassig, and so many others. The loss is profound. Rest in peace.

To Jeff Zucker for giving me my dream job. To Leora Kapelus, Deborah Rayner, and Tommy Evans and all my wonderful colleagues who have made CNN home. And to Hala Gorani and Max Foster for being the best office mates and for listening to me drone on about this book for a year!

To the gifted Ginny Smith Younce, who first encouraged me to write a book in 2012. Thank you for your incredible patience and grace, for holding my hand on this sometimes scary journey, for asking the important questions, and for shaping my words into something I am really proud of. To Caroline Sydney, whose hard work and positive energy and incredible efficiency were invaluable. To the ineffable Tim Lister for toiling over early drafts, for tirelessly "moving furniture," and for injecting his unmatched eloquence into my prose. To the elegant and erudite Sameen Gauhar for laboring to ensure that every fact and figure was correct and for providing incredible support and thoughtful commentary throughout. To Professor Jonathan A. C. Brown for taking the time to offer his thoughts and guidance.

To the brilliant Binky Urban, thank you for taking me on, for providing wisdom and support and honesty and for reminding me that "the train's gotta have tracks."

To the wonderful Louise Lewinton, who came up with the book title over dinner in Provence!

To my dear friend Prue Peiffer, a poet and writer whose talents are intimidatingly tremendous, thank you for reading an early copy and for offering your thoughts and for generally being a thoughtful and beautiful friend. Thanks also to Ben Plesser for offering insightful feedback as always.

To my sisters from other misters since childhood—Chiara, Alanna, Eddy, Victoria—you are a source of true joy in my life. I am blessed to have such wonderful best friends. And to my unofficial godmothers, Nancy and Liz, thank you for all your love and support.

To my parents, words fail me. Your love and generosity and humor and smarts and eccentricity and unerring support have made me who I am today. I am so lucky to be your daughter and I love you with all my heart.

To Philipp, my rock, my love, my best friend. Thank you for never failing to support and encourage me. Thank you for being kind and good and loving and noble and thank you for putting up with me.

Finally, to Ezzie and Caspar, there is no greater love. This is for you.

Photo Credits

Page 4, bottom: Courtesy of Christian Streib

Page 5, center: Georgia. Gori. August 14, 2008. Russian Army checkpoint at the entrance of Gori. © Thomas Dworzak/Magnum Photos

Page 6, bottom: Courtesy of Nasser Nouri

Page 7, top: Courtesy of Scott Munro

Page 8, top: © Taylor Jones, all rights reserved

Page 8, middle: Courtesy of the Tice family

Page 9, bottom: Courtesy of Adam Dobby

Page 10, bottom: Courtesy of Sebastiaan Knoops

Page 11, bottom: Courtesy of UNTV

Page 12, bottom: Courtesy of Christian Streib

Page 13, top: Courtesy of Adam Dobby

Page 14: Courtesy of Mark Phillips

Page 15, top: Courtesy of Salma Abdelaziz

Page 15, bottom: Courtesy of Salma Abdelaziz

Page 16, top: Courtesy of Scott McWhinnie

All other images courtesy of the author

Index